Inventing the 19th Century

The Great Age of Victorian Inventions

G. EASTMAN.
CAMERA.

No. 388,850.   Patented Sept. 4, 1888.

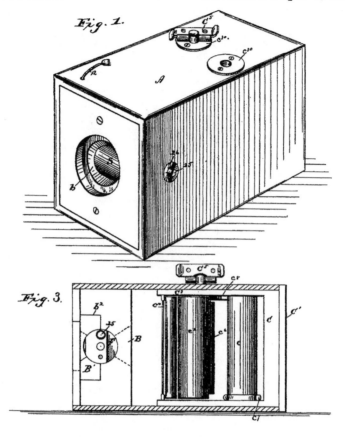

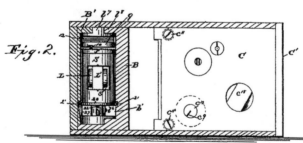

Witnesses.   Inventor.
Chas. R. Burr.   George Eastman.
A. B. Stewart.   by Church & Church
                                        his Attorneys.

Inventing the 19th Century

The Great Age of Victorian Inventions

Stephen van Dulken

SPONSORED BY

THE BRITISH LIBRARY

First published 2001 by
The British Library
96 Euston Road
London NW1 2DB

© The British Library Board 2001

British Library Cataloguing in Publication Data
A CIP record is available from the British Library

ISBN 0-7123-0881-4

Designed by Bob Elliott
Typeset by Hope Services (Abingdon) Ltd.
Printed in England by St Edmundsbury Press,
Bury St Edmunds

CONTENTS

CHRONOLOGICAL LIST OF PATENTS

1837	The electric telegraph
1839	Photography
1841	The cork-filled life preserver
1843	The facsimile machine
	Locomotive apparatus for the air
1844	Vulcanised rubber
1846	The multistage sugar evaporator
	The sewing machine
	The steam locomotive
	Sulphuric ether
1849	Buoying ships over shoals
	The safety pin
1851	The ice making machine
1853	The hand and draught carriage
1854	Machine for searching for gold
1855	The Bessemer process
1856	The junction interlocking railway signal
	Synthetic dyes
1857	The pocket protector
1858	The bowling machine
	The mirror galvanometer
1859	The school desk and chair combined
1860	The Winchester repeating rifle
1861	The safety lift
1862	The combined plough and gun
	The ironclad CSS *Virginia*
1863	Roller skates
1865	The clockwork dancing toy
	The Pullman sleeping car
1866	The bicycle
	The Checkered game of life
1867	Dynamite
	The pneumatic railway
	The square-bottomed paper bag
	The treadmill
1868	The typewriter
1869	The compressed air brake
1870	The can opener
	Celluloid
1871	Improvement in brewing beer and ale
1872	Blue jeans
	The moustache protector and trainer
1873	Barbed wire
1874	Lawn tennis
1875	The Big Wheel
1876	The cable street car
	The internal combustion engine
	The telephone
1877	Parlor baseball
	The phonograph

1878	The 'Resurgam' submarine
1879	The automobile
	The cash register
	The parachute fire-escape
1880	The electric light bulb
	The incubator
1881	Device for waking persons from sleep
1882	Indicating door fastenings for closets
	Safety apparatus for sea-bathers
1883	The automatic machine gun
	The fountain pen
	The vending machine
1884	Linotype®
	The mathematical divider
	Punched card tabulation
	The steam turbine
	The traveling thrasher and separator
1885	The dishwasher
	The (legal) liquor flask
	The tell-tale
1886	The comptometer
	Improved device for smokers
	The motion picture camera
1887	The alternating current induction motor
	Apparatus for treating diseases
1888	The pneumatic tyre
	The roll-film camera
	Tiddlywinks
1889	The automatic telephone exchange
	The perpetual motion machine
1890	Aerial locomotion by balloons
	The Ouija® board
	The veil that brings a blush to the cheek
1891	The clasp locker for shoes
	The crown top for bottles
	The Hardy Perfect fishing reel
1892	Apparatus for producing stage illusions
	The deliverance coffin
1893	The brassière
	Improved means for making tea
1895	Breakfast cereal
	The diesel engine
	The saluting device
	The Zeppelin
1897	The push-up player piano
1898	Aspirin
	Means for releasing draught animals
	The silent valveless water waste preventer
1899	The mousetrap
1900	The radio

INTRODUCTION

'I see you're admiring my little box', the Knight said in a friendly tone. 'It's my own invention—to keep clothes and sandwiches in. You see I carry it upside down, so that the rain can't get in.'

'But the things can get out', Alice gently remarked. 'Do you know that the lid's open?'

'I didn't know it', the Knight said, a shade of vexation passing over his face. 'Then all the things must have fallen out! And the box is no use without them.'

Lewis Carroll, *Through the looking glass* (1871)

THIS is the story of 100 patented inventions from the Victorian age, from Queen Victoria's accession to the British throne in 1837 to her death in 1901. Some were famous or important inventions of their time, while others have been chosen to represent interesting or quirky aspects of culture or life. I hope that the book will show that fact is indeed often stranger than fiction. Both Britain and the USA are extensively covered: other countries are also represented.

Inventions made up just one thread of life in Victorian times, but they were a distinctly colourful one. In this book all the inventions are represented by a page, normally a drawing, from the original patent. Patents provide a rich source for exploring the past which has been relatively little used, even though patents show the idea for an invention as it was 'at the beginning'. As is normal, some ideas that were put forward for patent applications were rejected at the time as impossible. The British clergyman Dr Dionysius Lardner, who was also a professor of natural history, said, 'No steamship could be built large enough to carry sufficient coals for a voyage across the Atlantic'. He forgot that the amount of coal which can be carried in a ship is proportional to the *cube* of the length of the ship while coal consumption is only proportional to the *square* of the ship's length. Two years later in 1837 two steamships succeeded in the first crossing. Lardner also said that railways were impossible as their speed would asphyxiate the passengers.

Of course, some suggestions for inventions were indeed silly or impracticable, but this is not always obvious except with hindsight. Many patented inventions were never produced. When you see some of them you can understand why. Just because someone secured a patent did not necessarily mean that there was money in the idea, or even that it worked (indeed, that has never been a requirement). The whole point of the patent system was to encourage invention by offering a temporary monopoly to an inventor in his or her country. Publication of a description and drawings of a patent also had the advantage of giving others an idea of what already existed. If the story behind the invention is known it is told here, although it has sometimes been necessary to compress a complicated story. The world of the common man or woman is relatively lacking here—as inventions are expensive to patent, usually only the wealthier classes could afford to patent them. Most stories behind inventions have stayed forever unknown after the death of the inventor, so that only the patents themselves remain as mute testimony. Some of the inventions may look odd but until electric power was widely available to domestic homes, which was after the end of the Victorian age, household machines were not powered by electricity.

It is easy to think of the Victorian age as a time when life consisted of over-stuffed armchairs in well-kept drawing rooms, and nothing ever changed very much. That world

certainly existed, side by side with the poor, who were always present in large numbers, but there were also huge advances in technology. The Victorian age saw railways replacing the canals as sources of work for large numbers of labouring navvies, and much money being put into speculative companies. Automobiles were beginning to replace horse-drawn carriages by 1901. First the electric telegraph (often referred to as the first Internet) and then the telephone made communications easier. The cheaper and more efficient postal system developed early in Queen Victoria's reign also helped communication with those far away.

This book tells the colourful tale of many episodes of villainy, folly and litigation. Several patents feature Thomas Edison, who strode his era like a colossus. He once said that genius was 1% inspiration and 99% perspiration. He is such a major figure that he is the only one whose life is briefly summarised further on in this introduction rather than opposite a drawing from one of his inventions. Ironically, most of his inventions were based on reading up on others' unsuccessful work and then getting his staff to experiment with numerous variants. This method was in fact very sensible and efficient. The phonograph was his only major invention not to be based on earlier work by others.

Side by side with the established world of Britain and the American East there was the exploration and settlement of the British Empire and of the American West. Britain's population grew from 20 to 41 million between the censuses of 1841 and 1901. The US's population grew from 17 to 76 million between the censuses of 1840 and 1900. Many of the inventors in this book either moved to the USA or, as native-born Americans, moved further west in obedience to Horace Greeley's famous 1851 editorial in his *New York Tribune* when he exhorted his readers to 'Go west, young man'—although he only meant Illinois, the western plains being considered a barren desert at the time. Britain, too, had its share of immigrant inventors, some from the USA, a fact that is not always recognised. What motivated these inventors was a variety of reasons, from a desire for wealth to making something which would help others. One thread brings together most if not all of them: they were obsessed with their ideas. Few people succeed in their professions unless they feel that way.

It was not until 1883 that a worldwide system of patenting was adopted. Those countries that signed the Paris Convention for the Protection of Industrial Property agreed to recognise the rights of those who had patented inventions in another Convention country for a limited period of 7 months, changed in 1902 to the current 12 months. Before then there were races to register patents in foreign patent offices by those who saw a potentially profitable patent filed in another country. Each country, while it could administer its own laws, was not to discriminate against foreigners in their applications, although in practice this was not always adhered to (especially in the USA).

Even before the Paris Convention patents were both contributing to technology and feeding off it. Patents were treated very differently in Europe and in the USA, although in both cases patents were supposed to be issued only for a new or improved product or technical process. In Europe patents were widely seen as a kind of protectionism, and free-traders bitterly opposed them as a restraint on trade. The great engineer Isambard Kingdom Brunel refused to take out patents since he felt that they were unfair monopolies, although his father Marc had been a prolific patentee. Journals such as the British *Economist* under its editor Walter Bagehot attacked patents, while the engineering press warmly supported reform, which to them meant making it cheaper and easier to secure patents for an idea for a limited period in a particular country. Charles Dickens also weighed in with his short story *Poor man's tale of a patent*, published in his magazine *Household Words*, where the hapless inventor had to wander London paying fees to such personages as the Deputy Chaff Wax. It was estimated that a patent for England and Wales alone would easily cost a skilled man's wages for a year. It was also necessary to be present during the procedure of applying for the patent, or else to appoint a representative to do such work, who became the actual applicant for the patent.

Another objection was a belief among British factory workers that innovation could cost them their jobs. Too early for this book, but the best known example of unrest for this reason, are the Luddites, who during 1811–16 destroyed textile machinery such as stocking frames. Textiles had been a very labour-intensive industry and the switch to factory production was virtually completed by the time Queen Victoria came to the throne, with the loss of many jobs, which is why there are no patents for textile machinery in this book. A later struggle was the destruction of threshing machines in 1830 in riots in the English countryside after a couple of bad harvests. Such disturbances have been dubbed by scholars 'collective bargaining by riot'.

However, some felt that there was insufficient support in Britain for innovation. Charles Babbage, who with his 'Difference engines' in the 1820s and 1830s devised (unpatented) forerunners of the computer, complained after the government stopped funding his work.

Propose to an Englishman any principle, or any instrument, however admirable, and you will observe that the whole effort of the English mind is directed to find a difficulty, or an impossibility in it. If you speak to him of a machine for peeling a potato, he will pronounce it impossible: if you peel a potato with it before his eyes, he will declare it useless, because it will not slice a pineapple.

Some of these difficulties were due to an aristocratic disdain for 'trade' and getting your hands dirty, although landowners were not averse to riches from renting out mineral rights if coal were found on their land. Consequently inadequate support was given to education (particularly at college or university level) in subjects like engineering or chemistry, as it was felt that such knowledge should be absorbed by working in a factory

environment. Meanwhile Germany and the United States were rapidly expanding educational provision in these subjects, the Germans mainly because of state intervention and the Americans because of demand. It is often felt that this negative attitude towards getting your hands dirty still persists today in Britain, allied with short-term goals in investment and profits. In spite of this the wealthy classes often did find new inventions interesting. Many newspapers and magazines, read largely by the educated and wealthy classes, covered technology and science at a level of illustrated detail that would today be considered astonishing. One of these was *Scientific American*, which paid much attention to inventions. This was perhaps not surprising as the owner, Alfred Ely Beach, ran a patent agent firm. He is to be found in this book for his unusual underground railway.

Prince Albert, husband and hence consort to Queen Victoria, was keenly interested in technology. The Great Exhibition of 1851, which publicised technology and which he enthusiastically backed, was probably a factor in bringing about a new Patents Act in 1852, which merged the three systems of England (and Wales), Scotland and Ireland, and cheapened and simplified the procedure. Elsewhere in Europe, France had a vigorous system from 1791. Unfortunately their drawings are small and grey and were not printed anyway (nor was the description) if the applicant did not pay the first year's renewal fees to keep the patent in force. Therefore this book does not properly reflect French invention. Germany had a small number of patents from Prussia, Bavaria, Saxony and the other states and although German unification was achieved in 1871 it was not until 1877 that a single German patent system was set up which, from the beginning, only accepted patents containing novel ideas. German applicants took to the patent system with great enthusiasm. By this time most other European countries had introduced patent laws, with Switzerland holding out until 1888, while The Netherlands tried not having patents from 1869 to 1910. The result was that the citizens of other countries were free to use Dutch inventors' ideas there, while no monopoly was possible for the Dutch in their own country.

The USA had a more positive view. Its Constitution in Article 1, Section 8 gave rights to the inventor for a limited period. Rights were assigned to the manufacturer or whoever hired the inventor and this information was recorded in the patent. There was relatively little opposition in the USA to patents, as they were considered to be a big help in encouraging innovation in a huge and relatively empty country (except for its original inhabitants) that had a constant labour shortage, and consequently high wages. Any ideas that would reduce the need for labour, and hence cut the cost of goods and services, and make American exports more competitive, were thought to be good.

This American enterprise caused concern among the more thoughtful, or perhaps chauvinistic, British press. Harold Evans, a British science writer, quotes an anonymous British commentator in about 1900, writing under the headline 'The American Invaders', as saying—

The average citizen wakes in the morning at the sound of an American alarm clock; rises from his New England sheets, and shaves with his New York soap, and Yankee safety razor. He pulls on a pair of Boston boots over his socks from West Carolina, fastens his Connecticut braces, slips his Waterbury watch into his pocket and sits down to breakfast . . . rising from his breakfast table, the citizen rushes out, catches an electric tram, made in New York, to Shepherds Bush, where he gets into the Yankee elevator. At his office of course everything is American. He sits on a Nebraskan swivel chair, before a Michigan roll top desk, writes his letters on a Syracuse typewriter, signing them with a New York fountain pen, and drying them with a blotting sheet from New England. The letter copies are put away in files manufactured in Grand Rapids.

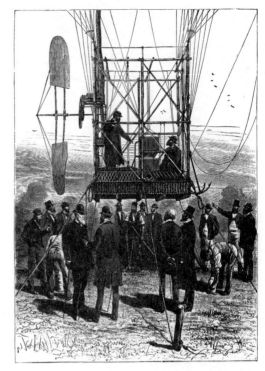

Slaves were in a strange position as befitted the South's 'peculiar institution'. This is illustrated by a true story. Oscar Stuart was a Mississippi planter who wanted a patent for a new cotton scraper plough by 'Ned'—the lack of any other name tells us much—who was one of his late wife's slaves. The application was made in Stuart's name. It was rejected by the Attorney General in a written opinion because Stuart was not the inventor and, as Ned was not a citizen, he was not allowed to assign his rights in an invention. The 1857 annual report states that there had been 'several' applications for patents by slaves in that year, which was apparently a new situation.

Those African-Americans who were free before Emancipation had a hard time securing patents. Henry Blair of Glenross, Maryland was responsible for corn planter patents granted in 1834 and 1836. He is described as a 'colored man' in a list of 1790–1847 American patents published in 1847. The first African-American patentee is thought to be Thomas Jennings, a New York City tailor whose patent from 1821 was for dry cleaning. He is said to have spent his earnings on buying his family out of slavery and in abolitionist activities. The Patent Office's 1900 annual report stated there were thought to have been 400 patents by 165 different 'colored' inventors, and gives some more details. This information almost certainly came from the researches of Henry Baker, an African-American assistant examiner, who sent circulars to patent attorneys asking if they were aware of any such patents. Baker collected references to 800 such patents, which he believed to be half of those actually existing. He is understood to have secretly coded patent applications so that they could be identified later.

Relatively few women were patentees although numbers greatly increased in late Victorian times. The first American patent for a woman inventor was that of Mary Kies of Killingly, Connecticut in 1809 with a patent for weaving straw with silk or thread.

However, two English patents, GB 401/1715 and GB 403/1716, the first for curing Indian corn and the second for making straw bonnets, were granted to Thomas Masters of Pennsylvania, variously planter and merchant, 'for the sole use and benefit of a new invention found out by Sybilla his wife'. The patents are indexed under his name alone.

The price of obtaining patents in the USA was low for US citizens, with the fees from 1836 being $30 for citizens but $300 for foreigners, unless they were British subjects, in which case the fees were $500. Foreign inventors who assigned their patents to US citizens still had to pay these higher fees. Canada, then a British colony, was so furious at being charged the $500 that the Canadian authorities only granted patents to those who had lived in Canada for at least a year. This provision was abolished in 1872 when a law leading to a single patent system for Canada was passed. No fees needed to be paid to keep an American patent in force. They lasted for 14 years until in 1861 the term was changed to 17 years, when the discriminatory fees ended.

There had been a new Patent Act in 1836, with the first under the new system issued to a senator from Maine, John Ruggles. He was an inventor and attorney as well as a politician, and his patent for a traction wheel was presumably pushed to the beginning of the queue as his reward for urging reform. All patent applications were now checked by examiners for novelty before being granted protection. An interesting feature of the American system was that those applying for patents were required to submit a miniature model of the invention, many of which still survive (but which are scattered in various collections). 'No model' on the American drawings in this book means that the applicant did not voluntarily send one in when compulsion ceased in 1880. Texas after independence in 1836 from Mexico had its own patent system until it joined the Union in 1846, while the Confederate States of America also had their own Patent Office based in Richmond, Virginia. Sadly their papers were destroyed by fire at the end of the Civil War.

Mark Twain is a good example of the American public's interest in patents. In his *A Connecticut Yankee in King Arthur's court* (1889) he has his hero set up a Patent Office when he travels back in time. His hero also said, 'A country without a patent office and good patent laws was just a crab, and couldn't travel any way but sideways and backwards'. Twain himself under his real name of Samuel Clemens had three patents: US 121992 in 1871, for straps for garments; US 140245 in 1873, for a scrap-book; and US 324535 in 1885, for a game based on historical dates. It was pointed out that his scrap-book sold very well for a book that had no words at all in it.

It is appropriate here to give a brief account of Thomas Edison, whose story would otherwise have to be repeated for several of the inventions described in this book. He was born in Milan, Ohio in 1847, son of a rooftile maker who had fled his native Canada in 1837 after taking part in an unsuccessful rebellion. Edison received little formal education, although his mother paid much attention to teaching him. In 1862 he saved a young boy from being hit by an oncoming train, and in gratitude the father, a telegraph operator, taught him Morse Code, essential for anyone working in that job. Many inventors during the Victorian period began their scientific schooling as telegraph operators, in much the same way that many electronics engineers in the late 20th century began as radar operators. For years Edison worked at a variety of places across the Midwest as a telegraph operator: a variety, because his interest in unauthorised experimenting with the equipment rarely met with favour. Meanwhile he read journals and handbooks in local public libraries and gradually increased his knowledge both of science and technology and of people of influence. In 1868 he obtained a patent, US 90646, for a vote-counting machine, the first of his 1,093 American patents. It did not sell because it removed the ability to filibuster, that is, to delay orally taken votes, as was patiently explained to him by a politician. He resolved to make inventions that would sell to industry or to ordinary people. At the age of 22, Edison moved to New York City, where he perfected a telegraph printer used by the New York financial community of the type later known as a 'stock ticker'. It caused great interest. Some brokers decided to buy Edison's patents on it. How much did he want, they asked. He stammered, thought of asking for $3,000, then said, 'Suppose you make me an offer'. They gave him a cheque for $40,000. It was equivalent to several million dollars today. Naively Edison kept the money at home at first, not realising that he could leave the money in the same bank that had honoured the cheque.

From 1869 Edison worked full-time as an inventor-entrepreneur. He began to gather together men to help him, specialists in a number of trades so that he would not have to make everything himself, or try out endless variations in a device, and could devote more time to thinking. His closest associate was probably the English immigrant Charles Batchelor, originally a textile mechanic. In March 1876 he set up at Menlo Park, New Jersey, which gradually expanded as workshops and storerooms covered the site. This was the first comprehensive industrial laboratory, and also included an extensive library, as Edison believed in reading what was available on a subject before trying to invent something. Edison, who was dubbed the 'Wizard of Menlo Park', was responsible for a stream of inventions covering telegraphy, telephones, electric lights, batteries, phonographs, cement, mining and so on. He intended to turn out a minor invention every 10 days and a 'big thing' every 6 months or so. Edison was heavily involved in patent litigation so that aspect too was not forgotten by him. When he died in Orange, New Jersey in 1931, lights dimmed round the world in tribute to him. He once said of invention, 'You've got to make the damn thing work . . . I failed my way to success'. His original laboratory has been reconstructed at the Henry Ford Museum and Greenfield Village in Dearborn, Michigan.

It is a myth that Commissioner Duell of the US Patent Office ever said that everything that could be invented had been invented. The various annual reports from the late 1890s which are supposed to have this statement do not include it. It is true that in the 1843 report Commissioner Ellsworth said, 'The advancement of the arts, from year to year, taxes our credulity and seems to presage the arrival of that period when human improvements must end'. Since then there have been 6 million American patents. *Scientific American* did say in its 2 January 1902 issue, 'That the automobile has reached the limit of its development is suggested by the fact that during the last year no improvements of a radical nature have been introduced'.

Japan is not mentioned elsewhere in this book but they too became involved with patents in the 19th century. This story is told in Kenneth Dobyns' *The Patent Office pony*. In 1886 the Japanese government sent Korekiyo Takahashi, who was later to be their first Commissioner of Patents, to Washington, DC to study how the American patent system worked. Takahashi had lived in the USA as a boy and spoke fluent English. He was provided with all the official literature and officials spent much time with him answering questions. One day an examiner asked if he in turn could ask a question, 'I would like to know why it is that the people of Japan desire to have a patent system'. The answer was—

I will tell you, then. You know that it is only since Commodore Perry, in 1854, opened the ports of Japan to foreign commerce that the Japanese have been trying to become a great nation, like other nations of the earth, and we have looked about us to see what nations are the greatest, so that we could be like them; and we said, 'There is the United States, not much more than a hundred years old, and America was discovered by Columbus yet four hundred years ago'; and we said, 'What is it that makes the United States such a great nation?' and we investigated and we found that it was patents, and we will have patents.

The rest, as they say, is history.

The patent system: an explanation of the finer points, plus some statistics

This section explains more details of the patent system. Until the Paris Convention of 1883 there was no proper system for patent owners in their own country to apply for patents abroad. This book gives the address details from the actual patents and tries to identify, and state, the patent numbers for both the USA and the UK plus those of any other country from which the inventor came, or where it was first patented. The drawing shown is normally from the first stated patent. The country codes quoted for each patent are not original and are added from modern, standardised usage, hence DE for Germany, FR for France, GB for Britain and US for the USA.

The 1852 Patents Act united the three previously separate patent systems of England (and Wales), Scotland and Ireland. The new Patent Office was situated in London and had simpler and cheaper procedures than the previous systems. It merely registered patents, and did not actually check to see if the ideas were new, until 1905. Any disputes were left to the courts. It cost £25 to obtain a patent but this was changed to only £6 by new legislation in 1883, which resulted in a trebling of applications. Renewal fees had to be paid at intervals to keep the patents in force. If all fees were paid the patent lasted 14 years from the application date.

The numeration of British patents was as follows. The English patents from 1617 to the 1852 Act were officially printed, and numbered, for the first time in a sequence from 1 to 14,359. Fresh sequences within each year were then used from October 1852 until the end of 1915 so that it became necessary to give the year in the format GB 2000/1867 to indicate that British patent number 2000 of the year 1867 was meant. The Scottish patents were not numbered or printed and still reside in Edinburgh while the Irish patents were destroyed in a fire in 1922. From 1916 all new patents were numbered in a sequence beginning with 100,001.

A patent reform in 1883, substantially lowering the cost of obtaining patents, meant that the number of patent applications climbed from several thousand a year to over 20,000. However, a change in the law meant that while previously applications which were 'abandoned' were still published, these now ceased to be published, but were still indexed in the annual name indexes until 1915. Hence we are aware of many applications that did not actually become patents. American patent law did not provide such useful (if misleading) information. One problem with the English (from 1852 British) patents is that until 1875 the drawings were on large sheets which opened out, sometimes to the size of a square metre.

The first American patents were not printed or numbered. They were destroyed in a disastrous fire in 1836, though some were recovered as copies in the following decades by appeals to inventors and others. Later that year it was decided to number the patents in a sequence beginning with #1 which continues to the present day, with the 6 million mark having recently been passed. Printing of the patents did not regularly occur until the 1870s. An attractive feature is the signatures on the drawings by inventors, attorneys and witnesses, as shown in this book. American patent drawings are often minor works of art and tend to be more attractive than the British examples.

American patents give details of 'assignors', which are those people or companies to whom the rights in the patent are partially, or totally, assigned. This could be to an employer or to a business backer. The inventor is always named. All such details are supplied in this book in the initial details for each invention above the patent drawings. British patents do not give the inventor during this period, but rather that of the applicant who personally turned up at the office in London. This could be a friend, business backer or purchaser of the rights. Many British patents originally stated that the application was on behalf of an un-named 'foreigner residing abroad' but later on the actual names tended to be given as well. The British patent usually gives the occupation of the applicant and this is given in most of these accounts.

'Reissues' are an American speciality and mean that the entire patent specification has been reprinted with corrections. The USA also has design patents, which are for the appearance of something and not how they work. (They do not appear in this book.) The largest such design is probably D11023 by Auguste Bartholdi in 1879 for the Statue of Liberty. In most other countries they are regarded just as designs and are never called 'patents'. The term 'utility patents' is often used in the USA to identify the kind of patents featured in this book.

Those who are interested in statistics will find much in the annual reports of the patent offices. The American reports were outspoken in their comments on the lack of space in their offices and on patent examiners being lured by higher pay to private industry (some things do not change). Perhaps the fact that the heads of the American office were political appointees, unlike their British counterparts, gave them more freedom to comment. Unlike the USA, Britain gave little statistical information on where the inventors came from until 1884. An exception is a (unique) survey of applications made during October 1852 to December 1853 which showed that out of 4,256 applications 1,833 were from London, 542 from Lancashire and 256 from Yorkshire. The very high London figure given above can be accounted for in part by the need for someone (not necessarily the inventor) to apply personally for patents, which in many cases must have meant inventors giving temporary London addresses.

Figures from the survey above and from the annual reports show the following numbers of foreign applications made through the British system.

	USA	Germany	France
Oct. 1852–Dec. 1853	57	13	263
1884	1,181	890	788
1901	3,246	2,844	948

In 1884 there were 17,110 applications in all and in 1901 there were 26,777. These may sound like high figures, but many were never granted due to a failure to send in the complete patent specification. It is obvious from the table how the USA and Germany leapt ahead while France made mediocre progress by comparison. From 1894 to 1965 Britain's Patent Office annual report gave the percentage of women inventors among all applicants. The highest percentage ever achieved was 2.4% in 1898. They listed the most popular topics among women applicants. These were usually clothing followed by cycling or cooking. Cycling liberated women and many inventions were for methods of preventing clothing from getting caught in the mechanism. The Married Women's Property Act in 1882 had already made it clear that women and not their husbands were entitled to rights from their own inventions.

The USA has collected statistics on patents from residents of the states or territories for many years, and from 1884 this included applications from abroad. These show the following figures:

	Great Britain	Germany	Canada	France
1884	592	298	284	138
1901	1,066	1,045	376	306

In 1884 there were 24,104 patents, of which only 1,549 went to foreigners. By 1901 the total number had only gone up to 27,202, of which 3,402 went to foreigners. The USA was clearly becoming a more attractive market to foreign traders.

The figures on the American states or territories also give the ratio of inventions in the population. This is of great interest in showing which areas were most intensively inventing (and which the least). In 1884 the leading American states were New York, with 3,924; Massachusetts, 1,917; and Pennsylvania, 1,863. The most active in population ratio were Connecticut, 1 to 694; the District of Columbia, 1 to 858; and Rhode Island, 1 to 909. The least active were North Carolina, 1 to 24,133; New Mexico, 1 to 19,927; and Alabama, 1 to 18,297. In 1901 the leading American states were New York, with 4,098; Pennsylvania, 2,837; and Illinois, 2,430. The most active were Connecticut, 1 to 1,198; the District of Columbia, 1 to 1,296; and Massachusetts, 1 to 1,472. The least active were Alaska, 1 to 31,796; South Carolina, 1 to 28, 517; and Alabama, 1 to 22,300. It is interesting that the most active states were less prominent than in 1884. By 1893 the number of patents had passed the 500,000 mark, and this rose to 1 million by 1911.

ACKNOWLEDGEMENTS

My grateful thanks to my patient editor, Anthony Warshaw; the designer, Bob Elliott; and above all to the inventors and their patents without which this book would not have been possible.

FIGURE 2.

FIGURE 1.

Aerial locomotion by balloons

Clara Louisa Wells is only known from her patent applications and will serve as an example of the Victorian eccentric. She was presumably British since she entrusted some of her applications to the care of the local British consul, and only used the British patent system (but she did use some Americanisms, and lived in Boston). Otherwise she lived on the Mediterranean shores. You can picture her as one of those highly determined women who, although living in voluntary exile from her country, continued to uphold in-bred traditions and standards while serenely marching through street markets filled with an excitable populace. Her first application was GB 13125/1887, 'Improvements in obtaining water from sea-water for supplying towns and for other purposes'. Declaring herself to be a spinster, the only address information she gave was that correspondence was to be sent care of Messrs. W. J. Turner & Co. of Naples, Italy. Salt water is boiled so that fresh water condenses and is then pumped into high towers. Pipes or canals would then channel the water to those places where it was needed. The cost of condensing and pumping the water was not discussed.

Next was the patent shown here. Unfortunately only one of four deliciously strange pages of drawings can be shown. Her address here was 'residing at Pompeii, Italy, to be addressed to the care of the English Consul, Mr Frederick Turner, No. 4, Monte di Dio, Naples, Italy, of no calling or profession'. The idea was that balloons should be attached to cables which connected with iron tubes running along the ground. Each balloon would preferably consist of a number of smaller balloons, each in the shape of a bird, with a 'conductor' seated in the 'chief' balloon. Two maps show how such a network could be adapted (with overhead cables) for the Bay of Naples, or the North Atlantic. 'My invention consists in the establishment of regular lines, for aerial locomotion, with stations, for the entrance and exit of passengers. Or for the placing and removal of luggage, with a similar system to that used on the funicular railroads ....'

Figure 11 shows a 'private car with luxurious or comfortable style', Figure 12 a 'balloon-station' in the middle of an ocean, and Figures 13 and 14 a mountain line using gravity to let the balloons descend (although lighter than air, balloons cannot benefit from gravity). Figure 15 shows a design for exploring the upper atmosphere, and Figures 16 and 17 depict a safety system. Many details were worked out in her six pages of description such as illuminating the lines at night and training birds 'to aid the balloon', which with eagles might help if the wind were against you. Clara Wells's remaining patent applications were two from Boston, Massachusetts in 1893 and 1894 (for ship-railways and distributing distilled water), both abandoned before publication; GB 13715/1896, again on aerial locomotion, when she was in Toulon, France; GB 12836/1897 on diverting molten lava into reservoirs for onward shipping; and GB 15679/1898, from Bordighera, Liguria, Italy. This was entitled 'Secure modes of exploring the cold and hot regions of the Earth by means of centers of elevation and depression, with reference to volcanic, aqueous, and meteorological forces, and of routes suspended with or without balloons'. A final application in 1899 from Bordighera was abandoned: it was about living upon and crossing water.

A.D. 1890. Oct. 7. N.º 15,850.
WELLS' Complete Specification.

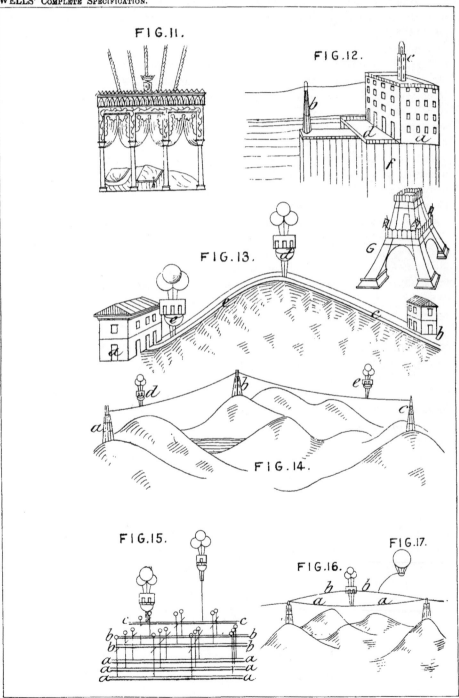

FIG.11.

FIG.12.

FIG.13.

FIG.14.

FIG.15.

FIG.16.

FIG.17.

The alternating current induction motor

Nikola Tesla's life sounds like something out of fiction. 'The wild man of electronics' was one of the most ingenious inventors ever, but he did have his eccentricities: he cleaned his cutlery with multiples of three napkins, feared women with pearl earrings, and calculated the cubic contents of his plate at dinner parties. He was also impractical with money, being more interested in patenting than in developing inventions and then making money out of them. Tesla was born in 1856 in what is now Croatia, son of a Serb Orthodox priest. He was trained as an engineer, and emigrated to the USA in 1884. Robbed on the boat, he landed with just 4 cents, only when walking up Broadway to come across some men trying to fix an electric motor, who paid him $20 to finish the job. He was one of the few people to have a unit of measurement (the tesla, a unit of magnetic flux density) named after him.

Tesla had a photographic memory, and was able to work out ideas in his head, down to testing them and correcting for faults before he built anything. His main achievement was in alternating current (AC), the electricity system we use today. This was known as an alternative to direct current (DC), which could only deliver low voltages for short distances, but the lack of a motor restricted its use. Tesla worked out that two AC sources, out of phase, could cause a rotating magnetic field and hence make an AC motor possible. The drawing shown is from one of seven patents applied for as a single application which the Patent Office split up, and which made Tesla's name in electrical circles. He was hired by DC advocate Thomas Edison, but they soon split, and a bitter quarrel began, with Edison claiming that AC was dangerous. In 1888 Tesla sold his patents on AC to George Westinghouse (for $1 million in cash plus royalties) who built the first power station on his principles at Niagara Falls. Edison meanwhile unwittingly popularised the (already invented) electric chair which operated by AC by demonstrating it on animals, saying that the unfortunate victims were being 'Westinghoused'.

In 1900 Tesla set up a 60 m high tower in Denver that shot huge bolts of lightning into the sky, which was meant to signal to other worlds. Residents angry at the noise and flashes (and blackouts) insisted that he move, so he did—next to an asylum for the deaf and dumb—and insisted that he had received replies before he stopped the experiment. He also performed on stage, wreathed with electricity, in what is still considered a baffling performance. Since few of his ideas led to working models his financial backers eventually gave up on him. Tesla had many other ideas such as transmitting energy without wires; death rays; creating an artificial aurora to light the world at night; and even an idea for transmitting pictures and text round the world in minutes using special terminals. In 1912 he was jointly offered a Nobel Prize with Edison but he refused it, so it was given to Nils Gustav Dalen instead. Tesla's last patents in 1928 were for vertical takeoff and landing aircraft. In his later years he was a recluse in the New Yorker Hotel in New York City, living with his beloved pigeons, and dependent on a small pension from the Yugoslav government. He died there in 1943, and FBI agents moved in to seize his papers. A few months later the Supreme Court declared that Marconi's radio patents were anticipated by Tesla's US 645576 and 649621.

Nikola Tesla, 'from Smiljan Lika, border country of Austria-Hungary', New York City, New York
Filed 12 October 1887 and published as US 381968

N. TESLA.

ELECTRO MAGNETIC MOTOR.

No. 381,968.   Patented May 1, 1888.

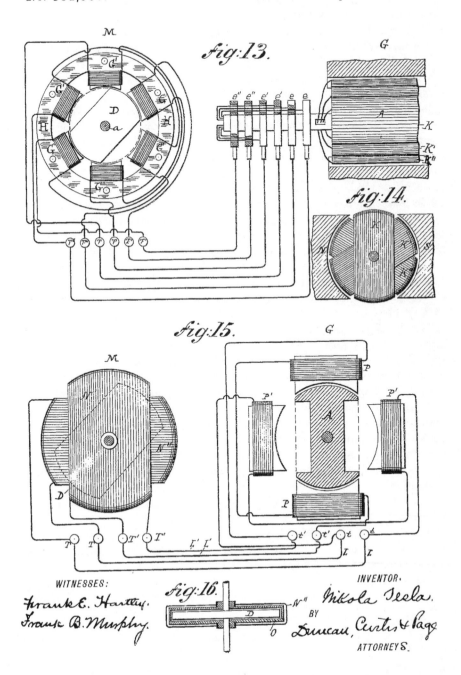

Fig:13.

Fig:14.

Fig:15.

Fig:16.

WITNESSES:
Frank E. Hartley.
Frank B. Murphy.

INVENTOR.
Nikola Tesla.
BY
Duncan, Curtis & Page
ATTORNEYS.

Apparatus for producing stage illusions

The Maskelyne family produced three generations of magicians. John Nevil Maskelyne Sr was born in Cheltenham, Gloucestershire in 1839 and worked as a watchmaker before he began practising conjuring professionally. The delicate work needed as a watchmaker is said to have given him the necessary sleight of hand. He first made his name when in 1865 he and his partner George Cooke exposed an American spiritualist act called the 'Davenport Brothers' Cabinet and Dark Séance'. He did this by standing up at the end of a performance and denouncing them as frauds, and promising to duplicate what they had done within 1 month. He campaigned against fraud all his life and billed Cooke and himself as 'Royal illusionists and anti-Spiritualists'. They toured for years with an act featuring box tricks (where people instantly changed places), juggling, escape work and (apparent) levitation.

In 1873 they stopped touring and moved to the Egyptian Hall on Piccadilly, London. Their work was popular and highly influential with younger magicians, and also with Georges Méliès, who used ideas in his own stage work and later as one of the first film-makers. Maskelyne Sr, or his son John Nevil Maskelyne Jr, with whom he is often confused, joined with David Devant, the greatest illusionist of his day (and first President of the Magic Circle) at the newly purchased St George's Hall from 1904. During his career Maskelyne Sr patented dozens of inventions. They included (with his son) GB 11424/1889, which allowed the shift key to be moved with the foot as well as with the hand, and which was the model for the first British-produced typewriter manufactured by his own company. It was a 'grasshopper' mechanism where the typebars were resting on an inkpad and 'hopped' up to print a letter. There were also several patents for the taking of money at shop tills; coin-freed doors for water closets; GB 1148/1880 for checking tickets; the 'Mutagraph' film projector with GB 11639/1896; and applications for stage illusions.

The idea of patenting a magic trick is paradoxical. An illusion is meant to baffle the audience, whereas a patent, although meant to prevent others from imitating the idea, reveals in the specification how the idea works. Many magicians think it very wrong to explain illusions. Maskelyne Sr's attempts were not granted protection as he did not send in the full specification, although a shorter 'provisional' application survives as GB 1804/1875 on an automaton. The illustration opposite is by his son, who was less well known. He and his collaborator Charles Morritt are described as 'illusionists' in the patent. The performer appears to be secured by hands and feet projecting beyond a screen while playing musical instruments and so on. The stout columns (B) were hollow and allowed confederates to project their limbs through the holes (D). The last generation was Jasper Maskelyne, son of Maskelyne Jr, who first appeared in acts from the age of 9 as a planted 'boy from the audience' for a famous trick by Devant with an egg. He joined the camouflage unit of the Royal Engineers in World War II and after producing an illusion of a German warship on the Thames was sent to Egypt, where men and materials were scarce, so that he could conceal and deceive. These included making the Suez Canal and the port of Alexandria disappear nightly so as to foil bombers.

John Nevil Maskelyne Jr and Charles Morritt, Egyptian Hall, London, England
Filed 12 May 1892 and published as GB 9033/1892

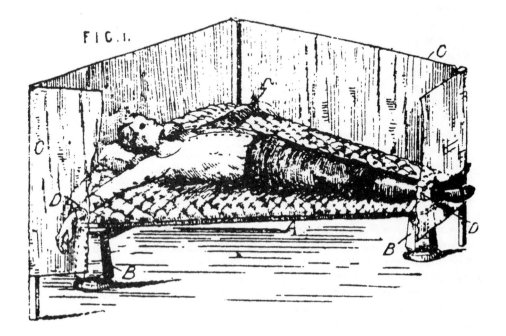

FIG. I.

Apparatus for treating diseases

Hercules Sanche had a total of four patents granted to him in 1897. The Patent Office took 10 years before accepting this patent. His other three give Detroit, Michigan as his address. All four patents were assigned to the Animarium Company with US 587612 involving 'thermal results', 588091 'therapeutic uses' and 588483 'treating disease'. All involved highly impressive equipment by this notorious 'quack', much of which is still available for purchase (but second-hand only). An extensive quote from this patent states his philosophy. 'My observation and experience justify the belief that most diseases, and especially those of a nervous character, are due to a disturbance of the electrical equilibrium of the body . . . the habits of civilised life—i.e., the wearing of shoes and clothing of non-conducting material and the insulation from the earth by dry floors and feather beds—prevent the body from partaking freely of the electrical equilibrium of the earth, and a preponderance of an electric tension of either a positive or negative character in the body produces by stimulation or suppression of chemico-vital function the abnormal condition of things the symptoms of which we call "disease". Hogs in the field, turtles, alligators, and the lower animals that lie in the mud and readily partake of or assimilate themselves to the electrical conditions of the earth are notoriously free from disease and nervousness. Man, the feathered tribe, and higher animals who are covered with a non-conducting coat and are more or less insulated from the earth are subject to these difficulties in marked contrast.'

Sanche's invention was meant to deal with this problem by artificially producing either a positive or a negative condition in the body with a small conductor linked to a very hot or very cold source. The illustration shows how it was used. As the mind seems to play a big role in fighting illness it is quite possible that users genuinely felt better. Many of Sanche's ideas were variations on the same theme. His earlier Electropoise was very popular. The device was placed in a bowl of water and wires led from it to little metal cylinders on the body and by 'Diaduction' oxygen was drawn into the bloodstream. The cylinders were sealed shut to protect the secret ingredients, which in this case was literally nothing at all. It cost $10. Later it was altered to the Oxydonor and sold for $35, reflecting the fact that the cylinder now contained carbon instead of just air. Relevant patents appear to be US 430974 of 1890 and US 476080 of 1892. Many surviving devices show signs of attempts to open the cylinders by their owners. It was available by mail order from Sears Roebuck. The actual production cost was $1.50. Supporters of 'Diaduction' set up the Fraternity of Duxanimae. In this way, Sanche solicited donations for his cause, hence making a contribution to modern marketing. In 1914 there was the first American court case leading to a conviction for sending quack devices through the mail. The perpetrator received a term of 18 months. Literature associated with such products was also stopped. In 1915 Sanche's company was denied access to the mail system. Sanche moved his company repeatedly to avoid conviction, first to two places in Chicago, then to Detroit and Montreal, where he was continuing to sell as late as 1946. Sanche was last sighted in 1952 running the Hydrotonic Company in Florida.

Hercules Sanche, New Orleans, Louisiana for the Animarium Company, New York City, New York
Filed 27 October 1887 and published as US 587237

(No Model.)   3 Sheets—Sheet 3.

H. SANCHE.
APPARATUS FOR TREATING DISEASES.

No. 587,237.   Patented July 27, 1897.

Fig. 4.

Witnesses: Inventor.
                                                  Hercules Sanche.
                                            By James L. Norris.
                                                        Atty.

Aspirin

Aspirin goes back to the Greek physician, Hippocrates, who in the fifth century BC used a bitter powder from willow bark to treat aches and pains. The substance was salicylic acid. During the 19th century sodium salicylate was used widely as a treatment. What is happening, as only proven in the 1970s by British scientist John Vane, who received a Nobel Prize, is that when pain occurs prostaglandins are produced which signal pain to the brain. Aspirin prevents the production of prostaglandins and, in effect, turns down the volume of pain experienced. Charles Gerhardt, a French chemist, synthesised what is now aspirin in 1853 but he did not think that it was important. Johann Kraut made a better formulation in 1869. Bayer was a fast expanding chemical company in the 1890s. Its pharmaceutical laboratory was run by Arthur Eichengrün, with Felix Hoffman as one of his chemists. Eichengrün wanted a version of salicylic acid with fewer side effects. Hoffman had the same motive as his father was crippled with chronic arthritis, and the son was begged to devise a way to make salicylic acid safer, as the sodium salicylic acid that he was taking was eating away at his stomach.

Hoffman modified Kraut's work, which he cited in the one-page patent shown, to make acetylsalicylic acid. What happens is that the acetyl group is added to shield the acidic effect. The new product was dubbed Aspirin after the German *Acetylirte Spirsäure*, acetylated spiraeic acid, plus the common chemical suffix '-in'. For a year the company ignored the compound, believing that it would endanger the heart (it was normal at the time to take massive doses of salicylic acid, and people's hearts would race). Bayer was more interested in selling another drug—heroin—a drug thought to have few side effects, which brought in massive repeat orders. Eichengrün insisted on trying the new drug on patients and found it was a great improvement on salicylic acid. Eventually the company executive who had blocked the new drug, Heinrich Dreser, wrote a glowing scientific paper, while omitting to mention his two chemists.

When they went into production sales quickly soared. This was despite the lack of a patent in Germany where it was not considered new. Dreser received royalties on it, and eventually died rich, as it was a product coming from the laboratory under his control but neither chemist received royalties as their contracts specified that patented products had to be involved. Eichengrün felt that his contribution had been neglected and (he was Jewish) was lucky in spending only 14 months in a concentration camp, only to die in 1949, the same month that he made a formal claim to aspirin's discovery. With such a lucrative product, Bayer made great efforts in foreign markets, particularly in the USA (despite contraband aspirin flooding in from Canada). Bayer Aspirin is still the best selling brand in the USA. The British patent was lost in 1905 in a court case because of Kraut's work. American prices were 10 times the European prices until the American patent expired. The word 'aspirin' was registered as a trade mark but (in a tangled history with so much money at stake) rights were lost because of World War I. Neither the UK nor the USA now permit Aspirin to be used as a trade mark as it is a 'generic' word, like a noun, but it does survive in many other countries including Germany. Usage continues to be high, with the latest medical advice being that patients with heart problems should take one every day and it is now proposed as a help to those with cancer.

Felix Hoffman, Elberfeld, Germany for Farbenfabriken of Elberfeld Company, New York
Filed 1 August 1898 in the USA and published as US 644077 and GB 27088/1898

UNITED STATES PATENT OFFICE.

FELIX HOFFMANN, OF ELBERFELD, GERMANY, ASSIGNOR TO THE FARBEN-
FABRIKEN OF ELBERFELD COMPANY, OF NEW YORK.

ACETYL SALICYLIC ACID.

SPECIFICATION forming part of Letters Patent No. 644,077, dated February 27, 1900.

Application filed August 1, 1898. Serial No. 687,385. (Specimens.)

To all whom it may concern:

Be it known that I, FELIX HOFFMANN, doctor of philosophy, chemist, (assignor to the FARBENFABRIKEN OF ELBERFELD COMPANY, of New York,) residing at Elberfeld, Germany, have invented a new and useful Improvement in the Manufacture or Production of Acetyl Salicylic Acid; and I hereby declare the following to be a clear and exact description of my invention.

In the *Annalen der Chemie und Pharmacie*, Vol. 150, pages 11 and 12, Kraut has described that he obtained by the action of acetyl chlorid on salicylic acid a body which he thought to be acetyl salicylic acid. I have now found that on heating salicylic acid with acetic anhydride a body is obtained the properties of which are perfectly different from those of the body described by Kraut. According to my researches the body obtained by means of my new process is undoubtedly the real acetyl salicylic acid

$$C_6H_4 \begin{cases} OCO.CH_3 \\ COOH. \end{cases}$$

Therefore the compound described by Kraut cannot be the real acetyl salicylic acid, but is another compound. In the following I point out specifically the principal differences between my new compound and the body described by Kraut.

If the Kraut product is boiled even for a long while with water, (according to Kraut's statement,) acetic acid is not produced, while my new body when boiled with water is readily split up, acetic and salicylic acid being produced. The watery solution of the Kraut body shows the same behavior on the addition of a small quantity of ferric chlorid as a watery solution of salicylic acid when mixed with a small quantity of ferric chlorid—that is to say, it assumes a violet color. On the contrary, a watery solution of my new body when mixed with ferric chlorid does not assume a violet color. If a melted test portion of the Kraut body is allowed to cool, it begins to solidify (according to Kraut's statement) at from 118° to 118.5° centigrade, while a melted test portion of my product solidifies at about 70° centigrade. The melting-points of the two compounds cannot be compared, be-

cause Kraut does not give the melting-point of his compound. It follows from these details that the two compounds are absolutely different.

In producing my new compound I can proceed as follows, (without limiting myself to the particulars given:) A mixture prepared from fifty parts of salicylic acid and seventy-five parts of acetic anhydride is heated for about two hours at about 150° centigrade in a vessel provided with a reflux condenser. Thus a clear liquid is obtained, from which on cooling a crystalline mass is separated, which is the acetyl salicylic acid. It is freed from the acetic anhydride by pressing and then recrystallized from dry chloroform. The acid is thus obtained in the shape of glittering white needles melting at about 135° centigrade, which are easily soluble in benzene, alcohol, glacial acetic acid, and chloroform, but difficultly soluble in cold water. It has the formula

$$C_6H_4 \begin{cases} OCOCH_3 \\ COOH \end{cases}$$

and exhibits therapeutical properties.

Having now described my invention and in what manner the same is to be performed, what I claim as new, and desire to secure by Letters Patent, is—

As a new article of manufacture the acetyl salicylic acid having the formula:

$$C_6H_4 \begin{cases} O.COCH_3 \\ COOH \end{cases}$$

being when crystallized from dry chloroform in the shape of white glittering needles, easily soluble in benzene, alcohol and glacial acetic acid, difficultly soluble in cold water, being split by hot water into acetic acid and salicylic acid, melting at about 135° centigrade, substantially as hereinbefore described.

In testimony whereof I have signed my name in the presence of two subscribing witnesses.

FELIX HOFFMANN.

Witnesses:
R. E. JAHN,
OTTO KÖNIG.

The automatic machine gun

Hiram Stevens Maxim was born in 1840 near Sangerville, Maine, son of a farmer, who at times was also a woodturner and millwright. His father was interested in ideas for automatic guns and flying machines. Maxim had little education, and after a variety of jobs settled down as a mechanic for his uncle in Fitchburg, Massachusetts. His first patent was US 57354 in 1866 for haircurling irons. In 1870 he moved to New York City and began working in the fields of gas lighting and engines. In 1878 he became chief engineer of the United States Electric Lighting Company, a rival to Thomas Edison. He invented a way of evening out the layer of carbon on light bulb filaments by 'flashing' them in a hydrocarbon atmosphere, an important concept, but he lost the rights to any patents.

In 1881 his company sent him to Paris, France to an exhibition. Someone said to him, 'If you wanted to make a lot of money invent something that will enable these Europeans to cut each other's throats with greater facility'. He began to think of an improved machine gun. There had been several attempts to enable automatic fire such as Richard Jordan Gatling with his US 36836 in 1862 and the later French Mitrailleuse and the Swedish Nordenfeldt gun. All these were handcranked guns with multiple barrels and ammunition stored internally. Maxim stayed on in France and then moved to England in 1883 and designed in Hatton Garden, London the first automatic machine gun. It was the first gun to use the recoil of the barrel to eject spent cartridges and then to load fresh ammunition. It was water-cooled and was fed by belts of ammunition. The American War and Navy departments were not interested, but the British Army adopted it in 1889, followed the next year by several European armies. Its first use in battle was by the British Army in what is now Zimbabwe in the Matabele War of 1893.

A factory was set up in Erith, Kent and the new Maxim Machine Gun Company was merged in 1888 with Nordenfeldt and then with Vickers in 1896. In World War I both sides used what to all intents and purposes were similar models of his machine gun, hence fulfilling his friend's suggestion. At the suggestion of Lord Wolseley, who was the original of Gilbert and Sullivan's 'modern major-general', he invented the first smokeless cartridges with GB 16213/1888. This meant that choking smoke was no longer created by firing, so that the gunners could see their targets. Wolseley also suggested that Maxim adapt the machine gun for different purposes.

Between 1889 and 1894, saying that 'if a domestic goose can fly, so can a man', Maxim built a steam-driven aircraft, which at its trial at Bexley, Kent actually took off for a second before crashing. It was far too heavy and in any case no provision had been made for controlling flight. Maxim predicted, correctly, that an internal combustion engine was needed for flight but did not attempt to build one. His estranged son called him a cruel eccentric, but Maxim called himself a 'chronic inventor'. He was vain, jealous of Edison and his own brother Hudson (another inventor), and hated lawyers and labour leaders. He was also ingenious and versatile, even inventing a bronchitis inhaler after suffering a severe attack, and charming in person. Maxim became a British subject in 1900, was knighted in 1901, and died in Streatham, Surrey in 1916 with over 100 patents to his name.

(No Model.)

H. S. MAXIM.
MACHINE GUN.

No. 317,161.

Patented May 5, 1885.

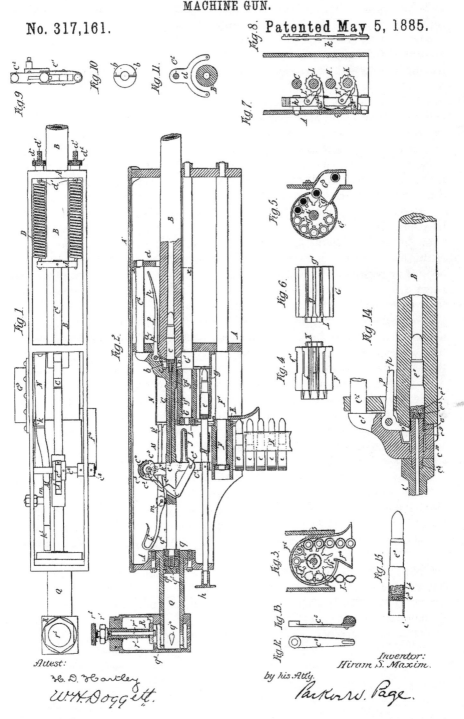

Attest:
H. D. Hartley
W. H. Doggett

Inventor:
Hiram S. Maxim.
by his Atty.
Parker W. Page.

The automatic telephone exchange

Initially telephones were designed so that direct connections were made between each pair. This obviously could not work for long as numbers built up, so in 1878 telephone exchanges began to appear in Connecticut. The user cranked a lever to alert and then speak to the operator, who would then either connect the call to another exchange or connect the user to another local telephone by plugging in jacks. The idea of automatic exchanges had been thought of earlier, as with the Connolly-McTighe apparatus patented in 1879 with US 221458, but they did not work properly. Almon Strowger was born in 1839 near Rochester, New York. He moved west, teaching and farming, until he saved enough money to learn embalming. He then purchased a funeral home in Topeka, Kansas in 1882. Strowger had a reputation for paranoia which was aided by his surprise when, on the death of a close friend, the family asked a rival firm to carry out the funeral. He was convinced that the operator was listening in on the call. According to legend she was either the wife or the daughter of his competitor. Nevertheless business was good and he sold out and purchased another business in the nearby booming cattle town of Kansas City, Missouri.

Strowger was determined to be a successful undertaker but he was convinced that the telephone company was trying to stop him. Kansas City *Star* reporter Joseph Popper wrote, 'In Topeka . . . he became convinced that the local telephone operators were conspiring to destroy him. . . . After his move to Kansas City, Strowger's torment seemed to become more intense. He was a frequent and unwelcome visitor at the phone company's office, shouting that his phone wasn't working and that the switchboard operators were falsely giving his customers a busy signal.'

He set out to invent a 'a girl-less, cuss-less switching device'. He was not mechanical so a jeweller was employed to make the model, but the jeweller was hardly more skilled than he was so Strowger spent much time correcting his work. The facing page shows the basic principle of what became known as the 'step by step' exchange. The insulated drum (A) was perforated with holes out of which came wires, each leading to a telephone. Electrically powered magnets supplied power so that the central axis (B) could rise and fall and rotate. This caused a sleeved arm holding a needle to make a connection to the right wire. The pulses heard while pressing buttons on the telephone told the system how far to move. The first model of the exchange was made from pins and a pencil inside Strowger's collar box. Later his nephew Walter Strowger helped him.

The first users were annoyed as they thought that pressing buttons was the operators' business. Strowger founded the Automatic Telephone Company in 1891 to exploit the idea but there was little interest at first. He sold out his patents for $1,800 in 1896 and his stake in the company for $10,000 in 1898 and retired to St Petersburg, Florida to run a hotel where he died in 1902. The massive Bell system was uninterested until the threat of a strike by operators, when they began to instal the exchanges in 1921 in Norfolk, Virginia. By then the original patent was long expired. As the numbers of telephones grew huge buildings were required where the same principle in modified form applied to the pulses for each dialled number on a rotary telephone telling the machinery how far to move to make the connection. The 'Strowger' exchanges still survive in some places but have increasingly been replaced by electronic exchanges.

(No Model.)
3 Sheets—Sheet 3.

A. B. STROWGER.
AUTOMATIC TELEPHONE EXCHANGE.

No. 447,918.   Patented Mar. 10, 1891.

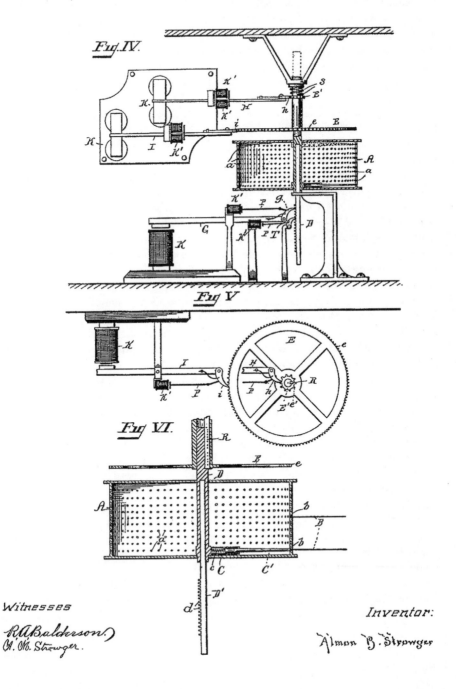

Witnesses
R. A. Balderson.
H. M. Strowger.

Inventor:
Almon B. Strowger.

The automobile

Maybe Karl Benz's DE 37435, from 1886, was the first practicable petrol-engined car but this story is too good to pass up. George Baldwin Selden was born in Clarkson, New York State in 1846. He initially began to study engineering, but gave in to his father's wishes and switched to law. He ran a patent lawyer practice in Rochester and handled George Eastman's photography patent applications (Eastman later signed the drawing shown as a witness). Selden spent a great deal of time experimenting in his basement workshop, and applied for many patents himself. He became increasingly interested in the idea of a self-propelled road vehicle. He decided that the answer would be a more powerful motor than any available and a light chassis. When he visited the Philadelphia Centennial Exposition in 1876 with his hoop-shaving inventions he looked at the displayed internal combustion engines and decided to adapt the design of the Brayton engine. He redesigned it by enclosing the crankcase and developed a much lighter engine weighing 168 kg (370 lb) with an output of 1491 watt (2 horsepower). He filed for his invention on 8 May 1879. It covered a compression engine (with a clutch) which would drive the wheels.

Selden knew the as yet unrealised automobile industry would be unlikely to bring financial rewards for many years. As American patents had a term of 17 years from the date of grant, and not from the date of filing, it would be to his advantage to delay publication. The law allowed a maximum of 2 years to reply to letters from the Patent Office, which he exploited to the full. Consequently the patent was published in 1895 when automobiles were beginning to appear. The claims seemed to cover the concept of such a vehicle. Failing to find anyone willing to manufacture his car, Selden sold the rights in 1899 to William Whitney of the Columbia Motor and Electric Vehicle Company for $10,000 plus royalties. This company successfully sued a manufacturer for patent infringement and the result was ten other makers banding together in the Association of Licensed Automobile Manufacturers to pay royalties at 1.25% of the retail cost. Such cars had a plate, 'Manufactured under Selden patent'. Royalties eventually totalled $2 million, of which Selden received $200,000.

Henry Ford of Detroit, Michigan had been making cars since 1896 and he asked in 1903 if he could pay royalties. He was turned down by the Association on the grounds that he was an assembler and not a manufacturer. He retorted 'Tell Selden to take his patent and go to hell with it'. A struggle erupted in the newspapers, with full-page advertisements by both sides. Ford offered to compensate anyone sued for driving one of his cars (50 people wrote in to enquire further). A court case dragged on until 1911, when it was held that the Selden patent was good but that Ford had not infringed it as he was using an Otto four-cycle engine which was different from the two-cycle compression engine which is, oddly enough, not mentioned anywhere in the patent. As everybody was using the Otto engine the royalties stopped (the patent was due to expire in 1912 anyway). Ford admitted that the court case gave his company a great deal of publicity. Selden later claimed that most of his money disappeared in the court case. He made a small number of cars between 1906 and 1914 with the slogan 'Made by the father of them all', although the only model made from his actual patent could hardly move. He died in Rochester, New York in 1922.

George Baldwin Selden, Rochester, New York
Filed 8 May 1879 and published as US 549160

G. B. SELDEN.
ROAD ENGINE.

No. 549,160.

Patented Nov. 5, 1895.

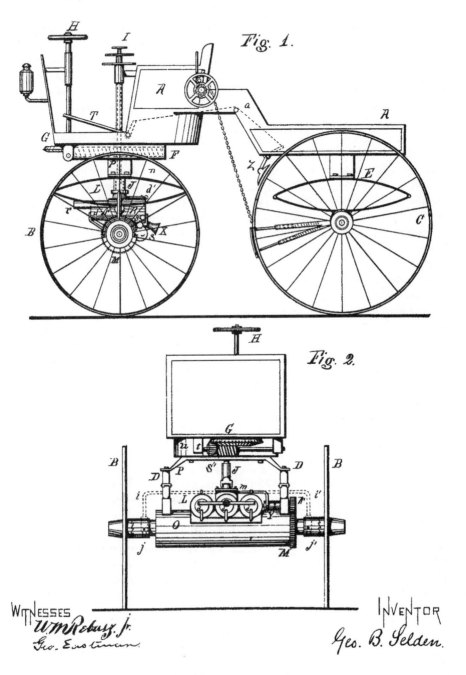

Fig. 1.

Fig. 2.

WITNESSES
W. M. Rebusy. Jr.
Geo. Eastman.

INVENTOR
Geo. B. Selden.

Barbed wire

Joseph Glidden was born in Charlestown, New Hampshire in 1813. He moved to De Kalb, 100 km west of Chicago, and bought a farm. In the summer of 1873 he and his friends Isaac Ellwood, owner of a hardware store, and Jacob Haish, a building contractor and lumber dealer, visited the county fair. Henry Rose of nearby Waterman Station was exhibiting his idea for fencing livestock with his US 138763, which had only been granted that May. It consisted of horizontal wooden slats with nails projecting on either side. All three men thought that they could improve it, Haish and Glidden thinking of an entire fence of wire. Glidden worked on the idea with his farmhand and filed the invention before Haish. In an 'interference' hearing the Patent Office ruled that Glidden had priority, meaning that he had thought of it first. Haish went on to patent a variant, the 'S' wire, which was published as US 167240. He was convinced that Glidden had stolen his idea and uttered the ominous words 'I'm gonna see him in court about this'. Like so many important inventions the Glidden patent seems so obvious. Two wires, twisted like rope, are joined in a knot and one end projects up and the other down. Next to the post is (C), a twisting key meant to tighten the wire if necessary (the idea was later dropped). Otherwise most modern barbed wire fences are the same.

Glidden offered to sell half the rights to a neighbour for $100, but was turned down. He managed to sell the half to his friend Ellwood, whose US 147756 was only a variant on the Rose patent, and who abandoned his own ambitions, for $265: possibly the best bargain in patent history. Both Glidden and Haish began manufacturing their wire and were soon working overtime. Vast quantities of wire were ordered from the East and were quickly made into barbed wire, had patent stickers put on them and were sold immediately through Ellwood's store. A supplier, Washburn and Moen of Worcester, Massachusetts, was puzzled by the sudden demand from De Kalb and sent vice president Charles Washburn out to investigate. He tried to buy Haish out, but was asked for $200,000. He then purchased Glidden's half share for $60,000 plus a royalty of 0.25 cent/lb (0.55 cent/kg) of wire. Ellwood promised only to sell his wire in the West, where he used colourful advertising based on Glidden as a folk hero to sell the product. Once one man fenced, his neighbours tended to do the same. Haish tried to compete but was less successful (but still made a fortune). Elwood bought a huge ranch in Texas and died in 1910 in De Kalb.

Haish did indeed take the Glidden patent to court, and several court cases ensued, to end in his defeat in 1892 at the Supreme Court, with Washburn and Moen v. The Beat 'Em Barbed Wire Company. Glidden died in De Kalb in 1906, a very wealthy man with many business interests. Barbed wire meant an end to the free range, with arable farmers being able to farm as they could keep livestock out of their crops. In Texas, particularly, there were the 'fence-cutting wars' with threats made by ranchers to farmers, and murders carried out in a vain attempt to hold back the wire. Barbed wire was used for the first time in war by Teddy Roosevelt's Rough Riders in 1898 in Cuba, in the Spanish-American War. The British used it in the Boer War to link up concrete blockhouses which were partitioning the country. A book has even been written listing barbed wire patents, Jesse James' 1966 *Early United States barbed wire patents*.

Joseph Glidden, De Kalb, Illinois
Filed 27 October 1873 and published as US 157124

J. F. GLIDDEN.
Wire-Fences.

No. 157,124.

Patented Nov. 24, 1874.

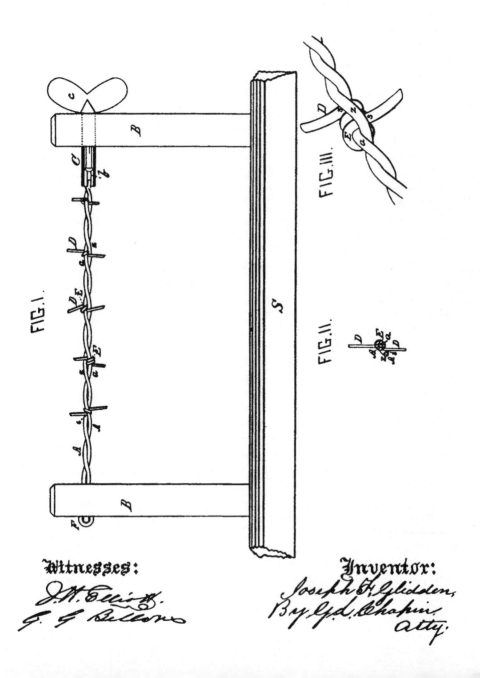

FIG. I.

FIG. III.

FIG. II.

Witnesses:

J. W. Elliott.
G. G. Bellows

Inventor:

Joseph F. Glidden,
By G. D. Chapin,
Atty.

The Bessemer process

Before the Bessemer process there were two methods of making iron. Cast iron was made by adding coke to iron ore in a blast furnace. This product was fine for uses involving compression. Wrought iron was made from cast iron by puddling it (stirring it to remove the carbon). As carbon makes iron brittle, the wrought iron was better for tension uses such as girders. It was, however, a slow and expensive way of making it. Henry Bessemer was born in Charlton, Hertfordshire in 1813, son of an engineer and typefounder. A self-educated man, Bessemer took out over 100 patents, mostly in metallurgy. He was able to fund much of his work by keeping a method of making 'gold' powder from brass for use in paints secret by using his three brothers-in-law to make it for many years, having realised the huge mark-ups that stores were charging.

When he devised a new shell for use by the French army in the Crimean War, they told him that the shell was too powerful for their cast iron cannons. He wondered if he could make a cheaper and better iron, and while ill in bed invented a way of refining molten iron with blasts of cold air. A cylindrical pot 6 m high had holes near the bottom through which the air moved, purifying and heating the iron still more to enable easy pouring. The 'mild steel' cost a fraction of the previous price and still retained 2% carbon, which made it hard and gave it valuable mechanical properties. In August 1856 Bessemer gave a lecture on his discovery in Cheltenham. There was much interest and the paper was translated into many languages.

Others who tried out the new method found that it did not work. In July 1858 Goran Göransson, a Swedish industrialist, worked out what was happening. Bessemer had used a Blaenavon iron which was low in phosphorus, whereas most European ores were high in phosphorus. It was not until 1877 that Sidney Thomas of Battersea, Surrey with his GB 4422/1877 found a way of using high phosphorus ore. Meanwhile, Robert Mushet of Coleford, Gloucestershire patented with GB 2219/1856 an improved Bessemer process. Owing to bad management by his partners Mushet's patent failed to have its renewal fees paid, but Bessemer nevertheless paid him some money as compensation for using the improvement.

Bessemer was not the first to invent his method. William Kelly of Pittsburgh, Pennsylvania had been working on the idea since 1846. He received his US 17628 in 1857 but was unsuccessful in getting Bessemer's American patent revoked. He did get an extension of 7 years to his patent in 1871 and died a rich man from royalties. In the 1860s the Siemens-Martin open hearth process began to supersede the Bessemer process and by 1900 production was about the same with the two methods. The open hearth process took longer, but could use scrap metal or phosphoric ores. Bessemer is still thought to have made £1 million from his process.

Bessemer was less successful in trying to suppress the motion of a ship, following an unpleasant trip across the English Channel. His splendidly illustrated GB 3707/1869 involved placing accommodation in a huge (and luxurious) tube suspended from two iron bolts within the hull. The idea was that the tube would stay level no matter how much the ship itself rolled. The ship was actually launched in 1875, but its maiden voyage to Calais on a calm day was a disaster, as the passengers were tossed unmercifully, and Calais pier was demolished by the ship. The passengers were not even able to flee the sealed compartment. Bessemer was knighted in 1879 and died in London in 1898.

Henry Bessemer, London, England
Filed 17 October 1855 and published as GB 2321/1855 and US 16083

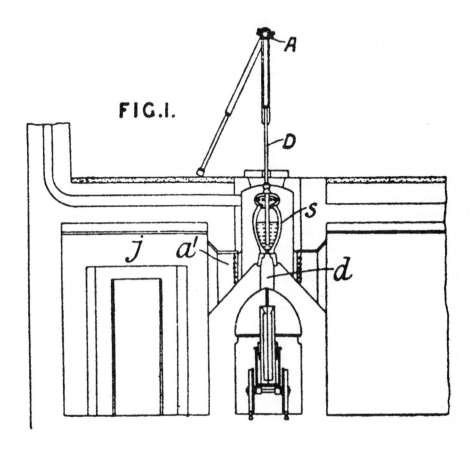

FIG.I.

The bicycle

There are numerous claimants to the invention of the bicycle, the most efficient way known of converting human energy to propulsion. Some say that the inventor was Baron Drais of Paris with his FR 869 (shown in detail in GB 4321/1818), the 'hobby-horse', which, although propelled by kicking your foot along the ground, added the idea of steering by changing the direction of the front wheel. Kirkpatrick Macmillan, a Dumfries blacksmith, improved the concept with his (unpatented) 1839 bicycle with pedals (on the back wheels). Such beasts were awkward and slow, and riding with metal or wooden rims over cobbled streets gave them the nickname of bone shakers, although they were properly termed velocipedes. It was only from about 1869 that they were called bicycles.

The Michaux father and son wheelchair and baby carriage workshop in Paris is often credited with inventing what looks reasonably like a modern bicycle, but their FR 80637 of 1868 was probably based on what they knew of the work of their employee Pierre Lallement. Born in 1843, he was a mechanic who in 1862 began thinking of an improved bicycle. There is evidence that the Olivier brothers, who later hired the elder Michaux to run a bicycle factory for them, had worked previously with Lallement. In 1865 he emigrated to America, and after refining his ideas in a machine shop, patented the invention shown here with the financial backing of James Carroll. The text says that he was 'temporarily residing' in New Haven.

For the first time the pedals or 'rocking treadles' are placed further forward even if not in the conventional position between the wheels (modern recumbents also place them forward). They worked like the cranks on tricycles for children. The front wheel was gripped by and pivoted within jaws. The patent explains that the 'guiding wheel' is used to move to left or right and that the greater the velocity the more able the bicycle is to stay upright. 'After a little practice the rider is enabled to drive the same at an incredible velocity, with the greatest ease.' Lallement did not take out any further patents and died in poverty in Roxbury, Massachusetts in 1891. The patent rights were sold several times and made a subsequent owner, Albert Pope of Boston, a fortune under the Columbia name.

Some refinements were still needed such as brakes. Many of these improvements were carried out in Coventry, Warwickshire. The story is that a sewing machine company decided to branch out into making 400 of the Michaux model for sale in France. The Franco-Prussian War of 1870–71 meant that they decided to sell them in England instead. The company foreman, James Starley, made many improvements such as GB 2236/1870 which had tensioned spokes coming at a tangent from the hub. His famous Penny Farthing design, sadly not patented, and also from about 1870, was excellent for speed if you knew how to handle it, as the gear ratio is higher if one wheel is bigger. It did cause fear in some riders and in many spectators because of the height of the rider, which made it unstable. The so-called safety bicycle emerged with Starley again with the first successful model being GB 3934/1879, which featured wheels with identical sizes with pedals between wheels and a chain and sprocket on the rear wheel. It also had brakes. Such bicycles did not need a stepladder so that the cyclist could mount. The real breakthrough that was to make cycling a mass sport was Dunlop's invention of the pneumatic tyre in 1888 (see page 148).

Pierre Lallement of Paris, France, assignor to himself and James Carroll of New Haven, Connecticut
Published 20 November 1866 as US 59915

P. LALLEMENT.
VELOCIPEDE.

No. 59,915. Patented Nov. 20, 1866.

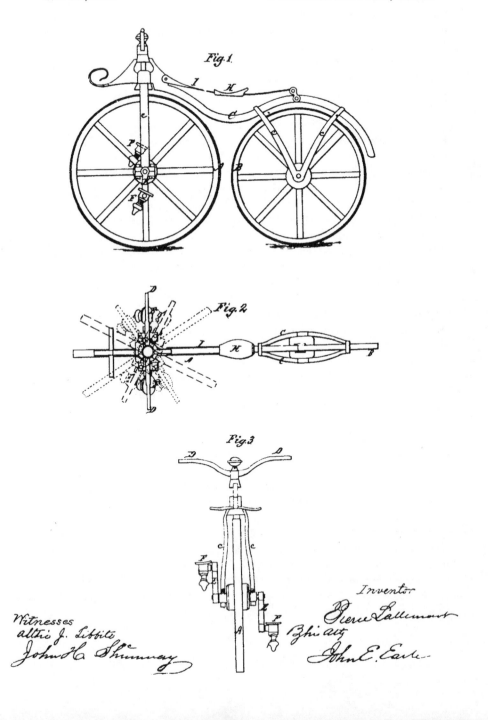

Fig.1.

Fig.2.

Fig.3.

Witnesses
altric J. Libbite
John H. Shumway

Inventor
Pierre Lallement
Bhi atty
John E. Earle

The Big Wheel

The origins of the 'Big Wheel' (or Ferris Wheel) are somewhat obscure, but this example is one of the very first to use the idea of a rotating vertical wheel containing cars. Isaac Newton Forrester liked the idea so much that four such wheels were provided. The drawing shows his invention from the side. Four separate wheels formed the sides of a square. They all operated off a vertical rotating shaft (B) which had four rotating arms (C) while the base itself could move. It was built in 1872 as the 'Epicycloidal Diversion' in Atlantic City, New Jersey and operated successfully for a time. There were eight cars in each wheel, each holding two passengers with a combined capacity of 64 passengers at any one time. In his patent Forrester mentioned his earlier US 70985 from 1867 which featured two wheels side by side, which is thought to be the very first patent for a Big Wheel.

Most of the early Big Wheels were built in Atlantic City. As it was then expensive and time-consuming to travel a long distance, resorts tended to be close to major cities. The origin of the (unpatented) 'Ferris Wheel' dates to Chicago's intention to host the Columbian Exposition in 1893. The planners wanted something big that would rival the Eiffel Tower, which itself dated from a fair held in 1889. Towers and a giant tent were suggested but the architect Daniel Burnham complained that they could not find something that 'met the expectation of the people'. Shortly afterwards George Ferris, when eating with fellow engineers, began to scribble a design down and he later claimed that he had worked out all the details by the end of the meal. It would be a huge wheel with 36 cars which would halt six times in an initial revolution to take on passengers, and then make a single revolution before halting six times again.

George Ferris was born in Galesburg, Illinois in 1859. In 1885 he devised a new profession: testing iron and steel from his Pittsburgh base before they were used in building bridges and railways. When they heard of his proposal the organisers were at first sceptical, but in December 1892 they approved it. Finance was somehow raised and the steel structure was built for $400,000. It consisted of two 42 m towers connected by a 13 m axle. The wheel itself was 76 m high and supported 36 enclosed cars each containing up to 60 persons, with 40 swivelling stools in each car. The wheel opened 6 weeks after the fair began on 1 May 1893 but was nevertheless a great success. An enthusiastic newspaper account described Ferris's wife standing on a chair at the top of the wheel toasting 'The health of my husband and the success of the Ferris Wheel' in champagne. A ride cost 50 cents and $726,000 was earned during the fair. What was new about it was its huge size.

That was what the Garden City Observation Wheel Company thought. William Somers of Atlantic City had filed in 1891 for US 489238, a 'roundabout', which was a wooden Big Wheel supported at its centre by a tripod arrangement. Each cabin was suspended from the outer rim of the wheel and, in the drawings at least, looked like swans. Most of the patent was taken up with explaining the driving mechanism. The company had built it under licence and fought a case against the Ferris Wheel Company for infringement but lost. Their Atlantic City Big Wheel burnt down in June 1892. George Ferris died of typhus in 1896, aged only 37. His Big Wheel was dismantled after the Chicago fair and the rusting remains were dynamited in 1906.

Isaac Newton Forrester, Baltimore, Maryland
Filed 6 October 1875 and published as US 169797

2 Sheets—Sheet 2.

I. N. FORRESTER.

ROTARY-SWING.

No. 169,797. Patented Nov. 3, 1875.

Fig. 2.

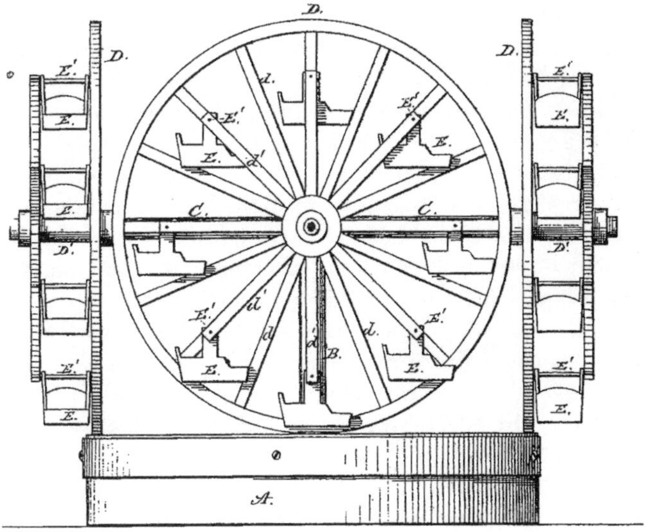

Witnesses:
E. C. Davidson
Joseph S. Layton

Isaac N. Forrester Inventor:

By his Attorney

Wm. D. Baldwin

Blue jeans

This is a bit of a cheat as the patent only applies to the rivets, but the company is proud enough of it to continue to refer to it on the back of its products. It is certainly a nice picture of a miner wearing a (beltless) pair of trousers. Levi Strauss was born Loeb Strauss in Buttenheim, Bavaria in 1829. His family emigrated to America in 1847, after the death of his father, and they worked at the dry-goods business in New York run by Levi's two brothers who had emigrated earlier. Strauss realised that the real money in the California Gold Rush was not in mining but in selling supplies to the miners. In March 1853 he moved to San Francisco and set up his own dry goods business. A miner is said to have suggested that he sell a line of hard wearing cloth, named denim for *serge de Nîmes*, the French city where it was originally made.

This business did well until a letter was received in 1872. A tailor in Nevada, Jacob Davis, had become a customer through buying bolts of cloth. He wrote to Strauss stating that he had worked out a way of making pockets stronger (and also the bottom of the button flies) by inserting rivets. He didn't have the money to patent it, but would share the profits with Strauss if he put up the money. Strauss was enthusiastic and did so. What may be an 'urban legend' is that a prospector who carried rock specimens in his pockets was thought by a blacksmith to have riveted them, and this may have sparked the idea. The patent claimed to be the first to think of applying rivets to 'the pockets of a pair of pants'. The rivets are shown by (b) on the drawing. Davis pointed out that placing hands in pockets tends to rip or 'start' a seam and the rivets would prevent damage. He mentioned being aware of rivets for shoes in US 64015 and US 123313.

Strauss brought Davis over to supervise manufacture of the improved jeans. At first the cloth was sent out to seamstresses to finish the jeans in their houses but demand grew so much that two factories had to be opened. At first two types were sold: indigo blue jeans and brown cotton 'duck' but the latter never grew soft and comfortable like denim and was dropped. Belts were later added. Strauss let his Stern nephews take over the business which was incorporated in 1890 and died in 1902 worth nearly $6 million, despite having dispensed much to Jewish charities during his lifetime. The San Francisco *Call* spoke of his 'fairness and integrity'. The famous label at the back of the jeans stating 'Quality riveted quality clothing' and showing horses trying to pull a pair of jeans apart, with 'PATENTED MAY 20, 1873' at the bottom was not registered as a trade mark until 1976. Apparently such a feat cannot be done. In 1943 a customer tried it with a pair of mules but the result was that one died from the effort.

Jacob Davis, Reno, Nevada, assignor to himself and Levi Strauss & Company, San Francisco, California
Filed 9 August 1872 and published as US 139121, and reissued on 16 March 1875 as Re 6335

J. W. DAVIS.
Fastening Pocket-Openings.

No. 139,121.

Patented May 20, 1873.

Fig. 1.

Witnesses
J. L. Borie
C. M. Richardson

Inventor
Jacob W. Davis
per Dewey & Co.
Attys

The bowling machine

John Wisden is a name renowned among cricket enthusiasts for his annual statistical almanac. Less well known is that he was jointly responsible for a machine to enable batsmen to practise against balls of a particular kind, especially when no experienced bowler was available. John Wisden was born in Brighton, Sussex in 1826, son of a builder. He played cricket for the Sussex side between 1846 and 1863. He was probably the leading fast bowler of his age, and was also a good batsman, despite being only 1.62 m in his socks. Cricket at the time was rough and primitive, with for example no padding to protect the batter's legs, and injuries were frequent. In 1859 he led the first major international tour of a selected cricket side—to Canada and the United States, where it was still played. The crowds were apparently enthusiastic.

In 1855 Wisden joined up with Frederick Lillywhite to open a cricket goods and cigar business on Coventry Street in the middle of London. Lillywhite, from a noted cricketing dynasty, was born near Goodwood, also in Sussex, in 1829. In this patent they describe themselves as 'cricketing outfitters'. The idea of a practice machine originated with 'Felix', another player, whose real name was Nicholas Wanostrocht. His father had asked him to take a pseudonym when he joined cricketing circles since the sport was considered rather risqué because of its associations with gambling. Felix devised a 'catapula' and described it in his *Felix on the bat*, the first edition of which appeared in 1849. It was so effective that when in one exhibition match it was allowed as a substitute for a human bowler it took six wickets (in baseball terms, struck six men out). The invention was adapted and improved by Wisden and Lillywhite.

The frame (a) was supported by (b) and held an inner frame which could be adjusted to change the height at which the balls were delivered. The wooden bows (d) were held in place by catgut cords (f). A spring catch was attached by strap (j) to a lever handle (k). Hook (i) on the catch engaged with (h). If handle (k) were depressed the sling (g) was drawn back to release the ball. With experience the mechanism could be adjusted to release balls with different length (before hitting the ground), pace and direction. An 1894 advertisement shows that even then the company was making it for sale, with a price of 12 guineas (£12.60). It stood 2 m high and took 5 minutes to erect. The wording includes 'Any servant could give his master as genuine *practice* (not, however, to include teaching) as any first-class professional bowler'. It could 'be well managed by a lady, if set at a moderate or medium pace'.

Lillywhite was apparently quarrelsome and difficult and in 1858 the partnership broke up and Wisden carried on alone. There is however today a large sports goods shop called Lillywhite's on the same street. In 1864 Wisden began the enterprise for which he became famous, the annual *Wisden's Cricketers' Almanack*, which was priced at 1 shilling (5p). Sports like cricket and baseball, with easily identified segments of action, lend themselves well to statistical analysis and 'Wisden' has vast amounts of information for analysts. It is considered a great feat (and an expensive one) to collect every single issue in the original edition. Lillywhite had been publishing a similar book from 1849 which was carried on by his family under other names until 1900. Upset at the success of his ex-partner, Lillywhite died in Brighton in 1866. Wisden died, prosperous from his business, in 1884 in London.

Frederick Lillywhite and John Wisden, both of London, England
Filed 24 April 1858 and published as GB 908/1858

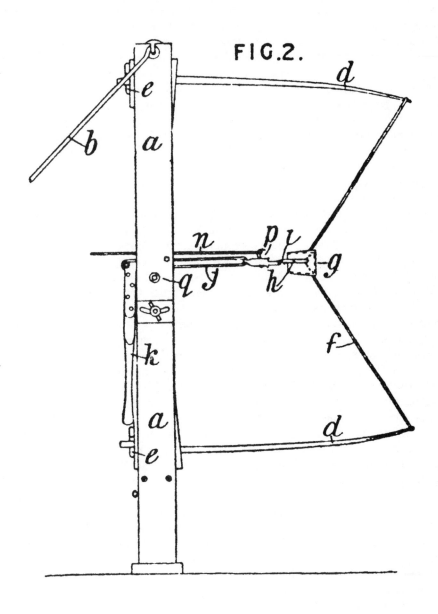

FIG.2.

The brassière

The famous whalebone corset, reinforced with steel and buckram, must have been agony to wear as a foundation garment. By the 1820s the styles available meant that the wearer no longer had to call on a husband or servants to haul in the laces, but that hardly made them easier to wear. Hooks, latches and laces were the order of the day, and numerous minor variations were patented. By the 1840s some corsets were appearing which featured individual pockets for the bust, and this became a dominant feature in patents. Other developments included using the new material, rubber, with Henry Lesher of Brooklyn's US 24033 in 1859 being an early use of—almost—the modern brassière. It had a connecting plate between each breast and looked more like body armour than anything else. In the 1860s there were minor rebellions against corsets by upper-class women in the USA, who only fell short of corset-burning in their agitations. An interesting, and popular, alternative to the corset was the Union Under-Flannel, patented by George Frost and George Henry Phelps of Boston in 1875 with US 161851. It was like an undershirt with support for the bust.

However the imaginative leap to the concept of a brassière seems to belong to Marie Tucek, as shown here. Instead of squeezing the bust from below, it was supported from the shoulders. With its straps and hooks and eyes this splendid creation could easily feature even today in a shop. She speaks in her patent of its being 'simple and durable in construction, designed to take the place of the usual corset, and to be worn more principally with loose dresses of the so-called "empire style"' (that is, those which came straight down without an obvious waist). The portion marked (A) was to be made of sheet metal, cardboard or other 'suitable material, and preferably covered with silk, canvas or other desirable fabric', and was to be bent to conform to the human shape. Perhaps it looks more comfortable than it would actually have been to wear. It attracted, however, little attention at the time. Tucek also patented a variation with US 525241 and then devices to help with making garment patterns with US 532613 and US 622092. Her last patent, US 628372, granted posthumously to her executor Frank Tucek in 1899, is, strangely enough, for a corset.

The patent granted to Mary Phelps Jacob in 1914, US 1115674, made more of an impact. She was a New York socialite who improvised one out of handkerchiefs, ribbon and cord with her French maid when impatient with the lines showing from her corset when dressing for a ball. The term brassière itself comes from the French for 'upper arm' and came into English in about 1907 (which is odd if the idea of wearing one was not known). Jacobs tried to sell the product under the name of Caresse Crosby but, disappointed with sales, sold out for $1,500 to the Warner Brothers Corset Company, which went on to make $15 million from the patent. The corset faded from history in the 1920s, perhaps helped by a drive by the War Industries Board in 1917 when they asked American women to stop buying corsets. This apparently saved over 28,000 tonnes of metal. A fashion for boyish figures among the 'flappers' in the same period may also have helped. There were also British patents for corsets, such as the intricate GB 15690/1894 by Thomas Williams of Landport, Hampshire. This involves 'back straps for drawing in the corset so as to afford additional support to the wearer's figure'.

Marie Tucek, New York City, New York
Filed 11 January 1893 and published as US 494397

(No Model.)

M. TUCEK.
BREAST SUPPORTER.

No. 494,397.   Patented Mar. 28, 1893.

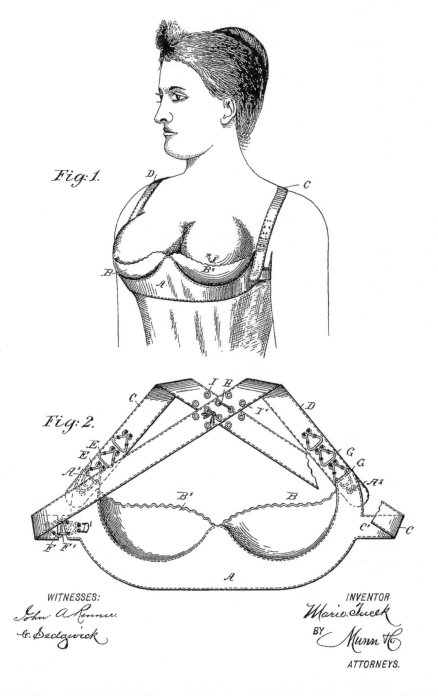

Fig:1.

Fig:2.

WITNESSES:
John A. Rennie.
C. Sedgwick

INVENTOR
Marie Tucek
BY
Munn &C
ATTORNEYS.

Breakfast cereal

Breakfast cereals actually started with Henry Perky of Denver, Colorado with US 502378 and there are many later patents for making what we now call shredded wheat. John Harvey ('J. H.') Kellogg was born in 1852 in Tyrone, Michigan to a farmer. His parents converted the same year to what in 1863 was organised as the Seventh Day Adventists. They moved to the small town of Battle Creek where their son Will ('W. K.') was born in 1860. The sect did not believe in alcohol or meat and favoured natural remedies. They founded what we would now call a health farm in Battle Creek and in 1876 J. H., who had just become a doctor, was asked to run the Battle Creek Sanitarium for a year. He stayed on for life. J. H. added to the regime some of his own ideas: counting calories, avoiding sugar, regular exercise and drinking 10 glasses of water daily. Tobacco, tea and coffee were banned. He called his health programme 'biologic living' and patients were put through a daily regimen of calisthenics from 7 a.m., after which came cold baths, enemas, swimming, electroshock therapy, and a vegetarian diet. The day would often end with J. H. leading the patients in a march for good health. Despite the hardy routine the numbers of patients rose considerably. J. H. was assisted as business manager by his shy brother W. K., whom he treated with condescension, always insisting on being called 'Dr Kellogg' by him.

Fixing, preparing, and even inventing foods was always important to the sanitarium's mission. J. H. believed that boiling food was good for digestion, so he tried cooking multigrain biscuits and then crushed them to serve raw to the patients, who did not like the new Granola. W. K. sometimes joined his brother in food experiments. During 1894 the two brothers fixed a mass of wheat dough, boiled it for different lengths of time, and put it through rollers to press it into large sheets. One night during these experiments, W. K. left the dough out overnight before he rolled it. When he later returned to the kitchen, he ran the dough through the rollers as before, but instead of forming a flat sheet, the dough broke up into flakes. W. K. was puzzled. The food had got moist overnight. He could have thrown the flakes out and mixed more dough. Instead, he took them to his brother and suggested serving them for breakfast. J. H. wanted to crush them into bits, but W. K. served the flakes whole. The patients happily ate them and asked for more.

This is the first page of the patent and from then on numerous patents flowed, mainly on food products but also on radiant-heat baths, inhalers and body-braces, and all by J. H. The process was soon adapted for corn and rice flakes. W. K. was in charge of production and began to sell the product. Imitators soon sprang up, many of whom moved to Battle Creek to set up factories. They included Charles Post, one of their own patients, who formed a company to make Grape-Nuts®. J. H. was not too bothered so long as people were eating more healthily, but W. K. was annoyed. He wanted to make money as well. The break between the brothers finally came when, in J. H.'s absence, W. K. added 'malt flavouring', a sugar, to the product. J. H. was furious. In 1906 W. K. bought J. H. out and formed what is now famous as Kellogg's®, out of his brother's shadow at last. Healthy living seems to have paid off as the brothers both lived to a ripe old age until their deaths in Battle Creek, J. H. dying in 1943, always wearing white and avid for publicity, and W. K., a noted philanthrophist, in 1951.

UNITED STATES PATENT OFFICE.

JOHN HARVEY KELLOGG, OF BATTLE CREEK, MICHIGAN.

FLAKED CEREALS AND PROCESS OF PREPARING SAME.

SPECIFICATION forming part of Letters Patent No. 558,393, dated April 14, 1896.

Application filed May 31, 1895. Serial No. 551,192. (No specimens.)

To all whom it may concern:

Be it known that I, JOHN HARVEY KEL-LOGG, of Battle Creek, in the county of Calhoun and State of Michigan, have invented
5 a certain new and useful Alimentary Product and Process of Making the Same, of which the following is a full, clear, and exact description.

My invention relates to an improved ali-
10 mentary product and to the process of making it; and the object of the improvement is to provide a food product which is in a proper condition to be readily digested without any preliminary cooking or heating operation,
15 and which is highly nutritive and of an agreeable taste, thus affording a food product particularly well adapted for sick and convalescent persons.

To this end my invention consists in the
20 new process and the new article of manufacture hereinafter described and claimed.

In carrying out my invention I use as a material from which to produce my improved alimentary product wheat, which is preferably
25 in its natural state, although it may be slightly pearled without materially affecting the desired result, barley or oats prepared by the removing of a portion of the outer husks, corn, and other grains.
30 The steps of the process are as hereinafter described.

First. Soak the grain for some hours—say eight to twelve—in water at a temperature which is either between 40° and 60° Fahren-
35 heit or 110° and 140° Fahrenheit, thus securing a preliminary digestion by aid of cerealin, a starch-digesting organic ferment contained in the hull of the grain or just beneath it. The temperature must be either so low or so
40 high as to prevent actual fermentation while promoting the activity of the ferment. This digestion adds to the sweetness and flavor of the product.

Second. Cook the grain thoroughly. For
45 this purpose it should be boiled in water for about an hour, and if steamed a longer time will be required. My process is distinctive in this step—that is to say, that the cooking is carried to the stage when all the starch is hy-
50 drated. If not thus thoroughly cooked, the product is unfit for digestion and practically worthless for immediate consumption.

Third. After steaming the grain is cooled and partially dried, then passed through cold rollers, from which it is removed by means of 55 carefully-adjusted scrapers. The purpose of this process of rolling is to flatten the grain into extremely thin flakes in the shape of translucent films, whereby the bran covering (or the cellulose portions thereof) is disinte- 60 grated or broken into small particles, and the constituents of the grain are made readily accessible to the cooking process to which it is to be subsequently subjected and to the action of the digestive fluids when eaten. 65

Fourth. After rolling the compressed grain or flakes having been received upon suitable trays is subjected to a steaming process, whereby it is thoroughly cooked and is then baked or roasted in an oven until dry and 70 crisp.

The finished product thus consists of extremely thin flakes, in which the bran (or the cellulose portions thereof) is disintegrated and which have been thoroughly cooked and 75 prepared for the digestive processes by digestion, thorough cooking, steaming, and roasting. In this respect it differs from any similar alimentary article which has been heretofore produced. 80

The preliminary cerealin digestion converts a part of the starch into dextrin, and thus causes the grain to become somewhat glutinous, whereby I am enabled to apply a high pressure during the rolling process with- 85 out any necessity of heating the rollers, and thus very thin flakes are produced which are not brittle and are readily roasted to assume a sweet flavor. The cooking before the rolling also assists in rendering the latter opera- 90 tion easier and more effective, and together with steaming or cooking after rolling brings the product into a condition in which it is readily soluble and digestible without any further cooking. The steaming or cooking 95 and baking or roasting processes may be effected in the same apparatus, the product being first subjected to the action of steam, and, after the steam is cut off, to the action of dry heat. 100

The product being perfectly sterilized will keep indefinitely. It is a perfectly cooked food and ready to be eaten at once with no preparation whatever. It is very palatable, and hence

Buoying ships over shoals

'To all whom it may concern: Be it known that I, Abraham Lincoln, of Springfield, in the County of Sangamon, in the State of Illinois, have invented a new and improved manner of combining adjustable buoyant air chambers with a steamer or other vessel for the purpose of enabling their draught of water to be readily lessened to enable them to pass over bars, or through shallow water, without discharging their cargoes. . . .' Abraham Lincoln is the only American President to have been granted a patent. He was born in 1809 in the famous log cabin near Hodgenville, Kentucky. The family moved to Indiana in 1816 and then on to Illinois in 1830. Conditions were primitive and Lincoln received little schooling; he worked as a storekeeper, postmaster and surveyor, and was elected as a state legislator in 1834, before he began to practise law in 1836. He was a Congressman from 1847 to 1849.

Lincoln travelled twice down the Mississippi carrying cargo on flatboats to New Orleans, first when aged 19 from Indiana as a hired hand helping the son of the owner to make the trip, and again in 1831. On that occasion he and several others were paid $12 each a month to build a boat and travel down the river. Before getting to the Illinois river, let alone the Mississippi, the flatboat became stranded on a mill dam at a village on the Sangamon. As the boat took on water, Lincoln had part of the cargo unloaded to right the boat. He then borrowed an auger from the village cooper and drilled a hole in the bow to let the water run out. Then he plugged the hole, helped move the boat over the dam, and they carried on.

Such experiences no doubt made him well aware of the problems of shallows. His lawyer partner, William Herndon, told the story that Lincoln as Congressman was on his way home to Springfield from Washington, DC when his boat became stranded on a sandbar. 'The captain ordered the hands to collect all the loose planks, empty barrels and boxes and force them under the sides of the boat. These empty casks were used to buoy it up. After forcing enough of them under the vessel she lifted gradually and at last swung clear of the opposing sand bar.' Lincoln keenly watched all this. He worked on the miniature model required by the law of the time with the help of a local mechanic and brought it into the office, whittling it with his own hands, telling Herndon that a great revolution in steam navigation was inevitable because of it. The model is now in the Smithsonian.

The invention worked by having chambers (A) stored within boxes (B). Ropes (f) connected the chambers with vertical shafts (D) and a shaft (C) down the length of the boat. By turning (C) in one direction the ropes inflated the chambers (A) which descended into the water to buoy the boat up. Turning (C) the other way deflated the chambers so that they could be put back in their boxes. The idea does not seem to have ever been tried out, if only because the extra weight would probably have made it even more likely that the boat would go aground. Lincoln continued to take an interest in the patent system. In 1858 Lincoln called the introduction of patent laws one of the three most important developments 'in the world's history', along with the discovery of America and printing. Just before becoming President, in 1859, he praised the patent laws for having 'secured to the inventor, for a limited time, the exclusive use of his invention; and thereby added the fuel of *interest* to the *fire* of genius, in the discovery and production of new and useful things'.

ABRAHAM LINCOLN

MANNER OF BOUYING VESSELS

No. 6,469

Patented May 22, 1849

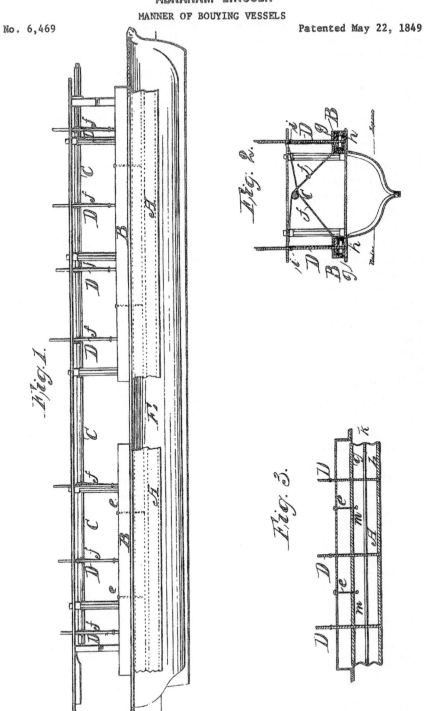

The cable street car

Andrew Smith (who later took the surname of Hallidie) was born in London, England in 1836, of Scottish parentage. His father, Andrew Smith, received patents for wire ropes. Hallidie was brought up to work by day and study by night and, becoming ill, was taken by his father when not yet 16 on a voyage to California in 1852 to recuperate. His father soon returned, but Hallidie stayed on as an (unsuccessful) gold miner, making 'just enough to starve on, with beans, pork and coffee, and pork, coffee, and beans for a change'. After a few years he became involved in implementing the use of wire ropes to build bridges or flumes across canyons. In 1857, still barely 20, he moved to San Francisco and set up his own business making wire ropes, the first in California.

This business was quite successful. In 1867 his US 66327 was a suspension bridge made of wire and his 'Hallidie ropeway', or rather wireway, a way of transporting freight over canyons or rough surfaces, received several patents in 1871. This caused him to think about ways to take passengers up San Francisco's steep hills. The city street cars of his time found it hard work as even with five horses they sometimes slipped, with catastrophic results. He suggested that a system of using endless wire ropes should be used to haul cars up and down the hills. There was much scepticism and only a few shares in the new business were taken up, mainly by friends. Hallidie himself contributed $40,000, all he had, and raised another $58,000 from shareholders and a bank loan. He had to design the whole system, and patented many aspects. Basically he had a tube buried under the street with two wire ropes. The ropes moved in opposite directions. A gripping device from the car held onto the rope, and the power to drag the ropes and hence the cars was provided by boilers in a power house. The patent shown is later than the actual beginning of operations, but summarises the features well, and is the only one which shows the cars.

An agreement was made to build an experimental line along Clay Street. The line would be 840 m in length with a rise in height of 92 m. The franchise was due to expire on 1 August 1873 if the system were not in operation by then. After frantic work, at 5 a.m. on that day the first car was boarded by a small party at the corner of Clay and Jones streets and Hallidie released the brake, a crude lever device. On reaching the turntable at the bottom it turned and went back up. There were no cheers, just handshakes in the silent city. A solitary Frenchman is reported to have thrown a faded bouquet in salutation from an open window. The idea spread to many other cities, and San Francisco is famous for still retaining three of the original lines, providing an exhilarating ride down hills, especially when hanging onto the outside. Andrew Hallidie died in 1900 in San Francisco, a wealthy and respected entrepreneur.

Andrew Hallidie, San Francisco, California
Filed 24 March 1876 and issued as US 182663

A. S. HALLIDIE.

RAILWAY.

No. 182,663.

Patented Sept. 26, 1876.

Fig. 1

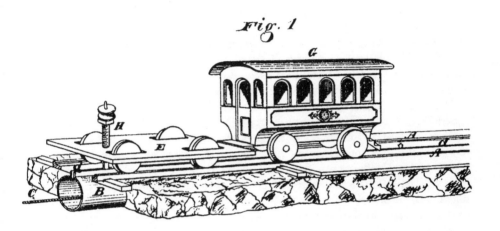

Fig. 2.

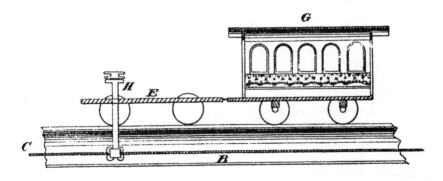

Witnesses

Jno. L. Boone

C. M. Richardson

Inventors

Andrew S. Hallidie
by Dewey & Co.
his attorneys

The can opener

The idea of tin cans dates back to GB 3372/1810 by Peter Durand of London 'for a foreigner'. The foreigner was almost certainly Nicolas Appert of France, a country with which Britain was then fighting a war. The French government had asked for a way of preserving food for use by the army and navy. Appert proposed sealing the food in bottles and heating them for a time. Although he did not realise it this was both killing, and keeping out, potentially dangerous micro-organisms. The idea was adapted to a can made of wrought iron with a tin lining for hygiene. The cans weighed ½ kg when empty and the sides were 5 mm thick—not much narrower than a modern ballpoint pen. By 1820 Durand had a good business supplying cans to the British armed forces and by 1830 they could easily be bought in the better English shops. It might have been thought that the invention of the tin can would result in the simultaneous, or at least swift, invention of the tin opener, but this was not so. The instructions for opening a tin of veal on William Parry's expedition to the Canadian Arctic in 1824 were 'Cut around at the top with a chisel and hammer'. Users were advised to open cans with whatever tools were to hand in the house. As late as the American Civil War hungry soldiers had to fire at tins in order to open them.

Ezra Warner of Waterbury, Connecticut patented one of the first inventions for opening cans in 1858 (US 19063). A pointed blade was pressed in for gripping and was prevented from sinking too deep by a guard. The guard was then swung out of the way and a second curved blade cut round the top. Although others described it as 'part bayonet, part sickle' he optimistically wrote, 'A child may use it without difficulty, or risk'. He also stated that 'the piercer will perforate the tin without causing the liquid to fly out, as it does in all those which make the perforation by percussion of any kind'. By percussion he meant those improvised tools. By this time iron cans were beginning to be replaced by steel cans. They were therefore thinner and so needed a raised rim to stiffen the can. The top and bottom were separate pieces joined to the can, having previously been wrapped over from the sides.

William Lyman had been patenting since 1858, mainly in the area of keeping fruit in cans or jars. His US 54929 in 1868 was for a hook lever for opening jars and other patents were for butter dishes, sash holders and tea and coffee pots. Lyman's can opener was a variation on Warner's and is shown by a side view in Figure 1 and a view from underneath in Figure 2. The revolving cutter was marked (a) with (B) as a pivot with its lower end (b) which cut into the can. The idea was that (B) was inserted into the middle of the can and then tilted until cutter (a) began to bite into the can. The cutter was then twisted round the edge. Its problem was that the exact centre of the can had to be pierced, and the opener had to be adjusted for different sized cans. William Lyman was presumably the same man who in 1878 founded a company at Middlefield to manufacture gun sights, with patents such as US 211753 for a gun sight and US 217626 for a pump. Despite its problems Lyman's invention was used extensively until, in the 1920s, someone thought of using the rim of the can for both gripping and cutting, with the now familiar rotary wheel can opener. It had taken just over a century for a practical can opener to be invented.

William Lyman, West Meriden, Connecticut
Published 19 July 1870 as US 105583

W. W. Lyman,

Can Opener.

No. 105,583. *Patented July 19. 1870.*

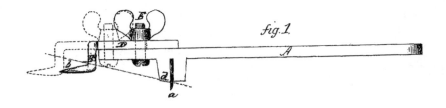

fig. 1.

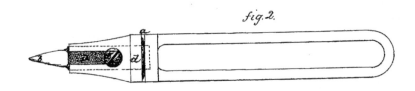

fig. 2.

Witnesses.
J. H. Shumway
A. J. Tibbits

William W. Lyman
Inventor
By his Attorney.
John E. Earl

The cash register

James Ritty was born in 1836 in Dayton, Ohio, son of immigrant parents from Alsace, France. He was running a Dayton bar called the Pony House when he noticed that, although he had plenty of customers, he never seemed to be making a profit. He was certain that, at a time when there were open cash boxes and account books to list sales, the bartenders were cheating him. He became so worried that in 1878 he took a steamship to Europe, hoping that he would feel better from a holiday. One day he went down to the engine room and noticed a machine which counted the number of revolutions that the propeller shaft made. An idea about using the concept to record sales in a store began to take shape. He cut short his holiday and, with his brother John Ritty, he designed a machine.

The Rittys' idea was to make a clock face with a keyboard showing amounts of money below it. The clerk tapped the right key showing the sale and the hands on the clock swung to indicate the sale amount. A bell sounded to alert the manager to the sale. Figure 3 shows what was happening internally: the wheel (O) marked cents and would move the correct amount each time a sale was made. Each fresh sale would make the wheel move again, and when it made a complete revolution it would trigger the next wheel to indicate '1', that is, $1, of sales. In this way the day's sales were steadily recorded. At the end of the day the manager removed the cover and simply noted the total sales and reset the wheels to zero. James patented with John Birch his improved US 271363 in 1883. In shape it was much more like the famous cash register and instead of a clock face 'tablets' sprang up to indicate the amount of the sale. The machines were made in a room over the saloon but business was not too good and Ritty sold out the business and patents for $1,000 to Jacob Eckert of Cincinnati, Ohio who in turn sold out to a consortium.

Then John Patterson, also of Dayton, came onto the scene. His coal supply business was in debt and when he heard of the new machine he bought two, sight unseen, and immediately began to make a profit. In 1884 he agreed to pay $6,500 for a controlling interest in the concern, which had 13 employees at the time. That evening other businessmen laughed at him: he had not realised that the company was making a loss. The next morning he offered $2,000 to be released from the contract but this was refused as a deal was a deal. He said, 'Very well, I am going into the cash register business and I will make a success of it'. He renamed the concern The National Cash Register Company. Patterson did suggest some improvements, such as sales receipts, but primarily he was a great salesman. He thought of the ideas of guaranteed territories for his salesmen (which were popular with them) and sales quotas (which were not), as well as sales conventions. When his brother-in-law improvised the idea of the standard sales pitch he had it printed in a 450-word booklet, which all the salesmen had to memorise. Patterson would make surprise visits and challenge a salesman to recite the sales pitch: failure to do so correctly meant that he was fired.

By 1888 the business had expanded so much that it moved to Patterson's old family farm south of Dayton. By this time there were already 1,000 employees. He offered free hot lunches for his employees but they refused 'charity', so he charged 5 cents. There were also programmes for their children, and well-designed and hygienic workshops, all in the name of getting more productivity. Patterson, a generous donor to local charities, died in 1922, James Ritty having died in 1918.

James Ritty and John Ritty, Dayton, Ohio

Filed 26 March 1879 and issued on 4 November 1879 as US 221360

J. & J. RITTY.

Cash Register and Indicator.

No. 221,360.   Patented Nov. 4, 1879.

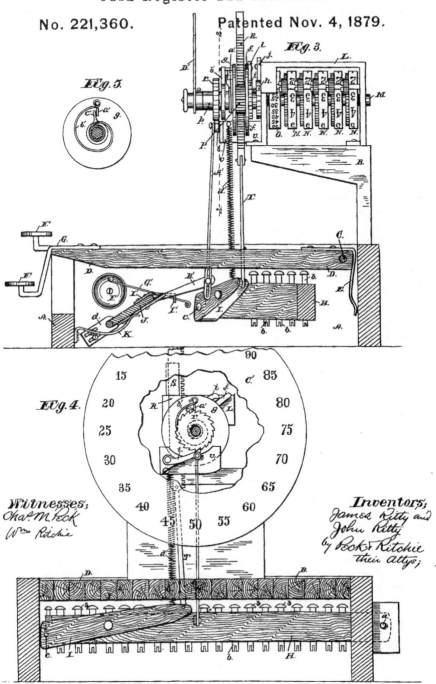

Witnesses;
Chas. M. Peck
Wm Ritchie

Inventors;
James Ritty and
John Ritty
by Peck & Ritchie
their attys;

Celluloid

John Wesley Hyatt was born in 1837 in Stalkey, New York, son of a blacksmith. He moved to Illinois and worked there as a printer and obtained his first patent, US 31461 in 1861, for sharpening knives. He moved to Albany and one day saw an advertisement by Phelan and Collander, a New York City firm, offering $10,000 to anyone who could invent a substitute for ivory in billiard balls. The price of ivory was rising as elephants were becoming scarcer, and 12,000 were dying annually so that their tusks could be made into billiard balls and piano keys. Although Hyatt knew nothing of chemistry he set up a shed at the rear of his boarding-house and with a printer friend experimented with making billiard balls out of pulverised wood, paper pulp, and shellac. The result was fine for making checkers and dominoes, but not for billiard balls. He and his two brothers set up a company to make those products.

Hyatt continued researching for a good substitute. Collodion was a substance known since 1847 which consisted of guncotton, dissolved in ethyl alcohol, which was then mixed with ether. It had applications in photography and surgical dressings. One day Hyatt noticed that an overturned bottle of collodion had formed a lump similar to ivory on the shelf. He heated and compressed his original mix and added collodion as a coating. Billiard balls were made in this way, but flames shot up if touched by a lit cigar, while there was the occasional small explosion when balls hit each other in play. A Colorado billiard saloon proprietor is said to have written to the Hyatts that he did not mind these noises himself but it was a trifle dangerous, as every man in his saloon would immediately pull a gun.

Finally the two brothers mixed pyroxline and camphor and pressurised and heated them to make what they called celluloid, a name which they registered as a trade mark in 1873. The one page patent is shown opposite. The mixture was soft enough to mould when it was heated but it set solid when cool. There are two possible British forerunners: Alexander Parkes of Birmingham, Warwickshire with his GB 3163/1865 and GB 2709/1866 for 'parkesine' and Daniel Spill of London for xyloidine. Spill had patented his substance in the USA as US 101175 just a few months before Hyatt, but the American courts decided that the two patents were different. There is no doubt that the Hyatts popularised the substance.

With financing from New York capitalists they began manufacturing in Newark, New Jersey. There is no evidence that they or anyone else ever collected the $10,000. Hyatt had many other patents, including equipment to make celluloid, water filtration, a sugar cane mill and a flexible ball bearing made out of a spring which could bend and slip (US 485938 in 1891). Hyatt continued to spend time improving billiard balls but when bakelite was introduced from about 1908 he was ready to acknowledge its superiority and immediately switched over from his beloved celluloid. Many other products had been made from celluloid including false teeth, knife handles, combs, brushes and (a major use) even collars and cuffs. With the development of superior solvents celluloid was made into flexible film for photography. However, it was still volatile and inflexible in some ways as it cannot be used in injection moulding or extrusion and so other plastics have taken over its role. Known for drinking half a bottle of champagne daily at lunch as a precaution against tuberculosis, John Wesley Hyatt died in 1920 at Short Hills, New Jersey.

UNITED STATES PATENT OFFICE.

JOHN W. HYATT, JR., AND ISAIAH S. HYATT, OF ALBANY, NEW YORK.

IMPROVEMENT IN TREATING AND MOLDING PYROXYLINE.

Specification forming part of Letters Patent No. **105,338**, dated July 12, 1870.

We, JOHN W. HYATT, Jr., and ISAIAH S. HYATT, both of Albany, in the county of Albany and State of New York, have invented a new and Improved Process of Dissolving Pyroxyline and of Making Solid Collodion, of which the following is a specification:

Our invention consists, first, of so preparing pyroxyline that pigments and other substances in a powdered condition can be easily and thoroughly mixed therewith before the pyroxyline is subjected to the action of a solvent; secondly, of mixing with the pyroxyline so prepared any desirable pigment, coloring matter, or other material, and also any substance in a powdered state which may be vaporized or liquefied and converted into a solvent of pyroxyline by the application of heat; and, thirdly, of subjecting the compound so made to heavy pressure while heated, so that the least practicable proportion of solvent may be used in the production of solid collodion and its compounds.

The following is a description of our process: First, we prepare the pyroxyline by grinding it in water until it is reduced to a fine pulp by means of a machine similar to those employed in grinding paper-pulp. Second, any suitable white or coloring pigment or dyes, when desired, are then mixed and thoroughly ground with the pyroxyline pulp, or any powdered or granulated material is incorporated that may be adapted to the purpose of the manufacture. While the ground pulp is still wet we mix therewith finely-pulverized gum-camphor in about the proportions of one part (by weight) of the camphor to two parts of the pyroxyline when in a dry state. These proportions may be somewhat varied with good results. The gum-camphor may be comminuted by grinding in water, by pounding, or rolling; or, if preferred, the camphor may be dissolved in alcohol or spirits of wine, and then precipitated by adding water, the alcohol leaving the camphor and uniting with the water, when both the alcohol and the water may be drawn off, leaving the camphor in a very finely-divided state. After the powdered camphor is thoroughly mixed with the wet pyroxyline pulp and the other ingredients, we expel the water as far as possible by straining the mixture and subjecting it to an immense pressure in a perforated vessel. This leaves the mixture in a comparatively solid and dry state, but containing sufficient moisture to prevent the pyroxyline from burning or exploding during the remaining process. Third, the mixture is then placed in a mold of any appropriate form, which is heated by steam or by any convenient method, to from 150° to 300° Fahrenheit, to suit the proportion of camphor and the size of the mass, and is subjected to a heavy pressure in a hydraulic or other press. The heat, according to the degree used, vaporizes or liquefies the camphor, and thus converts it into a solvent of the pyroxyline. By introducing the solvent in the manner here described, and using heat to make the solvent active, and pressure to force it into intimate contact every particle of the pyroxyline, we are able to use a less proportion of this or any solvent which depends upon heat for its activity than has ever been known heretofore. After keeping the mixture under heat and pressure long enough to complete the solvent action throughout the mass it is cooled while still under pressure, and then taken out of the mold. The product is a solid about the consistency of sole-leather, but which subsequently becomes as hard as horn or bone by the evaporation of the camphor. Before the camphor is evaporated the material is easily softened by heat, and may be molded into any desirable form, which neither changes nor appreciably shrinks in hardening.

We are aware that camphor made into a solution with alcohol or other solvents of camphor has been used in a liquid state as a solvent of xyloidine. Such use of camphor as a solvent of pyroxyline we disclaim.

Claims

We claim as our invention—

1. Grinding pyroxyline into a pulp, as and for the purpose described.

2. The use of finely-comminuted camphor-gum mixed with pyroxyline pulp, and rendered a solvent thereof by the application of heat, substantially as described.

3. In conjunction with such use of camphor-gum, the employment of pressure, and continuing the same until the mold and contents are cooled, substantially as described.

JOHN W. HYATT, JR.
ISAIAH S. HYATT.

Witnesses:
WM. H. SLINGERLAND,
C. M. HYATT.

The Checkered game of life

Milton Bradley was born in 1836 in Vienna, Maine, his father running a starch mill. In 1847 the family moved to Lowell, Massachusetts and in 1854 Bradley entered the office of a draughtsman and patent agent. In 1856 he became draughtsman at a locomotive works in Springfield, and when that went out of business he set up his own office as a draughtsman and 'patent securer'. He then took an interest in lithography, whereby wax impressions on stone are used in printing, and set up a lithographic works. He had an unfortunate experience when, having been asked to make and print thousands of copies of a photograph of a clean-shaven presidential candidate named Abraham Lincoln, the same candidate, after being persuaded to do so by a little girl, grew a beard, making them worthless. Business continued to be grim with the start of the Civil War.

Bradley thought he would change track again, and designed and made this 'social game' or 'Checkered game of life', although for some reason it was not patented until 1866. At the time board games were rare and were frowned on by many as frivolous. Bradley himself disapproved of gambling, but felt that chance and skill intermingled in life, and that life was a game and that games were life. It was 'A game peculiarly adapted to the home-circle from the fact that it can be played by two or more players, as the company may be, and also is susceptible of being so arranged as to impart useful or instructive facts, or to impress moral truths upon the minds of those engaged in the play'. Each person has a 'teetotum' which is spun to determine the moves. Each player starts from 'infancy' and hopes on achieving 'old age' to have accumulated the most points along the way. The hands in some squares force you off that square, like Snakes and Ladders. Unfortunately his illustration makes it impossible to play as the middle of the board is taken up by the teetotums. Bradley travelled around New York State selling the game and within a year had sold 40,000 copies. In adapted form it still sells as the Game of life® and is one of the most successful games ever. The modern version is somewhat different. The game ends in either a player going bankrupt or becoming a millionaire and 'unlike in real life, the player with the most money wins'.

Following this success Bradley devised a 'Wheel of life', which was a revolving drum with slits to show figures in motion. He also popularised croquet in the USA, including patenting 'Croquet bridge' (US 54848) which improved the design of the hoops. He also filed patents for a card game and a 'toy car and station' and some on other subjects such as engraving printing surfaces, a plaiting machine and what is thought to be the first one-armed paper cutter. The Milton Bradley Company was formed in 1864 and solicited ideas for games from others. The business continues to be active although now part of Hasbro, but still based in Springfield. From 1869 Bradley took a great interest in the idea of the kindergarten, which had been promoted by the German educationalist Friedrich Froebel, who had died in 1852. He published a translation of a book by Froebel (the first book in English on the subject), and produced many educational toys for use with small children. He also wrote about the use of colour in teaching children. These activities lost rather than earned money, but he thought that they were important, as children's activities were vital to their development. Milton Bradley died in Springfield in 1911.

Milton Bradley, Springfield, Massachusetts
Published 3 April 1866 as US 53561

M. Bradley,

Game Board.

Nº 53,561.

Patented Apr. 3, 1866.

Fig. 1.

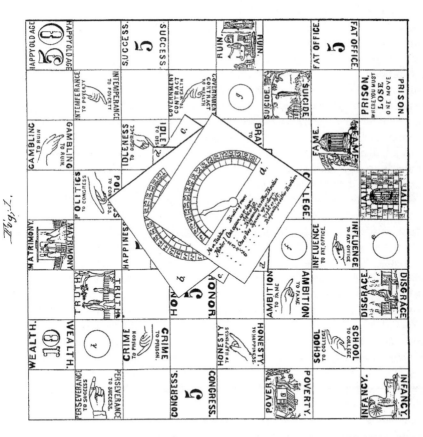

Fig. 2.

Witnesses;
Lewis Bradley
J. B. Gardner.

Inventor;
Milton Bradley

The clasp locker for shoes

Devising a secure and easy method of fastening clothes and other items has exercised the minds of countless inventors. What would be ideal would be a method of doing so in one operation. Elias Howe Jr, the sewing machine pioneer, had an 1851 patent for an 'automatic continuous clothing closure' with 'a series of clasps united by a connecting cord running or sliding upon ribs'. Such devices were in rows and had to be unfastened or fastened one by one, which was obviously tedious.

Whitcomb Judson began the long march towards the concept of the zip fastener with this patent. He lived in Minneapolis while patenting in the area of trams or streetcars in the late 1880s. These included US 402934 from 1889 for a tram propelled by a spinning tube. This was buried underground and used pneumatic power. It was clever but unnecessarily complicated. He founded the Judson Pneumatic Street Railway Company and an experimental line was built in Washington, DC. He then turned to the idea shown in the drawings. The wire hooks were pulled and locked together by the motion of the slider. The improved US 504037 was issued to him on the same day but was dated 18 months later. Both required the slider to be turned around to be ready to zip or unzip. Lewis Walker, a lawyer from Meadville, Pennsylvania, who had been interested in Judson's ideas for pneumatic trams, backed him financially. The new fastener was exhibited at the World's Columbian Exposition in Chicago in 1893. Walker had them installed on his own boots, and set up the Universal Fastener Company. Judson suggested its use for 'mail-bags, belts, and the closing of flexible seams uniting flexible bodies'—either a coy reference to clothes or a catch-all to ensure everything possible was covered. They were ideal for fastening mailbags but by the end of 1897 only 20 mailbags had been fitted with them. Their use in leggings was suggested, which pleased 'Colonel' Walker, so called because of his long service with the National Guard. Nobody seems to have suggested trousers or coats.

Judson kept on making his invention more and more complicated. Whatever he did the product was cumbersome, bulky, and difficult to manufacture. It had to be cheap to make or it was not going to sell. Walker remarked that 'Judson's way of meeting a difficulty was to add invention after invention to his already large supply'. Sales were good enough to raise hopes, but not enough to make a business. The problem was that it readily fell apart in use. In 1905 an improved fastener was thought to be the answer with hooks and eyes pointing along the seam to be closed. It was sold under the name of C-curity. A typical advertisement claimed, 'A pull and it's done! No more open skirts. . . . Your skirt is always securely and neatly fastened'. It was still apt to 'pop open' at unfortunate moments, with bending over being particularly risky. On such occasions the slider became stuck and the only way to remove the garment, if it were impossible to slip out of it, was to cut off the slider. It did work if gently used in the workshop, but not as customarily used in the outside world. Eventually Gideon Sundback, a Swedish immigrant, solved the problem for what was now the Hookless Fastener Company by filing a patent (US 1219881 in 1914) for the zip fastener. Judson had already died, in 1909 in Muskegon, Michigan. Walker once said of Judson, 'His inventive capacity was great; his practical utility of that capacity was almost nil'. Walker remained involved in the business until his death in 1938.

(No Model.)

W. L. JUDSON.
CLASP LOCKER OR UNLOCKER FOR SHOES.

No. 504,038.

Patented Aug. 29, 1893.

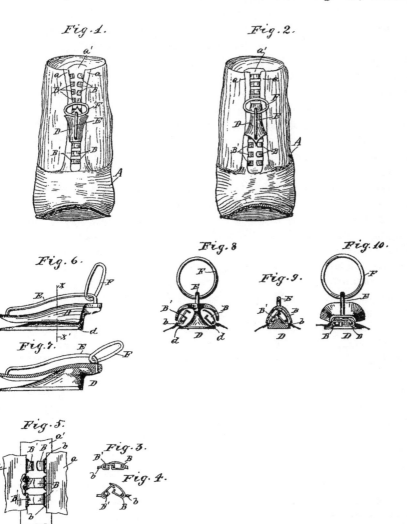

Fig. 1.

Fig. 2.

Fig. 6.

Fig. 7.

Fig. 8.

Fig. 9.

Fig. 10.

Fig. 5.

Fig. 3.

Fig. 4.

Witnesses.
A. U. Opsahl.
E. F. Elmore.

Inventor.
Whitcomb Judson
By his Attorney.
Jas. F. Williams

The clockwork dancing toy

The idea of 'automata' or mechanical toys has long fascinated toymakers and wealthy patrons alike. The German toymakers were particularly skilled, with human figures, as in DE 88335 or animals such as dogs, as in DE 78360. These used complex sets of balances, wheels, chains and so on to walk or crawl. The problem was that automata of this type were very expensive, and so few were made of each model. Rather more modest in cost was this example, some models of which survive. It is thought to be the first American patent for a toy operated by clockwork. Figure 2 shows the clockwork mechanism which causes the bar (D) in Figure 1 to tremble. This makes the jointed limbed dolls hanging from the bar appear to dance in turn. Figure 3 shows a view from above the stage with the line (x–x) being the cross-section shown in Figure 1 and the line (y–y) being that in Figure 2. James Cromwell states that the dancers 'have the grotesque motions peculiar to the ordinary Ethiopian or negro dancers'. Surviving examples have mirrors placed around the stage to give the impression that there are numerous dancers, which may be a later, unpatented improvement. The idea of a trembling bar was not new, as shown by Charles Thévenot's FR 4352 in 1858, which also provided sound effects.

In 1866 Henry Vrooman of Hoboken, New Jersey patented (US 58006) a horse operated by an eccentric clockwork mechanism. A famous clockwork toy was the savings bank with a crouching dog on the top. When you placed a coin before it, it sprang forward, grasped the coin, retired and deposited the coin. This was patented as US 206893 by Enoch Morrison of New York City in 1878. Although all these devices were meant to be toys for children one wonders if the parents were not enjoying them more.

Easily the most famous automaton was a spurious one. Baron von Kempelen of Pressburg (now Bratislava, Slovakia) invented in 1769 the 'Turk', who would play chess with all comers, even defeating Napoleon in a game in 1809. It is thought to be the first 'cabinet illusion'. The top half of a figure of a richly dressed Turk was fixed on top of a box full of mechanical movements. He would be wound up by the exhibitor and would then make exaggerated movements in playing opponents. There did not seem to be room for a person to hide, but the exhibitor would open first one side and then the other side of the box to show that there was nothing hidden. The real player, of course, would contort his or her body appropriately to avoid detection. After von Kempelen's death in 1804 the 'Turk' was sold repeatedly on to various showmen and had a tour of the USA in 1826. The crowds began to get suspicious—a certain member of the entourage was never around when the 'Turk' played, many candles of different sizes were placed near the 'Turk' to provide the occupant with light through the gauze on the chest, and so on—and finally in 1827 a man was seen getting out of the back by two boys after the show. The *Baltimore Gazette* published an exposé. The 'Turk' was finally sold to the Chinese Museum in Philadelphia in 1840 only to be burnt in a fire in 1854. By then various owners had published explanations.

James Cromwell, New York City, New York
Published 28 March 1865 as US 46997

J. M. Cromwell,

Automatic Toy,

№46,997.   Patented Mar. 28, 1865.

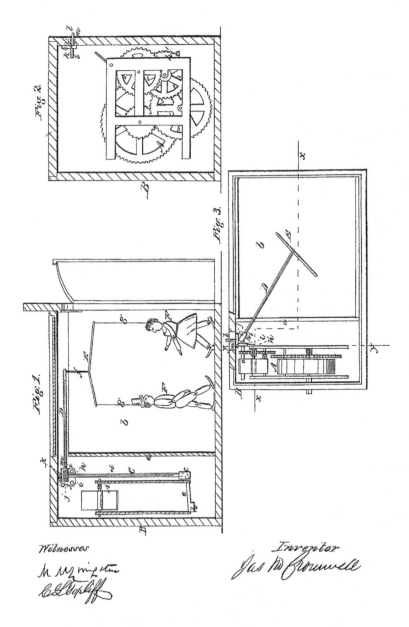

Witnesses   Inventor

Jas M Cromwell

The combined plough and gun

This 'New and Improved Ordnance Plow', patented by C. M. French and W. H. Fancher, was mainly a conventional plough, drawn by horses with the farmer using the handles to steer. The sharp end which penetrates the soil is called the share. Ideally the plough should be made of cast iron with wooden handles. The unusual part was marked in shading on Figure 2, with vent holes near the end of the barrel. 'As a piece of light ordnance its capacity may vary from a projectile of one to three pounds [0.4 to 1.4 kg] weight without rendering it cumbersome as a plow. Its utility as an implement of the twofold capacity described is unquestionable, especially when used in border localities, subject to savage feuds and guerrilla warfare. As a means of defense in repelling surprises and skirmishing attacks on those engaged in a peaceful avocation it is unrivalled, as it can be immediately brought into action by disengaging the team, and in times of danger may be used in the field, ready charged with its deadly missles of ball or grape.' The share could be thrust into the soil to anchor the plough and to resist recoil. The 'very slight expense' was considered well worth the trouble.

This invention may sound hilarious, but the inventors had serious reasons for devising it. The Civil War was in its second year and Southern cavalry were carrying out raids on Union-held territory. The problem for farmers using such a plough would surely be that the raiders would soon learn to shoot anyone using such a plough long before the plough was turned around and within range. The US Patent Office, incidentally, includes this invention under the classification 'Earth working: combined' without dividing this further into kinds of combined ploughs. Ploughs were of course of immense importance in agriculture. John Deere was the most significant inventor working in the area. He was born in Rutland, Vermont in 1804 and moved in 1837 to Grand Retour, Illinois as a blacksmith. Local farmers were very upset that their cast-iron ploughs, built to suit New England's light and sandy soils, were ineffective in the sticky Prairie soils as soil quickly accumulated on the ploughs. Deere thought that a properly shaped, polished mouldboard together with a steel share might solve the problem. He bent a broken sawmill blade over a log, used it as a cutting blade and combined it with a cast-iron mouldboard for lifting and turning with its upper surface polished. When he tried it on a local farm it worked: the first self-scouring plough. Together with the village's founder, Leonard Andrus, also from Vermont, he at first designed three new ploughs, but continuously worked to improve them.

Deere believed in making ploughs and then trying to sell them, when it was normal for a blacksmith to make tools 'to order'. At first Deere used any spare steel that could be found but in 1843 a shipment was sent out from England. By 1846 he had switched to a supply from Pittsburgh, Pennsylvania, when they were turning out 1,000 a year. In that year Deere sold out the existing business to Andrus and set up a new business in Moline, chosen as it was on the Mississippi river, which provided both transport and water power. By 1855 13,000 ploughs were being sold annually; by 1876 75,000. Deere did not actually take out a patent until his US 46454 in 1865, 'Improvements in landside and share plates for plows'. He died in 1886 at Moline by which time 800 men were working at his factory.

French & Fancher.

Plow.

Nº 36,600.   Patented Jun. 17, 1862.

Fig. 1.

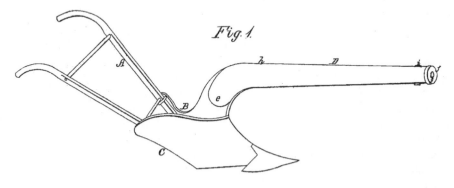

Fig. 2.

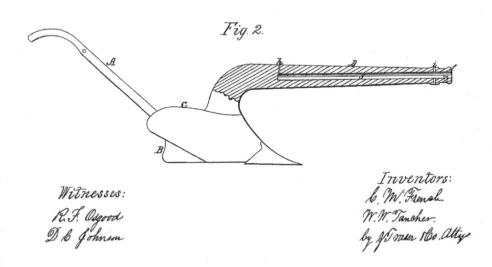

Witnesses:
R. F. Osgood
D. C. Johnson

Inventors:
C. M. French
W. H. Fancher.
by J. Fraser & Co. Attys

The compressed air brake

Except as a brand or company name the name of Westinghouse is little known today. Yet George Westinghouse was one of the most versatile and creative inventors ever. He was born in 1846 in Central Bridge, New York State, and his family moved in his boyhood to Schenectady, where his father ran a company making farm machinery. One day his father asked him to cut some pipe and he designed a powered device which would do this swiftly, possibly the same as his first patent, US 48857, a sawing machine, granted in July 1865 when he was only 18 years old.

One day in 1866 Westinghouse was riding a train when it suddenly came to a halt to avoid a wrecked train on the rails ahead. The brakes at the time were primitive. The driver would apply a brake for the locomotive and each carriage had a brakeman who would apply a hand-brake. Since they were unlikely to apply the brakes at the same time, or with the same pressure, derailments of part of the train at least could easily occur when stopping. Trains moved slowly to minimise the dangers. After he read about tunnellers in the Mont Cenis rail tunnel in Switzerland using compressed air for their rock drilling machinery, Westinghouse decided to use the same principle. An auxiliary engine supplies power to compress air which is passed through the couplings to each carriage. While the system is active the brakes are prevented from working but if a coupling breaks, or the driver applies the brakes, the air is lost or cut off and the brakes are instantly applied in each carriage. He was only 22 when the patent was issued.

Westinghouse was nicknamed 'Crazy George' when he tried to talk to people about his invention. It was unsound and nonsensical. He finally managed to persuade a friend, Ralph Baggaley, to provide some money to demonstrate the system. Railway officials watched but made no comment. Some months later a senior official, W. W. Card, managed to persuade his company to instal the equipment on one of their trains, although Westinghouse had to pay for it and to take on all risks. The train was boarded for a test run and as it emerged from the Great Hill Tunnel at Pittsburgh a horse-drawn wagon was seen blocking the track. In his hurry to urge the horses across, their driver fell onto the line. The train safely stopped—1 m from a much relieved man. The occupants of the train were bruised by being flung about by the unscheduled stop, and poured out to complain, only to be delighted when they realised the reason. The Westinghouse Air Brake Company was soon formed with Westinghouse as President, Baggaley as Vice President and Card as General Agent. The new concept was safer and meant that trains could travel much faster as there was less risk of derailment. From 1893 the system was made compulsory on American railways.

Westinghouse was responsible for 361 patents in all. Some were in railways, as with automatic block signalling, the concept still used today by which sections of track are controlled to avoid collisions. He also introduced the first way to transmit natural gas efficiently and ensured, in a ferocious battle, that alternating current rather than Thomas Edison's favoured direct current was used for electricity transmission. Westinghouse introduced many benefits for his employees such as only working for half a day on Saturday (in 1871), a pension fund (1908) and paid holidays (1913). However, many of his companies were lost as a result of the financial panic of 1907. Westinghouse died in New York City in 1914.

G. WESTINGHOUSE, JR

STEAM POWER BRAKE

NO. 88,929.

PATENTED APR. 13. 1869

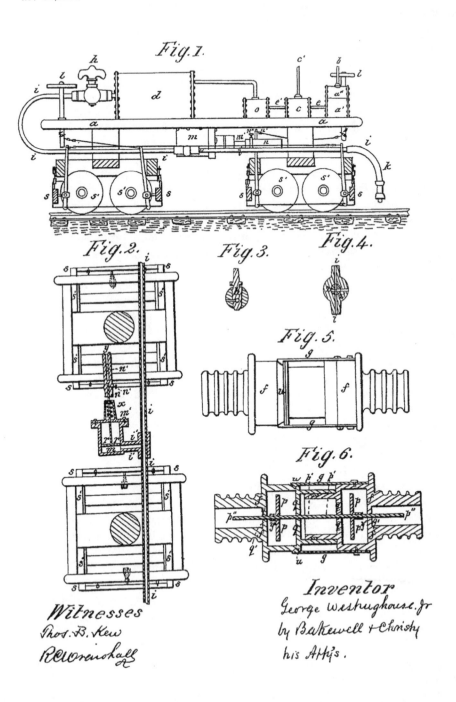

Fig. 1.

Fig. 2. *Fig. 3.* *Fig. 4.*

Fig. 5.

Fig. 6.

Witnesses
Thos. B. Kew
R.C. Wrenshall

Inventor
George Westinghouse. Jr
by Bakewell & Christy
his Att'ys.

The comptometer

Numerous calculating machines were invented in Victorian times. Frank Baldwin of St Louis, Missouri with US 159244 in 1875 invented the first which incorporated a flat pinwheel. This, however, is the story of the comptometer, a machine which (with numerous improved models) was used well into the 20th century by office workers. Dorr Eugene Felt was born in Rock County, Wisconsin in 1862, son of a farmer, and moved to Chicago in about 1882. He noticed while working in a machine shop how machines were used to control the depth of the cut in textiles and thought that the same idea could be used for a calculating machine. He financed his idea by getting a job with A. B. Lowther in exchange for rights in any invention. An old employer suggested that Felt buy out Lowther's interest, which he did by borrowing $800 from a cousin, Chauncey Foster. Meanwhile Robert Tarrant, another machine shop owner, offered work space and $5,000 for materials for a 50% interest. Foster wanted his money back, so that was covered by this money. In 1887 the two men founded the Felt & Tarrant Manufacturing Company, with Felt in charge.

Felt describes how he made the original model. 'It was near Thanksgiving Day of 1884, and I decided to use the holiday in the construction of the wooden model. I went to the grocer's and selected a box which seemed to be about the right size for the casing. It was a macaroni box, so I have always called it the macaroni box model. For keys, I procured some meat skewers from the butcher around the corner and some staples from a hardware store for the key guides, and an assortment of elastic bands to be used for springs. When Thanksgiving Day came, I got (home) early and went to work with a few tools, principally a jackknife. I soon discovered that there were some parts which would require better tools than I had at hand for that purpose, and when night came, I found that the model I had expected to construct in a day was a long way to be complete or in working order. I finally had some of the parts made out of metal and finished the model soon after New Year's Day 1885.' The model is now in the Smithsonian. Felt presumably spent longer working on the details as the patent was not filed until 18 months later. It was the first key-driven adding machine.

The digits one to nine (no zero was needed) were represented by keys on the top, with 11 windows at the front to display results. A lever cleared the results. Pressing keys moved the vertical rods; they ended in toothed segments which geared with toothed pinions. The machine carried automatically. Adding was easy, but subtraction was more difficult. Smaller or 'complimentary' digits on each key were for subtraction. Multiplication and division were initially not possible. The first machine was sold to the Equitable Gas Light and Fuel Company in January 1888. However, a court battle ensued with William Burroughs, a former bank clerk from St Louis, Missouri, whose US 388116-119 were thought to conflict, and some of whose features had been filed from January 1885. In some ways Burroughs's machine was better as, for example, it could print out the totals. Most of Felt's 46 patents were on improvements to the comptometer, a name which was registered as a trade mark in 1905 although used for many years from 1888. He died in 1930.

(No Model.)

5 Sheets—Sheet 2.

D. E. FELT.

ADDING MACHINE.

No. 366,945.

Patented July 19, 1887.

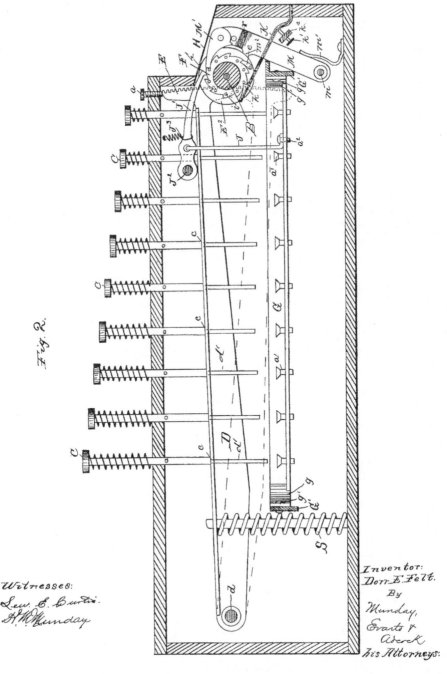

Fig. 2.

Inventor:
Dorr E. Felt.
By
Munday,
Evarts &
Adcock
his Attorneys:

Witnesses:
Lew. E. Curtis.
H. W. Munday

The cork-filled life preserver

This almost-heraldic set of drawings shows the first known attempt to have 'a jacket, waistcoat or coat composed of any kind of tissue in which is introduced a quantity of from eighteen to twenty quarts [20–22 litres] of rasped or grated cork'. Figures 4 and 5 show the rasp or grater. Nothing else seems to be known of Napoleon Edouard Guerin apart from his other patent, US 3019 of 1843, which involved hatching and rearing 7,500 chickens in a heated building. He was presumably of French origin but does not seem to have had any patents in that country. Just how useful this life preserver would have been in practice is not known. The first standard, circular cork-filled lifebuoy has been attributed to Mr Carte of Hull, Yorkshire, an ordnance storekeeper in an unpatented invention in 1848. To this day cork is widely used in life saving because of its lightness and the air pockets within it. There was much interest in means of preserving life at sea by using air in inflatable costumes, belts or cushions. Warren Simonds of Boston, Massachusetts with his US 16555 in 1857 shows a bearded man energetically swimming with an inflated belt round him. Leon Lejuste of Douai, France's GB 3079/1861 has a man in the water, with top hat and a cigar in his hand, wearing an inflated skirt and leggings round his legs. In another drawing he is aiming a rifle while floating, the inventor explaining that his invention can be used for military purposes.

Liborio Pedrazzoli of London with his GB 16923/1896 meant his apparatus to be used for helping swimmers but they would probably need some sort of life preserving aid. The drawing shows an understandably apprehensive swimmer in full bathing costume clutching a furled umbrella in each outstretched hand. Louis Grünfelder of Belfort, France with GB 3604/1887 has an excellent drawing of a debonair man with a boater on his head wearing an impermeable suit and a large, boat-shaped float worn round his chest. Plates were strapped to the feet. Best of all, perhaps, was John Banks of Northampton, Northamptonshire with his GB 619/1857 which involved a chest of drawers with a round hole running from top to bottom in the middle of the chest. In case of need the top was folded up in two sections and the chest of drawers divided to allow admission of the person who then snapped it shut again and closed the halves of the top to seal himself or herself in. The inventor does not seem to have thought of the difficulty of being flung into the sea in his device or, alternatively, of getting into it while in the sea. Saving life at sea need not be confined to life preservers. Besides many excellent ideas for lifeboats, including inflatable or collapsible lifeboats, Henry Hallock of Brookhaven, New York in 1858 with his US 20426 had an idea for saving several lives at once. This was his concept of 'self-detaching buoyant life-preserving state-rooms'. Each stateroom was in the shape of a cylinder which rested on short grooves on the deck. If the ship sank the cylinder slid off the grooves and floated to the surface. Every comfort and need was foreseen by Hallock in a detailed patent specification.

Napoleon Edouard Guerin, New York City, New York
Published on 16 November 1841 as US 2359

N. E. Guerin.
Life Preserver.

N.º 23.59.

Patented Nov. 16, 1841.

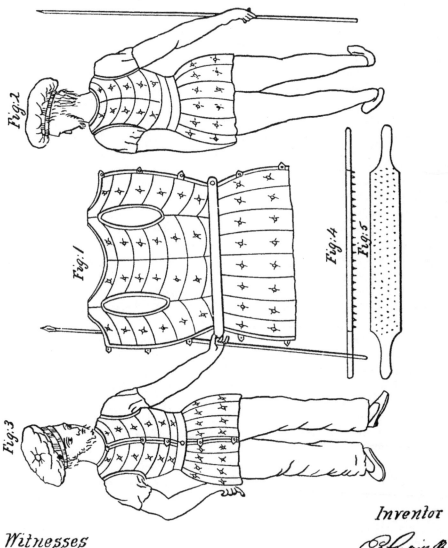

Fig. 2

Fig. 1

Fig. 4

Fig. 5

Fig. 3

Inventor

Witnesses
P. Morison
I. Coppinger

O. Guerin

The crown top for bottles

In early to mid Victorian times bottles were normally sealed with corks, but carbonated drinks such as many soft drinks, champagne or beer could force the bottle open. Making the entire stopper of cork was expensive and for many drinks the bottle had to be stored so that the cork was always kept moist. Stable contents were much easier, and a popular American method of storing stable contents such as preserves was using the famous 'Mason jar' by John Mason of New York with his US 22186 in 1858, which was not for the actual jar but rather the diagonal grooves in the neck which make a secure fit for the screw top. William Painter was born in Triadelphia, Maryland in 1838, son of a Quaker farmer. While working at a patent leather factory in Wilmington, Delaware he started to apply for patents, beginning with a method of giving change for fares with US 21082 in 1858 and then a railway car seat that could be converted to a couch, a counterfeit coin detector and a kerosene lamp burner. In 1865 he was offered the position of foreman of the Murrill & Keizer machine shop at Baltimore and stayed there for 20 years, inventing a variety of devices, but mainly pumps.

From 1880 Painter began experimenting with ideas for securely bottling carbonated drinks. In April 1885 he filed for US 315655 for a wire-retaining stopper which swung up to make a tight seal over the top. This was reusable. Painter and his friends organised a company to exploit this invention. However in June 1885 he filed for US 327099, which cost $1/10$ as much to make, although it could only be used the one time. So the company was reorganised to exploit this invention instead. Finally the drawings shown are for a single-use cap of metal with a cork liner, much used to this day, although often without the cork. The company was reorganised for the third time. Painter explained in the patent that the thin slice of cork was used for hygiene. He also invented the machinery to make the crowns and then to place them on the bottles. He did not invent a bottle opener although in this patent he suggests opening bottles with 'a knife, a screw-driver, a nail, an ice-pick'. Acceptance of the new idea was slow as a recession was in progress. As an experiment a brewer tried shipping a cargo of beer to South America and back and found that the beer was intact and in good condition when it returned. By 1905 25% of American bottlers were using the crimped crown tops (or bottle caps).

A little earlier Hiram Codd of Camberwell, Surrey had been working along different lines on the same problem. His key patent was GB 2621/1872 although he patented various improvements. He made a bottle with a glass marble stopper trapped within the neck of the bottle. Filling the bottle under gas pressure forced the stopper up until it met a rubber washer at the lip of the bottle. When opening the stopper was forced down projecting ridges in the neck so that the contents could be poured out. The term 'codswallop' for a poor drink may have come from badly made examples of his work being condemned by the consumer; 'wallop' is slang for beer. Codd's invention was the norm in Britain until the crown top superseded it in the 1930s. Painter once talked to a travelling salesman named King Camp Gillette and told him that a cheap product that was sold repeatedly would be an excellent idea. Gillette went on to patent the safety razor with US 775134 in 1905. Painter retired in 1903 with 85 patents in his name and died in Baltimore in 1906.

(No Model.)

W. PAINTER.
BOTTLE SEALING DEVICE.

No. 468,226.   Patented Feb. 2, 1892.

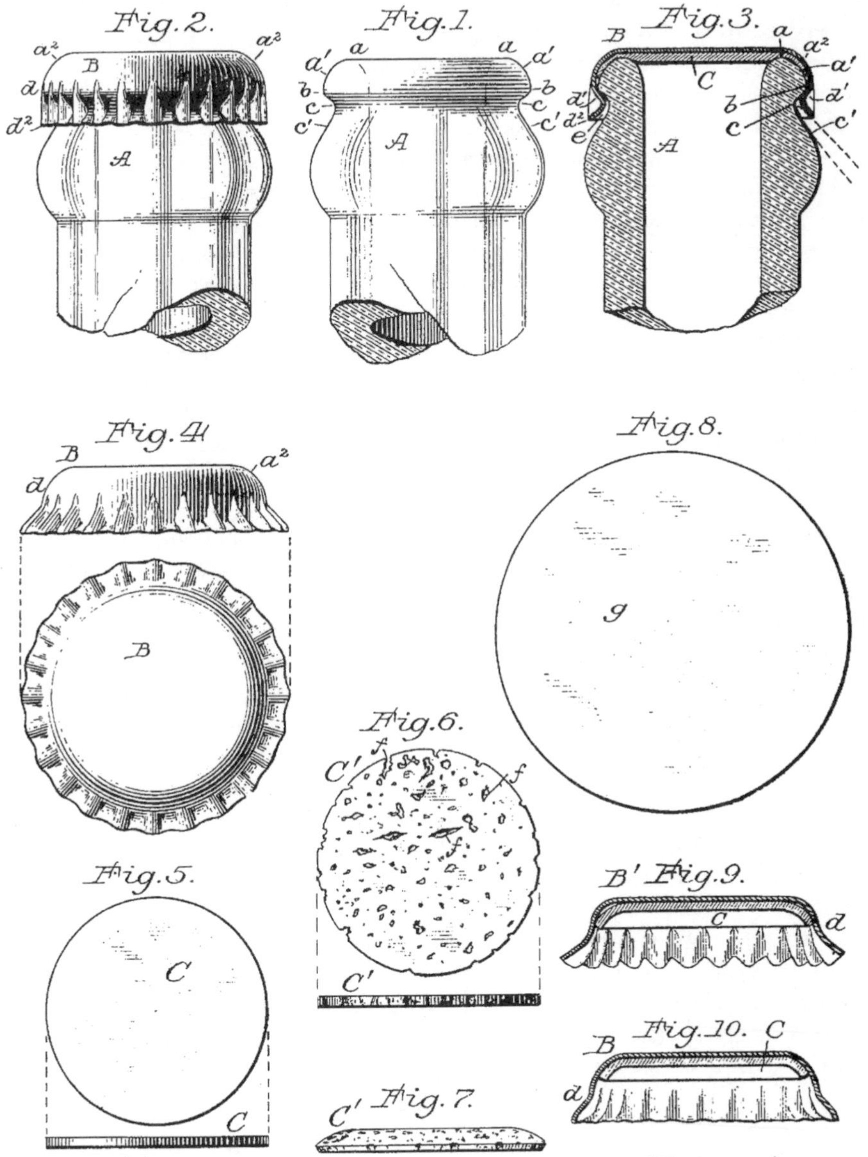

Fig.2. Fig.1. Fig.3.
Fig.4. Fig.8.
Fig.6.
Fig.5. B' Fig.9.
Fig.10. C
Fig.7.

Attest:
Philip F. Larner.
Howell Battle

Inventor:
William Painter
By Wm C. Wood attorney

The deliverance coffin

The title given above is a rough translation of the German *Rettungssarg*, while the British patent offers 'An apparatus for rescuing from the grave persons buried by mistake' and the American title is a concise 'Coffin-signal'. Premature burial was something that much preoccupied the Victorians, with Edgar Allan Poe's *The premature burial* just one contribution. Many asked that they be pricked to see if blood flowed, or to be buried only when the body was clearly going off, or to be buried with a vial of poison. It has been suggested that the idea of the 'wake' was to give the deceased one last chance to wake up. The subject is no joke: there is no doubt that some people have been mistakenly buried alive after fits and comas.

Adalbert Kwiatkowski's invention relates to 'safety-coffins'. 'Its object to provide a coffin with devices whereby in case of the burial of an apparently dead person an alarm will be given to the outer world by the slightest movement of the apparently dead body.' Figure 1 shows the vertical tube extending above the coffin. Figure 2 shows the tube when operating a signal. Figure 3 shows the 'bridle' resting on the forehead. Figure 4 is for the release of the signal while Figures 5 to 7 are details of the signal mechanism. Figure 8 is a view of the cap for covering the vertical tube. Figure 1 shows a rod (t) with a 'sheave or plate' (i). The spring (f) is compressed and releases the sheaf when the signal apparatus is actuated. The idea of the signalling is obvious: even if the person involuntarily stirs and is not conscious the mechanism is designed to work. The raising of the 'sheave', besides being a signal, allows air to enter the coffin. The cost of building in such precautions must have been considerable.

There are 23 American patents in the classification 27/31, 'Life signals', up to 1900. The first is US 81437 of 1868 by Frank Vester of Newark, New Jersey. Most work along the same lines as Kwiatkowski's but with a rope attached to the body ringing a bell on the surface. The modern International Patent Classification or IPC has a class A62B33/00 for 'Devices for allowing seemingly-dead persons to escape or draw attention; Breathing apparatus for accidentally buried person' which includes avalanche victims and the like. A complicated variation was by Michael Karnicki of Warsaw, Poland, who is said to have been Chamberlain to the Emperor of Russia. He covered with four American patents in 1896 and 1897 the idea of a spring-loaded ball that rested on the corpse's chest. Any movement of the chest released the spring, opening the box lid and allowing light and air into the coffin. In addition a flag sprang up, a bell rang for 30 minutes, and a lamp burned after sunset. A speaking tube connected with the surface. A complete reversal of the concept is represented by GB 4250/1818 by Edward Lillie Bridgman of London, tallow chandler, who had a cast iron coffin to discourage 'resurrectionists', those who dug up the dead to provide specimens for medical students. It turned out that his coffins could be opened by the determined with sledgehammers. Kwiatkowski's later GB 20444/1893 is for a more prosaic sleeping berth in a railway carriage.

Adalbert Kwiatkowski, Posen-Wilda, Germany
Filed 17 April 1892 and published as DE 66424, GB 8502/1892 and US 500013

ADALBERT KWIATKOWSKI IN POSEN-WILDA (Provinz Posen).

Rettungssarg.

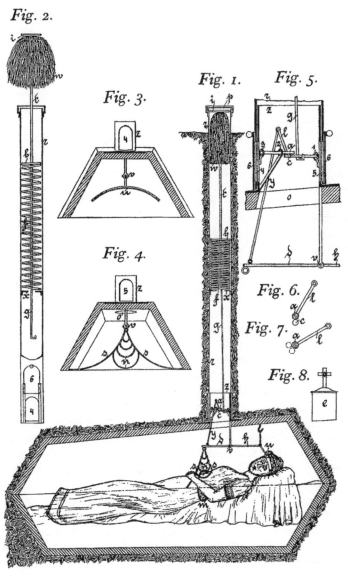

Fig. 1. Fig. 2. Fig. 3. Fig. 4. Fig. 5. Fig. 6. Fig. 7. Fig. 8.

Zu der Patentschrift

№ 66424.

Device for waking persons from sleep

Many people suffer from a chronic inability to get up in the morning. Samuel Applegate was determined that this should not be a problem with his device, which is the oldest in its class 368/12, 'Horology: combined with disparate device: external alarms'. It is unusual, and the inventor summed up his ideas so well that it would be a shame not to quote extensively from the patent. The inventor states, 'The object of my invention is to construct a simple and effective device for waking persons from sleep at any time which may have previously been determined upon, the device being also adapted for use in connection with an electric or other burglar-alarm apparatus, in place of the usual gong-alarms'.

Figure 1 shows 'the manner in which it is to be used' while Figure 2 is a side-view with Figure 3 showing more detail. Figures 4 and 5 are alternative 'releasing' devices. Applegate pointed out that 'Ordinary bell or rattle alarms are not at all times effective for their intended purpose, as a person in time becomes so accustomed to the noise that sleep is not disturbed when the alarm is sounded'. He wanted to 'provide a device which will not be liable to this objection'. 'In carrying out my invention I suspend a light frame in such a position that it will hang directly over the head of the sleeper, the suspending-cord being combined with automatic releasing devices, whereby the frame is at the proper time permitted to fall onto the sleeper's face.' Presumably the weight could be increased if the sleeper became 'accustomed' to the alarm, particularly as Applegate would 'prefer to limit the extent of fall of the frame (A) so that the bars (a) and (b) will not come into contact with the sleeper's face'.

The release mechanism could work in a variety of ways. The hour hand of the clock could strike the plate (h), or a magnet could be used with the hands completing the circuit, or a burglar alarm mechanism could be used. Applegate had tried to think through some of the details. A connection could be made between the cord (B) and a self-lighting gas burner so that the gas lighting could be lit at the same time. He had also thought about how to pack up the frame (A) to make it 'more compact for transportation'. What he had not thought about was the neighbours' reaction to someone installing the device.

The reference to using it as a burglar alarm is interesting, although this would only work if someone were lying in bed. No details were given. Many burglar alarm patents were eminently sensible, such as US 13157 in 1855 by Ephraim Brown of Lowell, Massachusetts whose device would both ring a bell and light a gas lamp if a protected door were opened. In an era when turning on a light involved striking a match this was useful. Quite a few patents involved a 'central station' being signalled if an attempt were made at illegal entry, which we regard as a modern idea. Most alarm clocks of the time were boringly practical. An unusual twist was given in GB 6118/1885 by Hans and Jens Jensen of London. Their suggestion was to have an electric circuit completed by the weight of a person in bed. When the hour hand of the alarm clock came around to the set time the alarm would go off and would only stop if the circuit were broken—by the occupant getting out of bed.

(No Model.)

S. S. APPLEGATE.

DEVICE FOR WAKING PERSONS FROM SLEEP.

No. 256,265.   Patented Apr. 11, 1882.

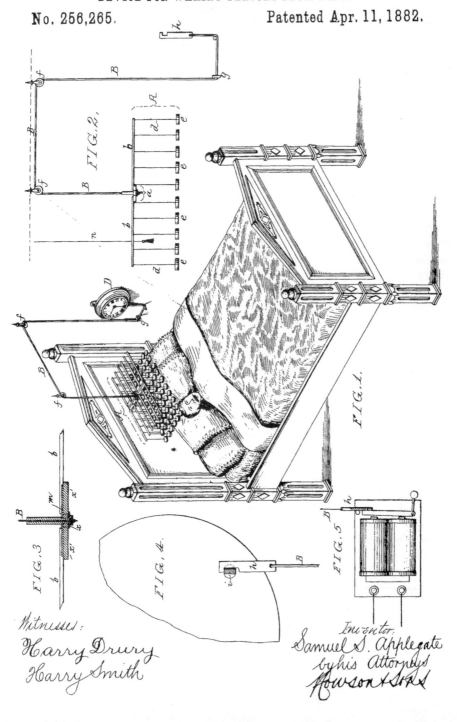

Witnesses:
Harry Drury
Harry Smith

Inventor:
Samuel S. Applegate
by his Attorneys
Howson & Sons

The diesel engine

Rudolf Diesel was born in Paris, France in 1858 to Bavarian-born parents. The family was deported to Britain when the Franco-Prussian War of 1870–71 broke out. They later returned and Rudolf completed his schooling in Augsburg and Munich. While attending engineering classes at the Munich Polytechnic he heard Professor von Linde lecture on the inefficiencies of steam engines. Only 12% of the heat supplied turned into useful energy. Diesel noted this on the margin of his notebook and this set him thinking about a new kind of engine. After graduation Diesel worked for von Linde's refrigeration firm in Paris and then in Germany.

Diesel began to study the Otto four-cycle internal combustion engine. He designed an engine that did not require electric ignition and which used a mixture of petroleum and air rather than petrol (refined petroleum) and air. In 1892 Diesel published DE 67207 before the engine was built. The patent and a book persuaded two companies to pay Diesel to build his engine, which was powered by coal dust. It exploded when it was tried out, but there was no doubt that heat from compression alone was enough to ignite the fuel. He redesigned and built a new engine (running on petroleum) and this worked satisfactorily in 1895 and was patented as the illustrated invention. Internal combustion engines work by taking in air and a fuel, compressing them, and igniting them with a spark. A diesel engine compresses air alone to a much higher degree, to a ratio of between 14:1 and 22:1 rather than the internal combustion engine's 8:1 to 12:1, and the heat generated by the compression is enough for ignition. The advantages of the diesel were greater fuel efficiency and a simpler design which meant that no spark plugs or carburettors were needed (and less wear on the engine). However, the heavier fuel required made it more polluting than the internal combustion engine, although this was unlikely to have been of concern then.

Diesel engines are either two-stroke or four-stroke models. 'Stroke' means the number of actions. Four-stroke models involve intake, compression, ignition and exhaust. The exact designs, for example of the fuel injector, will vary. A two-stroke engine involves just compression and exhaust and means a different design so that, for example, the exhaust valves are open all the time. The US rights for the patent were sold to the German-American brewer Adolphus Busch for $250,000. A single diesel was made and installed at the Anheuser Busch Brewery at St Louis, Missouri in 1898, the first ever commercial use. Production and usage of the new engines spread rapidly.

On 29 September 1913 Diesel boarded the mail steamer *Dresden* at Antwerp to attend a meeting in London of Consolidated Diesel Manufacturing Ltd. He seemed to be in good spirits, but was never seen alive after he turned in for the night. A few weeks later some German fishermen handed over a couple of rings that they said they had recovered from a well-dressed body in the water. This was just before a storm had broken which prevented them from retaining the corpse for burial. The rings were proven to be Diesel's. His death is still a mystery and an accident, suicide or murder have all been suggested.

Rudolf Diesel, Berlin, Germany
Published 30 March 1895 as DE 86633, GB 4243/1895 and US 608845

RUDOLF DIESEL in MÜNCHEN.

Vorrichtung zum Anlassen von Viertakt-Verbrennungskraftmaschinen durch Umwandlung derselben in Zweitakt-Druckluftmaschinen.

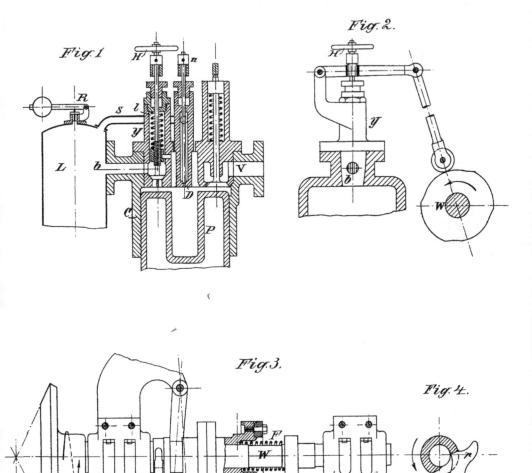

Fig. 1.

Fig. 2.

Fig. 3.

Fig. 4.

Zu der Patentschrift

№ 86633.

PHOTOGR. DRUCK DER REICHSDRUCKEREI

The dishwasher

Josephine Garis was born in Ohio in 1841, daughter to John Garis, a civil engineer who made a major contribution to the building of Chicago before the disastrous fire of 1871. She was also a descendant of John Fitch, the steamboat pioneer. She married William Cochran, a merchant and populist politician, and aspired to be a society lady, sometimes adding an 'e' to Cochran as it sounded posher. The china used at dinners was old and valuable and she was upset by the servants who sometimes chipped it when washing up. She tried washing the china herself but found this demeaning. So she thought of a wire rack holding the dishes with jets of water being directed at them. Her husband, meanwhile, was growing ill and asked her to come with him while he went away for a 'cure'. She refused and said that she wanted to work on her invention. He returned after the cure and died a few weeks later, heavily in debt. Somehow she managed to work on her idea for several years in a shed, assisted by loans from friends who believed in her idea.

The basic ideas are shown opposite by the drawing which is on its side. Not shown is the 'crate' holding racks for the dishes and cutlery with clamps keeping them in place. One of the cylinders at the bottom holds hot water, the other soap-suds. They are separated by barrier (5) as water is used in separate operations and drains back to the original cylinder. Each cylinder contains a pump-piston, with the water directed through the pipes (7). When the handle (17) at the left is moved the portion (15) (from which the 'crate' is suspended) engages with (19) or (18) alternately which actuates each pump. After the operation the water drains off to the bottom and back into the relevant cylinder through holes (6) assisted by a moveable bottom which slides to ensure that the water drains back to the right cylinder.

Cochran made some models for friends while larger models were powered by steam. At first her Garis-Cochran Dish-Washing Machine Company found it hard to make sales but gradually interest built up, especially in nearby Chicago. Manufacturing rights were acquired in 1889 by the Crescent Washing Machine Company. Large restaurants especially bought the new device. The dishwasher was exhibited at the 1892–93 Columbian Exposition in Chicago where it was also used in the massive kitchens. One newspaper wrote that it was capable of 'washing, scalding, rinsing and drying from 5 to 20 dozen dishes of all shapes and sizes in two minutes'.

At least 30 other American women patented dishwashing devices between 1870 and 1895 but this was the one that both worked well and which became popular. These other inventors included Margaret Wilcox of Chicago with her US 426486 in 1890 for a combined clothes and dishwasher, which involved a bowl being moved around within a larger bowl. It does not sound very hygienic. Cochran continued to work on her idea with US 391782 in 1888 (where Jacob Kritch of Cleveland, Ohio assisted her) and, as her last attempt, US 852419 in 1907. She later said, 'If I knew all I know today I would never have had the courage to start' and also commented that the hard part was not going from being a socialite to a mechanic, but from a socialite to a promoter. Josephine Cochran died in 1913 and her company was eventually absorbed into the Whirlpool Corporation. The automatic dishwasher as we know it was not invented until 1940.

(No Model.)

8 Sheets—Sheet 1.

J. G. COCHRAN.
DISH WASHING MACHINE.

No. 355,139.

Patented Dec. 28, 1886.

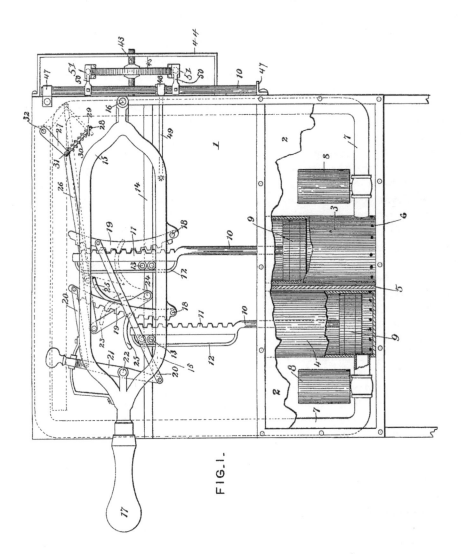

FIG.1.

Dynamite

Alfred Nobel was born in Stockholm, Sweden in 1833. His father, the inventor of an early torpedo, was asked to build and run a torpedo factory in St Petersburg, Russia and so Alfred from the age of 10 lived there. He was educated at home by tutors and experimented in chemistry. When he was 18 his father sent him for several years around Europe and to the USA to learn about engineering, and he added fluent English to Russian, French and German. When he rejoined his family he found his father was experimenting with explosives. Explosives were needed in mining and road building and for many other engineering projects. There were many types such as guncotton and saltpetre. The problem was not how to cause an explosion but how to prevent one, as these materials were liable to explode if poorly handled or stored. It was also necessary to control the actual explosion safely. Father and son began to work on the problem by looking at nitroglycerine, which had been discovered by Ascanio Sobrero, a professor from Turin, Italy in 1847. It is said that one of Alfred's own tutors suggested the subject by pouring some drops onto an anvil and then hitting them with a hammer, causing a satisfactory if modest bang.

The family moved back to Sweden in 1859 after the end of the lucrative Crimean War meant the bankruptcy of the family firm. Swedish investors would not put money into a factory to make a product that might make the factory blow up. The Nobels managed to raise money from a French banker so that a factory was built at Heleneborg in 1862. In September 1864 the factory did blow up, with Emil, Alfred's brother, being one of the five victims. The Nobels were soon told that they could no longer work with explosives in populated areas. Therefore a barge was moored in Lake Malaren, and work was carried on there. Here Alfred made two discoveries. A mixture of nitroglycerine and kieselguhr, an absorbent sand, made a dough-like material that could be handled safely. A blasting cap of mercury fulminate would mean that it could be set off safely. Nobel called it dynamite after the Greek *dynamis*, power, rejecting a German colleague's suggested 'blasting putty' as sounding like window cleaning. Now money came in to finance the building of factories in many countries.

One day in April 1888 Nobel looked in the newspaper for an obituary of his brother Ludvig, who had just died. To his shock he read his own obituary as the newspaper had confused the two. It called him a 'merchant of death' and the 'dynamite king'. There was no mention of his philanthropic activities. He decided to form his famous foundation. Nobel died at San Remo, Italy in 1896 with over 300 patents to his name. His will attracted great attention as it provided for annual 'prizes to those who, during the preceding year, shall have conferred the greatest benefit to mankind' in five subjects. He was very suspicious of lawyers and did not involve them either in writing his will or in arranging the award of prizes. As a result there was controversy, with some relatives contesting the will, and many Swedes suggested that eligibility should be limited to Swedes. In addition the Swedish king opposed the idea. Nevertheless the prizes were awarded from 1901 and continue to be awarded annually.

Alfred Nobel, Paris, France
Filed 7 May 1867 and published as GB 1345/1867 and US 78317

A.D. 1867, 7th MAY. N° 1345.

Explosive Compounds.

LETTERS PATENT to William Edward Newton, of the Office for Patents,
66, Chancery Lane, in the County of Middlesex, Civil Engineer, for
the Invention of "IMPROVEMENTS IN EXPLOSIVE COMPOUNDS AND IN THE
MEANS OF IGNITING THE SAME."—A communication from abroad by Alfred
Nobel, of Rue St. Sebastien, Paris, in the Empire of France.

Sealed the 15th October 1867, and dated the 7th May 1867.

PROVISIONAL SPECIFICATION left by the said William Edward Newton
at the Office of the Commissioners of Patents, with his Petition, on the
7th May 1867.

I, WILLIAM EDWARD NEWTON, of the Office for Patents, 66, Chancery Lane,
5 in the County of Middlesex, Civil Engineer, do hereby declare the nature of
the said Invention for "IMPROVEMENTS IN EXPLOSIVE COMPOUNDS AND IN THE
MEANS OF IGNITING THE SAME," to be as follows :—

This Invention relates to a method of modifying the nature of nitro-glycerine
in a manner which renders it much safer for use than heretofore. Nitro-
10 glycerine if mixed with porous inexplosive substances, such, for instance, as
charcoal or silica, becomes very much altered in its properties ; thus, for instance,
nitro-glycerine alone is not inflammable by a spark, but may be got to explode
by submitting it to a very rapid shower of sparks. Nitro-glycerine absorbed
in porous substances, on the other hand, easily catches fire from a spark, but
15 burns away slowly and without explosion, except under very close and resisting

The electric light bulb

It will be surprising to many that Joseph Wilson Swan is given the credit for the electric light bulb but there is no doubt that he thought of it before Thomas Edison. At the time gas was piped in from outside to light well-off households and offices. Gas was smelly and a health hazard, and soot readily collected on furniture and carpets. Nor could gas power appliances. Many inventors were working on the idea of electric power providing efficient lighting. It was understood that a good vacuum was needed so that the filament did not burn up, but it was thought that low-resistance filaments were vital, rather than the high resistance filaments that were later used. High-resistance means that the filaments 'incandesce', or glow white (a mixture of all colours, rather than say red if cooler), and the light is a by-product of the heat.

Swan was born in Sunderland, Durham in 1828. He became an assistant and later a partner in a Newcastle firm of manufacturing chemists. In 1860 he worked out the principles of using carbonised paper in an evacuated bulb, but this produced poor light and did not last long, due to both the vacuum and the electric supply being inadequate. Swan announced his invention on 18 December 1878 in a lecture and first demonstrated it on 18 January 1879 in Sunderland. He had worked out that a horseshoe shape was the most efficient. Cotton thread was treated with sulphuric acid and then carbonised. In the drawings of variants the electricity is conducted up (c) through clips (b) to the filaments. He set up a factory to make the bulbs at Benwell, a Newcastle suburb, later that year. German glassblowers were imported to blow the bulbs as local expertise was not available, and each bulb sold for 25 shillings (£1.25). The first street to be lit by electric light was Mosley Street in the centre of Newcastle.

Unfortunately for Swan he delayed filing for a patent. Edison was independently working on similar lines, and on 22 October 1879 after countless experiments with different materials successfully tested a lamp with a carbonised sewing thread. Swan's bulb was in fact better. The patent was swiftly filed on 1 November and was published as US 223898 in January 1880. Thread was found not to be robust and was soon replaced by carbonised paper, one of many improvements. Edison also worked on inventing equipment such as screw sockets, meters, switches and fuses to make a complete system. The problem was not only that the bulbs cost $2.50 each but that an infrastructure for supplying and distributing the power was needed, and people would not sign contracts unless the system was already there. Therefore big initial investments were needed. During 1879–82 only 3,144 bulbs were sold to 203 customers in Manhattan but by 1900 there were 3 million customers. Edison's mistake was to use direct current rather than the modern alternating current, which Westinghouse championed.

When Edison applied for a British patent an action was brought against him for infringement and the two were forced to merge as the Edison & Swan United Electric Light Company. In October 1883 Edison lost his American patent too as the Patent Office ruled that prior art by William Sawyer and Albon Man prevailed. Swan went on to invent bromide paper in 1879 and in 1883 he patented a method of squeezing nitrocellulose material through holes to form fibres while working on the threads idea. This is used in the textile industry. He was knighted in 1904 and died in 1914 at Warlingham, Surrey.

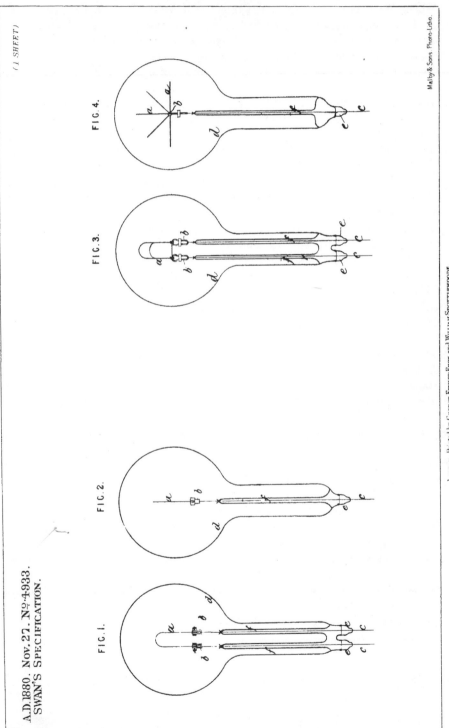

(1 SHEET)

A.D.1880. Nov. 27. Nº 4933.
SWAN'S SPECIFICATION.

FIG. 1.

FIG. 2.

FIG. 3.

FIG. 4.

Malby & Sons. Photo-Litho.

LONDON: Printed by GEORGE EDWARD EYRE and WILLIAM SPOTTISWOODE,
Printers to the Queen's most Excellent Majesty. 1881.

The electric telegraph

William Fothergill Cooke was born in 1806 in Ealing, Middlesex and was an officer in the East India Company army while Charles Wheatstone was born in 1802 near Gloucester. The idea of using an electric circuit to transmit noises was known when Cooke attended a lecture in Heidelberg on the concept, became interested, and was referred once in London to Wheatstone, a professor of electricity at King's College, for help. They devised the invention for which just one of many drawings is shown. It shows 20 letters and any two of five needles pointed to each letter to show which was meant.

A railway line was built in 1841 from Paddington station in London to the village of West Drayton 20 km away, later extended to Slough. In January 1845 a sensational incident publicised both its utility and a flaw. Early one morning a woman named Sarah Hart was found dead in her home. A man had been noticed leaving her house some time before. The police knew that she was visited from time to time by John Tawer, an Australian chemist. On enquiring at nearby Slough they found that a person answering his description had earlier boarded a train for London. The police telegraphed at once to Paddington asking for his arrest. 'He is in the garb of a Quaker,' said the message, 'with a brown coat on, which reaches nearly to his feet.' There was no 'Q' in the telegraph alphabet, and the clerk at Slough began to spell the word 'Quaker' with a 'kwa' but was interrupted by the clerk at Paddington, who asked him to 'repent'. The repetitions were rejected until a boy suggested that Slough should be allowed to finish the word. 'Kwaker' was understood, and Tawer was shadowed on his arrival by a detective, who later arrested him in a coffee tavern. Tawer was hanged for the murder of his lover.

Samuel Morse independently made a better version which was adopted as the standard with his US 1647 in 1840, which included his famous Morse Code. Born in Charlestown, Massachusetts in 1791, he thought of the concept while on a six-week Atlantic voyage in 1832. He first demonstrated it in September 1837 and begged for money to build an experimental line covering the 65 km from Washington, DC to Baltimore. Congress reluctantly granted him $30,000 and the line was built, with the first message being 'What hath God wrought', as suggested by the daughter of the Commissioner of Patents. The operators needed to be skilled, unlike in the English patent, to key the dots and dashes of the code, which was heard by the operator at the other end. In this way the entire alphabet was available. In 1861 a line reached California (which put the short-lived Pony Express out of business) and in 1866 the first successful submarine cable was laid across the Atlantic, a huge task involving the *Great Eastern* steamship laying out cable. Thomas Edison perfected the 'duplex' whereby two messages could be sent in opposite directions. The huge impact of the electric telegraph in enabling messages to be sent swiftly across vast distances is now difficult to comprehend, and it has been compared to the Internet. Morse grew wealthy and won numerous patent cases and died in New York City in 1872. Wheatstone died in 1875 in Paris, having also, improbably, invented the concertina with his GB 5803/1829 among other achievements, while Cooke died in 1879 in Farnham, Surrey.

William Fothergill Cooke, Hastings, Sussex and Charles Wheatstone, London, England
Filed 12 June 1837 and published as GB 7390/1837

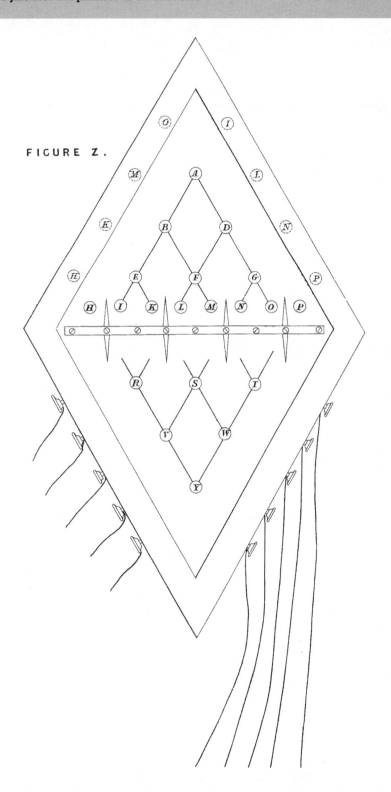

FIGURE Z.

The facsimile machine

Astonishingly the idea of sending images by electricity was patented in 1843. Alexander Bain was born near Thurso, Caithness, Scotland in 1811. He became a watchmaker and moved to London, having become fascinated by science when he attended a lecture and had to walk many kilometres home afterwards. He patented 10 inventions beginning with GB 8783/1841, the first electric clock. Most were on telegraphs or timepieces but they included GB 10450/1844, for determining the direction ships were taking and taking soundings.

The idea behind his facsimile machine was based on a discovery by Edmond Becquerel, a French physicist. He had discovered that if two pieces of metal were immersed in an electrolyte, an electric charge developed when one of the pieces was illuminated. He had discovered the electrochemical effects of light, but did not make any suggestion on how to use them. Bain suggested electrifying raised metal letters and, using a stylus attached to a pendulum, following the shape of the letters as the pendulum moved slightly on each passage. The electric currents so generated on contact were transmitted along a telegraph line where an exactly synchronised pendulum in contact with paper soaked in potassium iodide printed out the image as brown stains when electricity passed through. It was an ingenious idea, but required exact synchronisation at both ends. The drawing shows two identical telegraph apparatuses, one for sending and one for receiving, with permanent magnets (A) at the top and coils of insulated wire (B) between them, in theoretical operation.

Frederick Bakewell of Hampstead, Middlesex, 'gentleman' (actually a physicist) with GB 12352/1848 replaced the metal type with tinfoil wrapped round synchronised rotating cylinders, which meant that drawings could be sent. The pendulum was still used as well. A model was demonstrated at the Great Exhibition of 1851. Normal use awaited the work of Giovanni Caselli. He was born in Siena, Italy in 1815. He became a Catholic priest and, after becoming involved in revolutionary activities in Parma in the 1848 upheavals in much of Europe, fled to Florence where he taught physics at the university. His GB 2395/1861 for a 2 m high 'Pantelegraph' incorporated ideas from both Bain and Bakewell. The sender wrote a message on a sheet of tin in non-conducting ink. The sheet was then fixed to a curved metal plate and scanned by a needle, three lines to the millimetre. The signals were carried by telegraph and at the other end the message was marked out in Prussian blue ink, the colour produced by chemical reaction as the paper was soaked in potassium ferro-cyanide. To ensure that both needles scanned at exactly the same rate, two extremely accurate clocks were used to trigger a pendulum which, in turn, was linked to gears and pulleys that controlled the needles.

The French government was very interested, and after trials actually set up a line from Paris to Lyons from 1865, which was later extended to Marseilles. It was used mainly for stock market information, but drawings were also sent. The Franco-Prussian War in 1870 interrupted the service, and it was never resumed. Caselli died in Florence in 1891. As for Bain, he received £7,000 for his telegraphic inventions but lost it all under threats of litigation. In 1873 a number of well-known inventors asked the British Prime Minister, Gladstone, to grant Bain a pension of £80 annually. This was agreed but it was difficult to locate him at first. Bain died in 1877 in Kirkintilloch near Glasgow.

Alexander Bain, London, England
Filed 27 November 1843 and published as GB 9745/1843

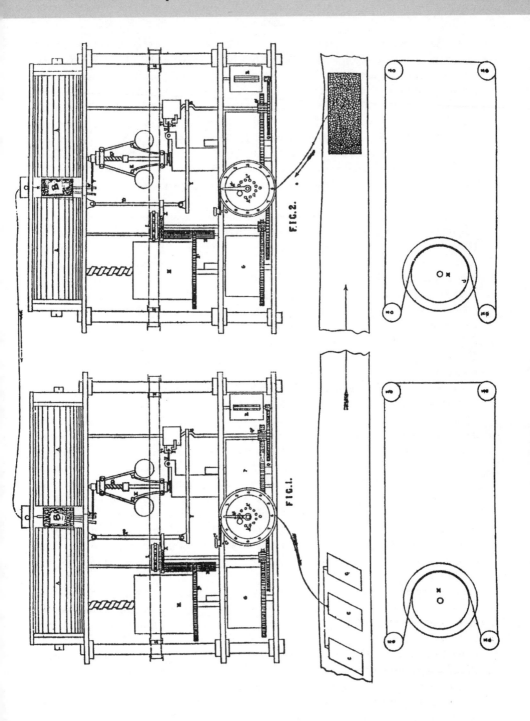

FIG.2.

FIG.1.

The fountain pen

Lewis Edson Waterman was born in Decatur, Otsego County, New York State in 1837. He was the son of a wagon builder. For a while he taught or sold books until in 1862 he took to selling life insurance, from 1870 travelling for most of the time. One day he decided to impress a client by lending him a new fountain pen to sign a contract. Such pens had been known for a long time, and needed to be dipped frequently into an ink well, so that the ink well had to be carried around by the writer. This model promised to store a reliable supply within the pen itself. The client tried to sign, but no ink flowed. He tried a second time, a third. Then the ink did flow, but so much that a large ink blot was left on the contract. Waterman did not have any blank copies and he rushed to his office and hurried back with a fresh contract, but too late. Another salesman had beaten him to it.

Waterman realised what the problem was. The air pressure from where the ink was flowing was different from the air pressure where it came out: air locks could develop. His solution was simple and elegant. A piece of hard rubber, (B) in Figure 1, was inserted into the open end of the pen. It was shaped to fit within the screwed barrel of the inside of the pen. Three tiny fissures allowed ink to flow down by both gravity and capillary action, but at the same time air could go up through the other fissures so that the pressure was equalised. The steel nib (P) was protected by a cap (E). By pressing on the nib while writing the thin gap between the halves of the nib widened to allow the ink to flow, which would vary in thickness (unlike ballpoints). Refilling was carried out with a glass eye dropper. Years of work by a man unfamiliar with the business were needed to perfect it.

He decided to start manufacturing fountain pens but needed capital. Asa Shipman, a wholesale stationer, lent him $5,000 secured on the patent itself. Waterman opened a business behind a cigar shop on Broadway and made pens by night and sold them by day. Sales were not good and he had to default on his loan. Shipman claimed the patent and started to make his own. He also sued Waterman for infringement of the patent that he now owned. Waterman lost and had to pay a licence to use his own invention. About the same time E. T. Howard, an advertising salesman, approached Waterman and asked him to buy advertising space in a new magazine, the *Review of Reviews*. Waterman was short of cash but Howard offered to lend him the money and agreed only to ask for the money back if the advertisement paid for itself in sales. It did, and from then on there was heavy advertising in newspapers and magazines. The outside of the barrel was handsomely engraved by machine, something that was expected by his wealthy clientele.

The company prospered but did not expand out of the United States until the Paris Fair of 1900. Frank Waterman, Lewis's nephew, went there to exhibit the pen. A gold medal was awarded and L. G. Sloan of London purchased the European rights. Lewis Waterman himself died in 1901 in Brooklyn and by then sales were 350,000 annually at prices from $2 each. The addition of a clip to the pen in 1905, so that it could be easily stored in a jacket pocket, added 25 cents to the price of the pen, but sales rose. David Lloyd George, the British Prime Minister, signed the Treaty of Versailles in 1919 with a Waterman pen, and in the 1930s the company introduced the new idea of ink cartridges so that ink wells became unnecessary.

Lewis Edson Waterman, Brooklyn, New York
Filed 19 September 1883 and published as US 293545 and GB 3125/1884

(No Model.)

L. E. WATERMAN.
FOUNTAIN PEN.

No. 293,545.   Patented Feb. 12, 1884.

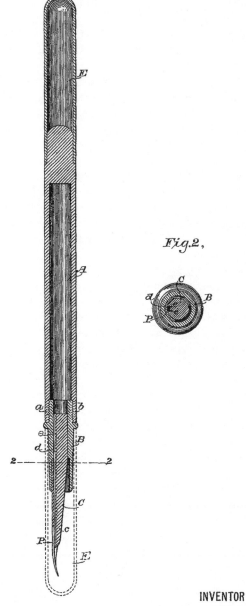

Fig.1,

Fig.2,

WITNESSES

Wm A. Skinkle.

Jos. S. Latimer.

INVENTOR

Lewis E. Waterman

By his   Attorneys

Pope Edgecomb & Butler.

The hand and draught carriage

The concept behind the perambulator or pram goes back to an invalid vehicle designed for the Duke of Devonshire by William Kent in about 1733. The 'Bath chair' was named after the town where its inventor James Heath lived. It had superseded the 'Sedan chair', which was suspended on poles borne by two sturdy men, by 1830. The basic design of a vehicle with three wheels (the smallest being in front), designed for an invalid or child sitting in it, and usually with a hood at the back, remained until about 1850. In that year two rival London concerns began making similar models which differed radically in one important respect from the earlier models: they were meant to be pushed rather than pulled. Dragging meant that a mother or nurse could not keep an eye on her baby, who sometimes fell out. These prams still had three wheels, as four-wheeled vehicles were only permitted on the road, which explains why the British Patent Office indexed perambulators under 'Road vehicles'. The front wheel was always smaller to enable a tighter turning circle.

The patent illustrated seems to be the first for anything resembling a pram. Charles Burton emphasised that his two improvements enabled it to be pushed from behind with the long curving handles, and for his 'hand carriages for children' to be taken to pieces and packed. His drawings show different models, with Figure 7 being for infants and Figure 9 a light draft carriage. The screw shown went in at (p) and its removal enabled the carriage to be taken to pieces and folded. We do not know the origins of this 'carriage manufacturer', although one source claims that Burton invented it in 1848 in New York, and on receiving a hostile reaction from busy pedestrians moved to London. By 1855 the concept was popular in London at least. The Rev. Benjamin Armstrong of rural East Dereham, Norfolk noted in his diary after a visit to London, 'The streets are full of Perambulators, a baby carriage quite new to me, whereby children are propelled by the nurse pushing instead of pulling the carriage'. The Queen (who had nine children) purchased three models from Hitchings Baby Stores for 4 guineas (£4.20) each which must have helped to set the fashion.

In Britain, especially, there were numerous variations of the same concept until in the 1880s the wickerwork 'bassinette' model arrived from France. This allowed the infant to be laid flat as it had space between its four wheels. Some were prosecuted in Britain for using them on the pavements, but it is thought that seeing babies in what initially looked like a cradle on wheels made even hardened policemen hesitate to make an arrest, so that eventually they were left alone. As late as 1888, though, licences had to be applied for in Germany before taking a (named) child out in a pram. The licence had to be carried so that the police knew that the user had permission to be on the pavements (provided, that is, that the pram kept to the right). The USA was less active in this market. The British *Pram Gazette* sniffed at an American version of the bassinette model as 'An inartistic, uncomfortable vehicle, its body made of cane or other vegetable product . . . That class of pram scarcely suits British tastes'. Other designs were for 'sociable' prams for more than one infant, some being for three, two sitting side by side and one in front. The 'mailcart' model was a low cart based on the vehicle used for delivering mail in which the infants sat back to back.

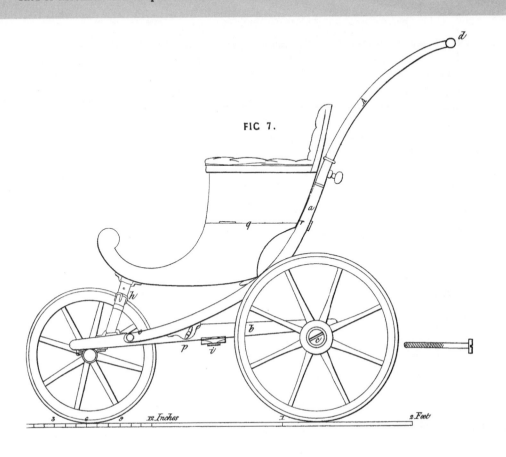

FIC 7.

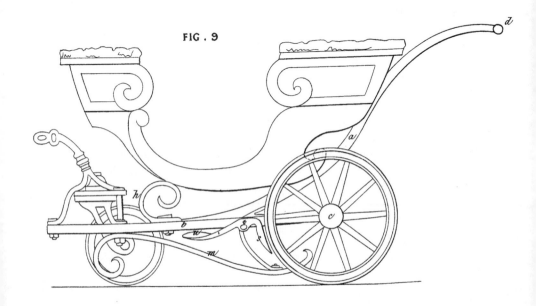

FIG . 9

The Hardy Perfect fishing reel

Hardy fishing reels are famous among anglers. The Hardy Brothers firm was started in 1873 by William and John James Hardy who were later joined by other brothers and sisters (there were seven in all). The business initially sold guns, knives and tin goods in what was only a large village. The two brothers were only 20 and 19 and were probably only able to set up in business with the backing of their mother, who had been widowed 2 years before. The brothers soon began to supply items that they had invented themselves. The first of these was a preparation for cleaning guns and fishing equipment. The brothers were keen on both river and sea fishing. GB 1766/1881 for a reel fitting by William was the first of many patents, mostly with John James as a co-inventor. It was however a third brother, Forster Hardy, who invented the 'Hardy Perfect' fishing reel with GB 18373/1888 (where he described himself as an 'extra 1st class marine engineer') and then the improved GB 612/1891. Fishermen need to cast their reels as far as possible, for which the smooth and fast running of the reel from its casing is vital. Forster's idea was to use ball bearings. Figure 5 shows the 'barrel' casing for the reel with ball bearings arranged in a circle. It was marketed as the Hardy Perfect reel with the lozenge stating, 'Hardy Bros. Makers Alnwick' and continues to sell well. It was first exhibited in the British Sportsman's Exhibition of 1890. They seem to be Forster's only patents for the company.

Other innovations included a split bamboo rod instead of a traditional greenheart rod. The light yet strong rod made it ideal for dry-fly fishing and a newspaper commented that it would 'allow ladies to enjoy angling for the first time because the rods require less exertion to cast'. Every aspect seemed to be covered by their inventions, such as a creel for storing caught fish (GB 2597/1891), a method of mounting artificial flies (GB 4551/1894), dish hooks (GB 3851/1895) and a landing net (GB 29084/1896) as well as many patents for the rods. One idea allowed the rod to be shortened by sliding the last section in the handle while another was to regulate the balance by placing weights in the handle.

The brothers realised that they had to publicise the company and so exhibited extensively. By 1884 they employed four men and in 1886 a small catalogue was replaced by a handsome, full-sized catalogue of their wares, which included much relevant to hunting and other country pursuits. Rods were the main expense for an angler, with prices up to £15, so the catalogues emphasised them. By 1888 the catalogue talked of export and wholesale terms so the company was obviously keen to expand from its remote base. Recruitment was a problem and advertisements were placed in Birmingham, Warwickshire to hire skilled craftsmen. Royal families from Italy and Spain began to patronise the business. Zane Grey, the Western writer, was also an enthusiastic customer and a reel was named after him when he requested the 'best big game fish reel in the world' (quoted in their advertising). He also wanted the reel to be the most expensive, but the company did not publicise this. William patented his last invention in 1906 and John James in 1927, but Laurence Robert, William's son, carried on the tradition of innovation from 1909. The firm, renamed in 1985 House of Hardy, continues to thrive at its factory at Willowburn near Alnwick. The Hardy family's involvement in the company's management only ceased in 1992.

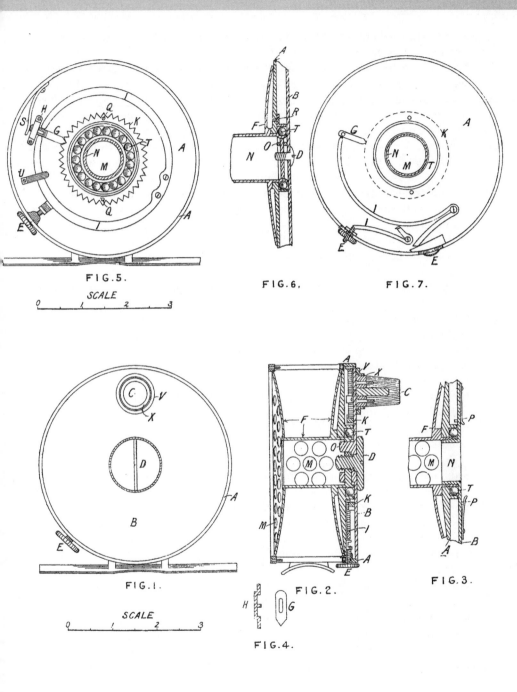

FIG.5.

SCALE

FIG.6.

FIG.7.

FIG.I.

SCALE

FIG.2.

FIG.4.

FIG.3.

The ice making machine

John Gorrie was born in 1803 in Charleston, South Carolina. He trained as a doctor and settled in Apalachicola, then a flourishing cotton port, on the Gulf of Mexico coast of Florida. Here he worked with those suffering from yellow fever or malaria. He noticed that these diseases were contracted at night, and that few were affected when it was cold. It was after 1900 before scientists discovered that mosquitoes were the vectors of both these diseases. He reasoned that if the wards were kept cold at night then few would contract the diseases (although if they had already contracted them it would only help keep them cool). Gorrie tried putting ice in basins suspended from the ceiling, which melted so that the denser, cold air sank down to floor level. There was an extensive trade of ice arriving by steamer from New England, where it was harvested in winter from ponds and kept underground during the summer, insulated with straw. The ice was sold at the quayside to all comers for moderate prices but sometimes the steamers did not arrive.

Gorrie gave up his practice in 1845 to work on his idea. He gradually moved from the idea of cooling generally to working out a way of making ice in hot climates. When he had finished designing the first mechanical refrigerator he went to New Orleans and secured backing from a Bostonian. The basic principle is of heat being taken up by a surrounding medium, the same way that refrigerators work today. Pump (A) first compressed (heated) and then expanded (cooled) air, a combination which results in even cooler air than there was at the beginning. After compression some water was added to cool it. The compressed air was placed in tank (B) submerged in coils surrounded by a circulating bath of cooling water. The water condensed out into a holding tank (C), with valves controlling the amount admitted, and the air expanded into tub (I) which had lower pressure and which contained brine. This lowered the temperature of the brine to freezing point and brick-sized, oil-coated metal containers of non-saline water, or rainwater, in the brine resulted in ice bricks. The cold air was then released into the atmosphere.

Gorrie made ice publicly at Apalachicola, although with some problems owing to leaks and irregular working, but he failed to interest other Southerners in setting up factories to produce ice across the South. There was also furious opposition from the ice-making interests. He published *Dr John Gorrie's apparatus for the artificial production of ice in tropical climates* and then, after a nervous collapse, died in 1855.

The key to improving Gorrie's concept was in using a medium that could absorb more heat than water. Alexander Twinning of the USA used sulphuric ether which was improved by James Harrison of Geelong, Australia, engineer, using ether vapour. His GB 747/1856 and GB 2362/1857 meant that in the 1860s Australian exports were no longer confined to products such as gold and wool with the development of refrigerated ships. Ferdinand Carre of Paris, France with FR 41958 in 1859 used ammonia. Meanwhile in Britain, American visitors complained that they could rarely obtain ice for their drinks. Stately homes relied on their own subterranean ice-houses storing ice during the summer, often unsuccessfully, and always at great expense.

John Gorrie, New Orleans, Louisiana
Published 6 May 1851 as US 8080 and GB 13234/1850

J. GORRIE
ICE MACHINE.

No. 8,080.

Patented May 6, 1851.

Fig:1.

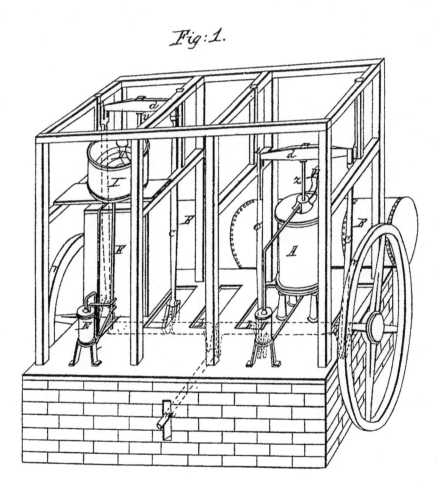

Improved device for smokers

This splendid 'improved device for containing pipes, matches, and other requisites for smokers' depicts Trajan's Column, which is the best-preserved of all monuments in Rome. The Emperor Trajan made his name conquering the Romanians in two campaigns in AD 101–102 and AD 105–106, and the reliefs on the column recorded the events of the campaign. Unfortunately someone blundered, possibly the patent agent, Henry Lake, as the specification talks of the 'Trojans Column', which is unknown.

Cesare Orsini clearly wanted something unusual and striking that would still be useful for hiding away tobacco products. He mentions in the patent that the concept could be applied to any other similar column, and that the one shown was merely an example. Part (A) of the column was a match box and was hinged so that the statue formed a lid. Part (A) could also be removed in which case (B) was a base for a candle or lamp. Part (B) in turn could be removed exposing lid (c) above part (G) which contained pipes. The spring at the bottom allowed the pipes to lift up when the lid was raised. Drawer (G) at the base of the column held cigarette papers as users were clearly expected to roll their own cigarettes. The base held four doors marked by (D) and (E) which stored different kinds of tobacco in (F), although it is not clear how a single container held several kinds. The opened door (D) shows some articles fastened to the inside, 'adapted to hold cigars, mouthpieces, scissors, a penknife and other articles that are necessary to render the article complete for a smoker's use'. Clearly the column must have been of some size although this is not stated. Orsini's title at the top of this page says it all. All the smoker's requisites—apart from an ashtray—were provided for by his invention.

There were numerous patents related to tobacco covering 'combination articles', where more than one function was carried out. Another monumental invention was GB 5882/1890 by Samuel Skerritt of Sheffield, Yorkshire. A domed receptacle was on a base. A depression at the top of the dome allowed matches and other articles to be stored. A column rose out of this depression with a 'call bell' and a button—presumably to summon servants or waiters. The dome's surface was roughened so that matches could be struck on it, and the base could be used as an ashtray 'and may be provided with advertising tablets'. Other combination patents were for smokers who wanted to keep score in billiards or cards and needed somewhere to store their cigars temporarily. A very unusual invention was GB 1304/1869 by Oswald Moseley of London which was for a chalk holder for billiard players. It was meant to be attached to the bowl or stem of a pipe. Most patents were however for sensible concepts like keeping matches and cigarette papers close together. What is noticeable is that of the 100 to 150 patents related to tobacco annually in the 1890s, most of the British patents involved cigars or pipes and not cigarettes (or snuff, which was going out of fashion). Perhaps this reflected the patentee's wish to target the more affluent users of tobacco.

A.D. 1886. Nov. 25. Nº 15,402.
LAKE'S COMPLETE SPECIFICATION.

(1 SHEET)

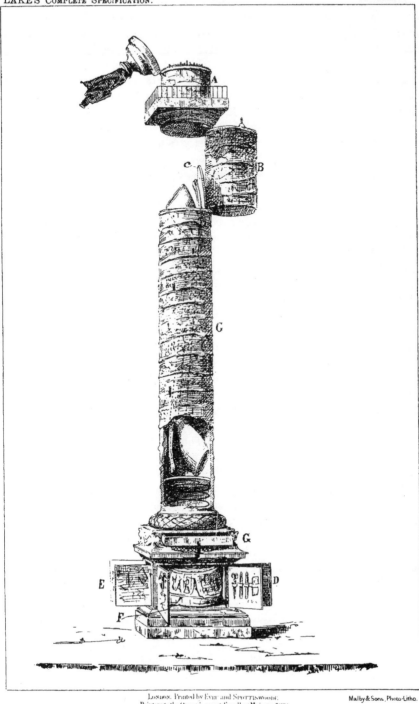

Lonpon. Printed by Eyre and Spottiswoode,
Printers to the Queen's most Excellent Majesty. 1886.

Malby & Sons, Photo-Litho.

Improved means for making tea

The full patent title is 'The improved means for boiling water and obtaining an infusion of tea or other beverage at any prearranged time without the aid of an attendant'. John Thomas Hardman described himself as a clerk while James Alfred Greenhalgh was a tinman. It is an early version, possibly the first, of a device much loved by generations of British householders, who are accustomed to waking to a terrifying sound as the tea is automatically made in their bedroom. 'The object of this invention is primarily to enable a person who requires to attend work or other business, at any early hour in the morning to have a cup of tea or the like prepared without attendance and ready for consumption previous to departure, but the same apparatus may be employed for domestic purposes at other times.' The mechanism is ingenious if bulky. Figure 1 shows the apparatus from the front while Figure 2 is a side view. The kettle (h) has a fixed nozzle (h^3) and a nozzle pipe (u). A bunsen burner (j) is pivoted on a cock on the pipe (k) and is held in the upright position by an extension (j^1) which engages a slot (d^4) in the lower cross-bar (d) of the frame (A) when that is depressed by the weight of water in the kettle. A cock (m) is provided with a weighted lever (m^1) which is supported, so that the cock is slightly open, by a lever (r^1) on a rod (t). This rod has an arm (r^2) put in the way of the alarum handle of a clock (q) which is set for the time when tea is required. When the alarum handle moves it turns the rod (t) so that the lever (m^1) is freed and falls, turning the gas full on. When the water boils it is forced over into the teapot, and the weight on the frame (A) being lessened the bar (d) rises and frees the burner. This then falls over on its pivot and turns off the gas.

The invention worked broadly in the same way as many versions, but was much larger. The first compact automatic tea-maker is GB 15170/1902 by Frank Clarke of Birmingham, Warwickshire, gun maker. The best known trade mark, Teasmade®, was not registered until 1949 by the British Vacuum Cleaner and Engineering Company, which had plainly diversified. The trade mark was chosen in preference to the chairman's suggested 'Cheerywake'. Considering its apparent simplicity there were a surprising number of patents for teapots. Britain had about 10 annually in the 1880s, many being a means of improving or speeding the infusion or a means of straining the tea so that the leaves did not join the tea in the cup. Thomas Powell of Hampstead, Middlesex suggested GB 5088/1884 which moulded one pot upside down above the other pot. The idea was that the tea infused in the higher pot and dripped down to the second. GB 3429/1886 by Vincent Tyzack of Sheffield was for what looks like a beer barrel with taps around it, each for pouring off the suggested tea, coffee or cocoa. A hot iron was placed in the middle to keep the drinks warm. Perhaps it was meant as encouragement to join a temperance meeting. Meanwhile the USA in the period to 1873 had about 60 patents for teapots and another 40 for those pots meant for either tea or coffee, which may sound a surprisingly large number after the reception given to tea at the Boston Tea Party in 1773.

John Thomas Hardman and James Alfred Greenhalgh, Salford, Lancashire, England
Filed 17 August 1893 and published as GB 15604/1893

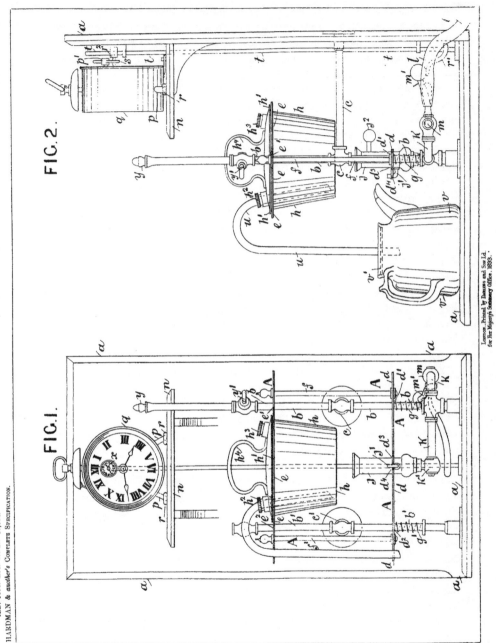

A.D. 1893. Aug. 17. № 15,604.
HARDMAN & another's Complete Specification.

London. Printed by Darling and Son Ld.
for Her Majesty's Stationery Office. 1893.

Improvement in brewing beer and ale

Louis Pasteur was probably the greatest ever microbiologist. He was born in Dole, France in 1822, son of a tanner, and from 1848 was a professor at various French universities. His first major achievement was the introduction of pasteurisation in 1861, where heating milk or another food product preserved it for longer. He deliberately did not patent the method as he wanted others to benefit. In 1865 a crisis broke out in the French silk industry. Something was killing the silkworms. Pasteur offered to help and spent 3 years identifying the parasite, although at first he knew nothing of the industry. This experience caused him to suggest that there were such things as germs and that different germs caused different diseases: a novel idea. The decomposition of food, for example, was not due to some innate quality in the food, but rather because of micro-organisms, which were living creatures that multiplied by breeding.

While he was a professor at Lille an industrialist asked him if he could make alcohol from grain or beet sugar. This led to his first studies of fermentation, and he showed that yeast could reproduce itself without oxygen. A major problem in the beer industry was beer going 'off' if kept for a long time. Pasteur showed that this was due not to the beer itself but rather to exposure to micro-organisms, in this case air-borne. No-one had previously realised that fermentation was caused by micro-organisms. Sometimes the presence of micro-organisms is beneficial, as in this case if controlled, while sometimes it is not. This patent resulted from research both in France and in England. Pasteur visited a sceptical London brewery and after examining a sample of their yeast through a microscope predicted that the day's production would be undrinkable. This was shown to be true. When he paid a second visit a week later he found that they had already purchased a microscope.

Traditionally malt was made from barley and its wort was ground up, stirred in water, cooked, and cooled in open barrels. In his patent every precaution was taken to exclude germs. The drawing shows a cylinder designed to hold boiled wort. Cooling water was fed into gutter (p) and ran down the outside through perforations (t). When enough cooling had occurred yeast was introduced through cock (R^1) or (R^2). The fermented wort (now beer) was drawn off at (L) and the yeast at (K). His insistence on removing all germs to make a pure drink initially resulted in a mediocre, flavourless beer, as he had not realised that other factors were involved in making a pleasant drink. The Carlsberg brewery in Denmark was one of the first customers. Pasteur's work was also the origin of the British drink 'India pale ale', a beer which could for the first time be shipped to India without spoiling. Pasteur hoped that his invention would 'have the result of harming those German blackguards, whose superior skills as brewers are unquestioned at this time'. This followed the Franco-Prussian War which resulted in the loss of beer-making Alsace. It was a 'beer of revenge'. The British patent, incidentally, proudly states that he was a member of the Institute of France and of the Royal Society of London. Pasteur was the first to use vaccination against rabies in 1885. The Institut Pasteur was set up in 1888 to continue his work and he directed it until his death in 1895 in St Cloud near Paris.

Louis Pasteur, Paris, France
Filed 21 August 1871 as FR 91941 and GB 2225/1871

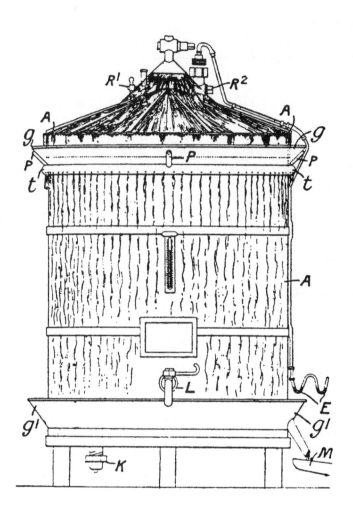

The incubator

The idea of an artificial incubator for hatching chicken eggs had been known for a long time, with the young Princess Victoria being presented with chicks so hatched in 1824, but nobody had thought of using the idea for babies. One day in 1878 Stéphane Tarnier, a doctor at a children's hospital in Paris, visited the nearby Jardin d'Acclimation (the zoo) and saw an apparatus designed by Odile Martin for the artificial hatching of chickens. Tarnier suggested that he might adapt it for prematurely born babies, who are very vulnerable and need to be kept warm. Martin designed a box and in 1880 brought it to Tarnier at the Paris Maternity Hospital. In August 1883 the British medical journal *The Lancet* had an enthusiastic editorial describing the concept in detail. The illustrated patent is actually an incubator for eggs but Martin's 'Improvements in incubators, partly applicable for other purposes', which seems to be his sole patent, can at least stand here as a tribute to his work, and was presumably applied for because of his work for Tarnier. The patented design was different as it involved double walls containing hot water as an insulation layer. *The Lancet* describes the baby incubator as containing in its lower half a reservoir with 60 litres of water. The water was heated in one of various ways. The upper portion of the box was large enough for two infants, who could be withdrawn from the side, while a double glass covering at the top enabled both the infants and the thermometer next to them to be watched to ensure a stable temperature. Small apertures allowed air to enter. The temperature was kept at 30 °C.

The results were dramatic. The death rate for babies with a birth weight of less than 2 kg fell from 66% to a still high 38%, although it was not until 1893 that Tarnier's colleague, Pierre Budin, started a special unit for premature babies. To popularise what they were doing Budin sent six incubators to the 1896 Berlin Exposition. Martin Couney, the assistant in charge, added realism to the exhibit by borrowing six premature babies from a nearby hospital. Their chances were thought so slim that the risk was considered worth taking. The new *Kinderbrutanstalt* was a great success, and even at the price of 1 mark the incubators were more popular than the Congo village or the Tyrolean yodellers. Fortunately all six infants survived. An attempt to repeat the success in London the next year initially failed, as nobody would trust their children to a French invention, so premature babies had to be imported from France. *The Lancet* in May 1897 commented that the use of incubators was not yet 'general in England' and that they were available only for the rich or the poor. The 'attendant' still had to be watchful to ensure that the incubators maintained the right temperature as there was no automatic mechanism. The article explained that an incubator which automatically adjusted the temperature had just been installed (probably at the same fair) using a bimetallic strip, a well-known concept in plumbing by which the properties of two metals enables switching on or off if the temperature changes.

Couney continued the formula of charging to show infants inside incubators at fairs until the 1939–40 World's Fair in New York. Yet another article in *The Lancet* (in February 1898) had asked 'Is it in keeping with the dignity of science that incubators and living babies should be exhibited amidst the aunt-sallies, the merry-go-rounds, the five-legged mule, the wild animals, the clowns, penny peep-shows, and amidst the glare and noise of a vulgar fair?' More to the point, perhaps, they wondered why on this occasion the air surrounding the infants had been that of an agricultural show.

Odile Martin, Neuilly, France
Filed 9 April 1880 and published as FR 136015, US 237589 and GB 4308/1880

(No Model.) 3 Sheets—Sheet 3.

O. MARTIN.
Incubator.

No. 237,689. **Patented Feb. 15, 1881.**

Fig. 5

Fig. 12.

Fig. 6

Fig. 13.

Fig. 14.

Witnesses.
1 Robt M Hooper
2 Jean-Baptiste Rolland

Inventor:
Odile Martin
A. v. Briesen
attorney

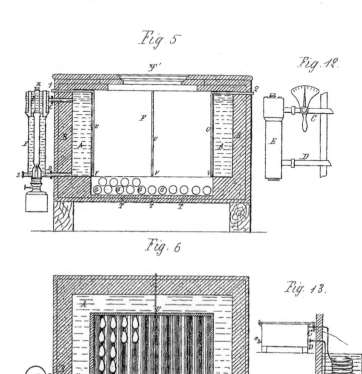

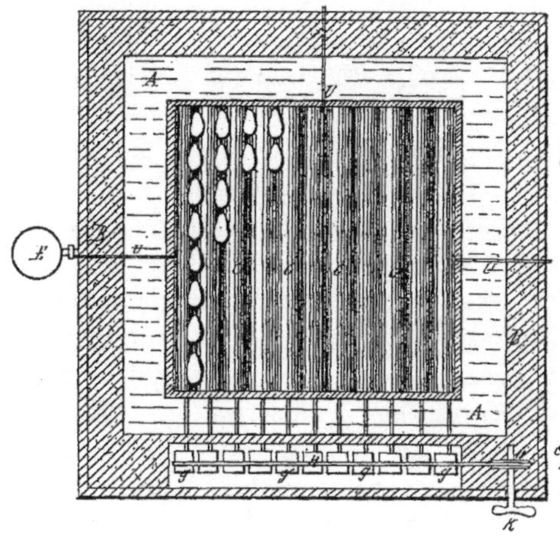

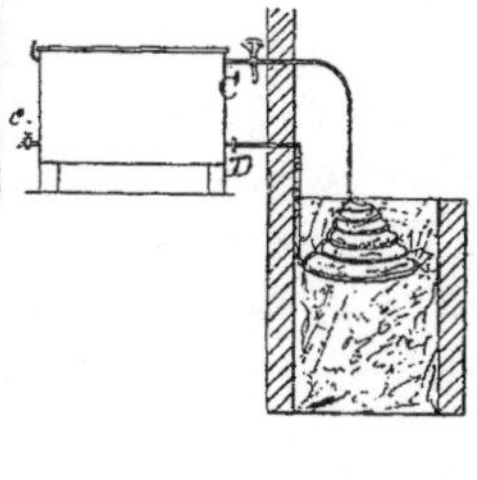

Indicating door fastenings for closets

This is thought to be the first workable patent for indicating if a room is 'engaged'. 'The invention is particularly applicable to consulting rooms, bathrooms, water closets and lavatories.' The proud patentee included his claim to a patent on the actual drawing. The invention was simple but effective, and certainly very useful when applied to public lavatories, discouraging hearty tugs on the door handles. Figure 1 shows the outside of the door and Figure 3 is a cross-section through the door. Drilling through the door to accommodate the spindle would be needed to adapt an existing door. The staple (A*) was fixed to the door jamb. The occupant slid bolt (A) across to lock the door. The bolt had racked teeth which geared on a pinion (B). The pinion was mounted on a spindle (C). Disc (D) was mounted on the outer end of the spindle with a glazed cap piece (E) attached by screws and transparent where the word 'ENGAGED', on porcelain, was visible when brought into position.

Arthur Ashwell stated, 'I would remark that I am aware that indicating door fastenings have been designed and carried out with some success but none have to my knowledge offered sufficient facilities for their application, as the cost of manufacture, the want of a positive action, or the necessity for cutting into the door has rendered their use prohibitory, under ordinary circumstances'. In GB 6928/1885 Ashwell, a 'gentleman' and Chester Cross of Herne Hill, Surrey, 'druggist', improved the apparatus. They simplified the construction and made it 'less liable to breakage from rough usage'. It was also easier to put on an existing door. The pinion and spindle were no longer made from separate pieces but rather from a single casting. There were other changes. The main problem was displaying the word 'engaged' because of careless workmanship in installation by the 'uninitiated'. 'It often works loose so that sometimes half the word only appears or disappears, and the object of the indicating bolt was thereby frustrated.'

There were other inventions in this field, which the British Patent Office allocated to their 'Signalling' class under the heading 'Indicators, "Engaged", and the like', which included doctors' surgeries and other purposes. Henry Taylor of London, 'marine artist', seems to have been the first in Britain to patent a mechanism like Ashwell's with GB 1096/1865, which worked in a much more cumbersome way as the entire disc, instead of the word 'Engaged', swung out and into position. The signalling class lists many ways of making a signal, including balloon, bell, colour, flag, flash, foghorn, heliograph, pneumatic and pyrotechnic. Most intriguing is the solitary entry for 'touch' in one index, which turns out to be a bit of a cheat. George Quarrie of the Colonnade Hotel, Birmingham, Warwickshire with his 9920/1887 had a device for waking guests in hotels. The guest turned a dial from inside the room to indicate outside at which time he or she was to be woken by the 'attendant'. Quarrie vaguely says that a bell, whistle or the telephone could be used to wake the sleeper, or there could be a 'mechanism for waking the sleeper by touching him'. He called his invention 'The early call'.

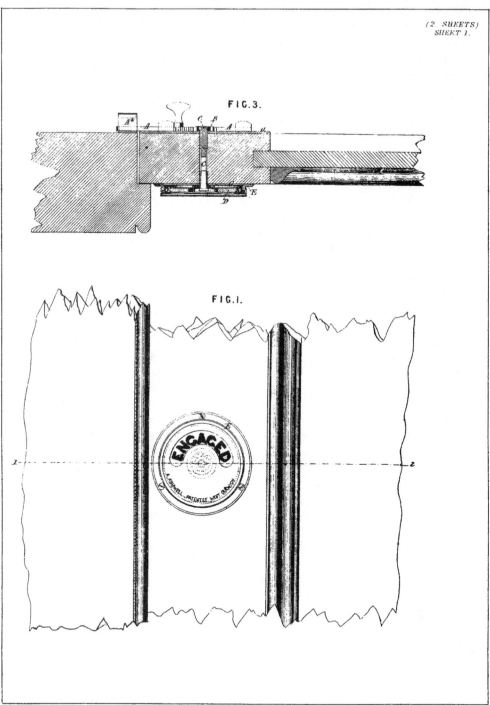

The internal combustion engine

Nicolaus August Otto was born in 1832 in Holzhausen auf der Haide, Germany. He dropped out of school at 16 and worked in a grocery store, as a clerk and as a travelling salesman. He heard about a gas engine that had been invented (FR 43624) and built by Jean Joseph Etienne Lenoir, a Luxembourg-born engineer, in 1860. It was a primitive internal combustion engine which consumed a great deal of fuel and required a great deal of cooling, or the engine would seize up. Otto built a two-stroke gas engine in 1861, the 'rattling monster'. 'Two stroke' meant that there were two actions in every cycle. Otto and his partner Eugen Langen built a factory and worked on improving the engine. It was not until 1876 that they built a four-stroke piston cycle internal combustion engine, still running on gas. The first application was made in Britain, and the Alsace-Lorraine application was later transferred to the newly unified German patent system.

The American drawing shows a view from one side. (A) was a water-jacketed cylinder open at both ends with a working piston (a) and a loose piston (B) inside it, the latter being connected by a rod (B) to a piston (c) within a hydraulic cylinder (C). Two flywheels (W) on either side were connected by a shaft. The 'combustible gaseous mixture' was admitted through a slide (D). The four strokes were admission, compression, combustion and discharge. Although crude it was the first practical alternative to the steam engine. Over 30,000 were sold in the next decade, which were used for producing power in factories rather than to move vehicles. The factory's hot-headed production manager, Gottlieb Daimler, together with August Maybach adapted the engine to make it lighter and quicker. Otto had thought that revolutions of 160 to 200 per minute could not be exceeded. By building a lighter engine with revolutions of 800 a minute they substantially improved performance with GB 4315/1885. Karl Benz of Mannheim with DE 37435 in 1886 soon built an entire, three-wheeled vehicle using a petrol-driven motor. A few months later Daimler produced a four-wheeled vehicle also using a petrol-driven motor, but he mounted it on a (horse-drawn) carriage. Petroleum was still quite new, having first been exploited for power in the late 1850s, so it is not surprising that gas was not thought of as a fuel by Otto. Daimler and Benz later joined forces as Mercedes-Benz.

Repeated attempts to get around Otto's patent had failed due to misunderstandings by nearly everybody of exactly how the engine worked. Basically, anyone trying to use in-cylinder charge compression was taken to court. In 1883 a civil engineer wrote to a German journal pointing out that in 1862 Alphonse-Eugène Beau de Rochas, a French engineer, had published a booklet describing a four-stroke cycle engine. It was later discovered that he had also filed FR 52593, although it was never published as he failed to pay the renewal fees. He did not build his engine, which was thought close enough to Otto's for the German courts in 1886 to revoke Otto's German patent. A huge amount of work by rival engineers quickly began to emerge in Germany. The British patent ran its full term to 1890 as the court pointed out that although the booklet had been acquired by the British Museum, it had never been on the open shelves, and hence was not considered 'part of the public stock of knowledge'. Otto died in 1891 in Cologne.

Nicolaus August Otto, Dietz, Germany
Filed 17 May 1876 and published as DE 532, US 178023 and GB 2081/1876

N. A. OTTO.

GAS MOTOR ENGINE.

No. 178,023.

Patented May 30, 1876.

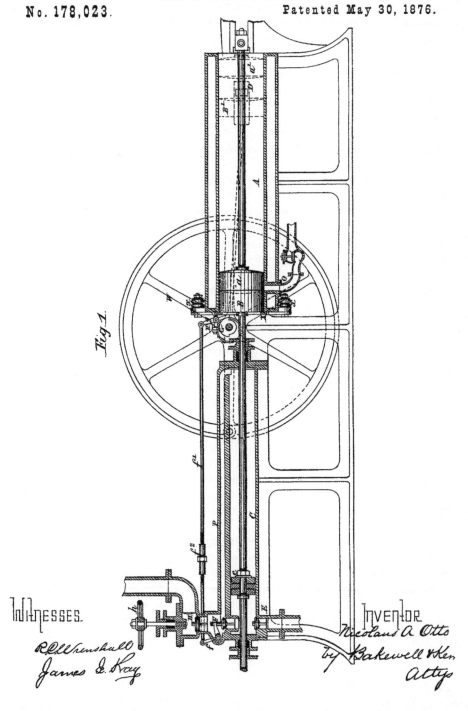

Fig. 1.

WITNESSES.

R. C. Wrenshall

James E. Kay

INVENTOR

Nicolaus A. Otto

by Bakewell & Ken

Attys

The ironclad CSS *Virginia*

John Mercer Brooke was born in 1826 at Tampa Bay, Florida, son of a Brigadier-General from a Virginia family, He became a lieutenant in the US Navy where he was involved in hydrographic work and invented a deep-sea sounding apparatus. He resigned in April 1861 and joined the new Confederate Navy with the same rank. He was invited by Confederate Secretary of the Navy Stephen Mallory to make a plan for raising the hulk of the steam frigate USS *Merrimac* (which had been scuttled by retreating Union forces) and reconstructing her as an 'ironclad'. John Porter, a naval architect, worked with Brooke and made technical drawings and supervised the work, although with much help from Brooke. Brooke also supervised the making of the armour (which was composed of railway tracks) and the 10 guns at Richmond's Tredegar Iron Works. An iron ram was also added to the ship.

On 8 March 1862 the CSS *Virginia* set off on its trial voyage into Hampton Roads at the mouth of Chesapeake Bay. Its commander Franklin Buchanan instead put the workmen ashore and while under heavy fire attacked and sank two Union frigates. The situation was grim for the blockading Union forces, but by sheer chance that very night the ironclad USS *Monitor*, one-third the size and with just two guns in a small (but revolving) turret, arrived. The next day they fought an inconclusive battle, with the USS *Monitor* eventually retreating into shallow water where her rival could not follow. Shells were bouncing off both ships' armour. This was not the first time that ironclads had gone into combat, as the Union navy had built some for the Mississippi theatre of war, but it was the first fight between two such vessels. When Britain heard of the two battles she immediately began to adapt a warship to be an ironclad.

These were the only battles the CSS *Virginia* ever fought. The Union forces, even with the USS *Monitor*, fled whenever she appeared. Some weeks later the Confederacy evacuated Portsmouth, and the CSS *Virginia* was set on fire by its crew on 11 May. The USS *Monitor* did not survive much longer, sinking in rough weather when being towed out to sea on New Year's Eve with the loss of 16 men. After the battle there was controversy in the newspapers about who had designed the CSS *Virginia*. In order to end the argument Brooke decided to file a patent application for the ironclad. The drawings shown are copies of those by Porter but he did not dispute the application, and a patent was granted in July 1862. It shows the hull (B) with a 'shield' (C) of wood covered with iron inclined at an angle of 40° to 50°. This as Brooke pointed out meant that projectiles would bounce off. The bottom of the shield was to be below the waterline shown as W.L. The patent explains that the *Merrimac* was used because her boilers could be repaired and there was not time to build a totally new vessel. Brooke was later Chief of the Navy's Bureau of Ordnance and Hydrography and while there designed the 'Brooke' rifled cannon.

The argument about who was responsible for the design of the CSS *Virginia* rumbled on and as late as 1891 Brooke, now a professor at the Virginia Military Institute, published a pamphlet in his own defence. It is only because of the pamphlet that we know the details of the patent, since the Confederate Patent Office burned down with all its records in April 1865 when Richmond surrendered to Union forces. 266 patents in all had been granted (many for weapons of war), only a few of which survive as copies. Brooke died in 1906 in Lexington, Virginia.

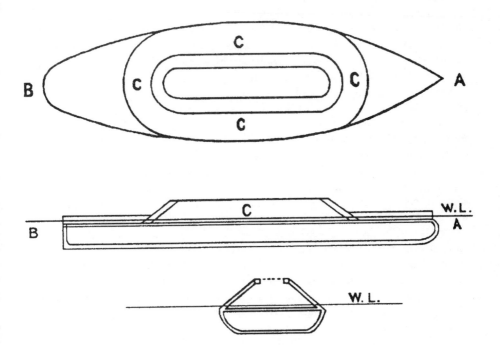

The junction interlocking railway signal

Railways became increasingly important as a means of transport in Victorian times, enough for one of the 146 classes of British patent abridgments to be devoted solely to railway signalling. Methods had to be devised to move railway trains safely and quickly without the risk of collisions. The private companies were reluctant to spend much, but the many disasters were terrible publicity. Initially there was reliance on flags and lamps. Signals were at first always positive ('You may proceed') rather than negative ('Do not move until further notice'), so that if a signal fell down or was obscured a disaster could occur. There were also problems with single-track lines, where movement was restricted by requiring the possession of a baton, which was handed to the train driver at, say, one end of a tunnel and handed back to another signalman at the other end. In 1858 it was made compulsory in Britain to place switching equipment close together rather than scattered along the track. John Saxby was the first person to move the equipment into a raised, enclosed signal box in 1857. The telegraph was much used so that signalmen could send warning messages, but here too mistakes sometimes occurred, if only because nobody thought of working out the exact wording for warnings. An important change was the introduction of block working where trains ran in separate 'blocks', at first separated by time and then after disasters when trains caught up with others at night or in fog separated by space. Controlling distance between trains by having blocks of empty space between them is still the main system used on railways, and a British statute in 1889 made this system compulsory.

John Saxby was born in Hurstpierpoint, Sussex in 1821. He was apprenticed to a carpenter but joined the local railway company in 1840 and rose to become foreman of their workshop in Brighton. One day in 1855 Saxby witnessed an error by a signalman which meant that trains were permitted to go in one direction although the points were set so that a collision could have occurred. He tried out the apparatus shown for one day at another junction and then applied for a patent. The drawing shows semaphore signals (D) and the lamp (E) for the 'up' and 'down' main line while the signals (F) and lamp (G) were for the branch line, red and green being used as traffic lights. The signal rods were attached to levers (H^1) which were linked to the points for changing the route of the trains. By a single action the signalman changed both the lights and the points. By 1860 Saxby was describing himself as a signal manufacturer, and with his partner John Farmer set up a factory in Kilburn in London. Together they patented GB 16101/1871 which adapted the idea so that less wear or damage was liable to occur. A curved and slotted casting transmitted motion from the catch handle and lever to the bar and stud locking of the interlocking apparatus. This was used for decades in much of Europe and the USA and is the system seen in countless films. There was, however, a flaw: Saxby's 'simultaneous locking' meant that a wrong signal could be set by the signalman. Austin Chambers of Bow, Middlesex with GB 31/1860 provided for 'successive locking' where any attempt to set the points at variance to what the signals said was prevented by the mechanism. Saxby died in Hassocks, Sussex in 1913. Engineers were then planning to remove the last of his signals, which was situated just 5 km away.

John Saxby, Brighton, Sussex, England
Filed 24 June 1856 and published as GB 1479/1856

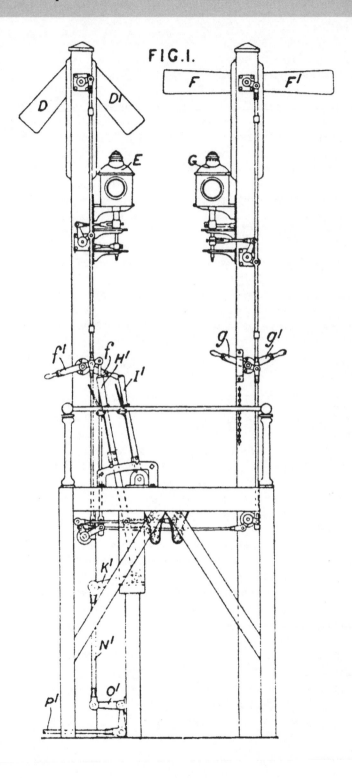

FIG.I.

Lawn tennis

The origins of tennis are thought to go back to ancient times. By the Middle Ages a French game called jeu de paume, or in English real or royal tennis, was being played in rectangular indoor courts. It was a little like tennis played in a squash court, with balls being played off a low roof taking up one side of the court. It is still played at some surviving courts today. Walter Clopton Wingfield was born in 1833 and was a major in the King's Dragoon Guards. His pamphlet *The game of sphairistike: or, lawn tennis*, which was published in at least five editions, is dedicated to 'the party assembled at Nantclwyd in December, 1873', the house near Ruthin in north Wales where the game was first tried out. A delightful engraving of ladies (wearing bustles) and gentlemen watching a game of mixed doubles features further on, and there are many amusing reviews from journals at the end. The name sphairistike (from the Greek, playing ball) was quietly dropped in favour of lawn tennis when it was pointed out that nobody could remember the name (or pronounce it, perhaps).

The illustrations from the patent show that his idea was somewhat different to the modern game. His 'portable' version of the 'ancient game' made it easy to set up and it was ideal for all ages and both sexes. The court was in the shape of an hourglass with a net 6 m wide. The patent does not state other dimensions but his pamphlet advocates a baseline 11 m wide tapering to a net 6 m wide and 1 m high. The court was to be 26 m long. Wingfield suggested using paint, coloured cord or tape to make the boundaries, the latter being easy to trip over, and later he recommended chalk. Scoring was as in badminton, and the designated areas for serving into were the same as they are now. There were just six rules. The side netting can now be seen as superfluous and dangerous and was soon discarded.

Wingfield advertised his idea in the newspapers on 7 March 1874 and produced a box holding all the equipment to play the game. It measured 91 by 15 by 30 cm and cost £6 in 1876. It was considered a good rival to croquet, which was too 'scientific', and to the new sport of badminton, which required a windless day. It could also be played by both sexes as mixed doubles. It soon spread to America after Mary Outerbridge watched British officers playing the game in Bermuda. She purchased the kit and showed it to her brother, who was the Secretary of the Staten Island Cricket and Baseball Club, and the American game was first played there.

There were five different versions of the game by 1877, when the first All-England Lawn Tennis Championship was played at Wimbledon (for men only, women not having a championship until 1884). The rules were standardised for the first tournament with a rectangle 24 m long by 17 m wide and the net 1 m high. Royal tennis scoring was adopted and is the same as now. The main change since is that modern nets are 0.9 m high. The first American championship was in 1881 at Newport, Rhode Island. Wingfield made another attempt to invent a game with a book on bicycle gymkhana in 1897, but this was not so successful. He also patented a scoring board for bridge with GB 13409/1900. There have been many changes in equipment since, but the biggest difference is that tennis is now rarely played on grass except at Wimbledon, a variety of hard courts being used instead. Wingfield retired to Rhysnant Hall, Montgomeryshire and died in 1912. His obituary in *The Times* did not mention tennis.

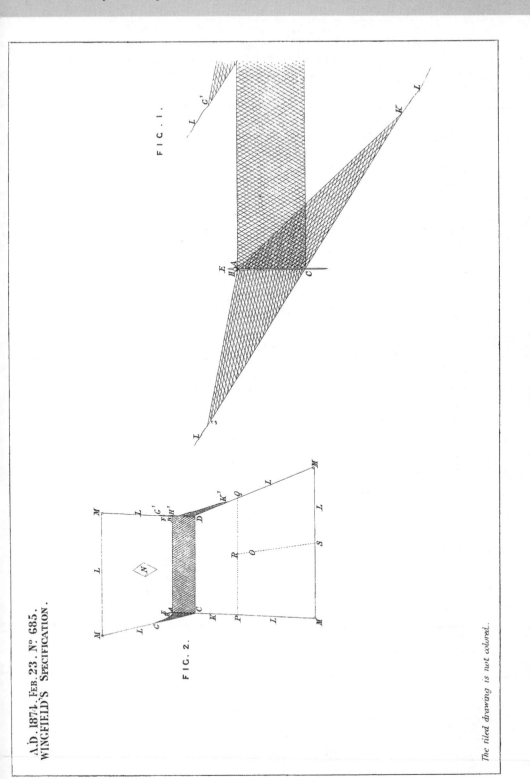

A.D. 1874. FEB. 23. Nº 685.
WINGFIELD'S SPECIFICATION.

FIC.1.

FIC. 2.

The tiled drawing is not colored.

The (legal) liquor flask

Only the British patent for this invention gives Herbert William Torr Jenner's occupation, 'patent solicitor and mechanical expert', besides adding that he was a British subject. He obviously had spent too much time getting bored in court rooms. As one might expect from a patent expert it is full of exact wording. 'This invention relates to liquor-flasks; and it consists of making the outer covering of the flask in the form of a book or other similar article large enough to entirely cover the whole of the flask, including the neck and stopper, and having a hole in the said covering beneath the bottom of the flask, so that it can be pushed upward and the neck made to project through an opening in the covering.' He added that the outer covering was designed so that 'the top of the flask-stopper may be concealed from observation'. He claimed that it was the first time that the stopper had been both concealed and made to provide easy access. In the drawings (E) was the opening through which the top of the flask projects. Figure 1 shows one variation whereby a spring allowed the top to come out while Figures 3 and 4 showed (e) which could slide back and forth beneath (E). By pressing on the bottom the flask was forced up through the opening.

Jenner suggested that the title on the spine of the disguised flask 'may have printed thereon any suitable title more or less suggestive of the contents behind it'. A title like 'Legal decisions', whether Volume I or II, was therefore hardly in the right spirit. He suggested that the contents could also consist of 'drugs, chemicals, perfumery, or any other substance or liquid'. Thomas Helm of Danville, Virginia was working along similar lines with his US 490964 in 1893, a 'Combined clothes brush, flask, and drinking cup'. The 'desired object' was apparently that you could pause while brushing down your clothes and have a drink. One end of the back of the brush slipped off to act as a cup and to reveal a spout. What must have been a modest amount of, presumably, hard liquor was held within the rest of the back. He did not explain why there was a need for such an invention, but John Carter was keen enough to have half the rights assigned to himself.

There were many patents for wine coolers, such as GB 1775/1868 by Julius Nuellens of Torquay, Devon and Matthias Neuhaus of London. This involved wedging the bottle in an insulated bucket. The unusual twist was shown in one of the drawings with the bucket resting on a tray that was supported by gimbals. Two vertical arms extended from the tray to the bucket. The drawing shows the bucket pivoting on its arms to pour into a low wine glass—presumably the apparatus was adjusted for taller glasses. Finally, Frederick Flint of Mount Airy, Georgia with US 408607 in 1889 suggested an 'Electric drinking-vessel'. He believed that electrifying drinks would be of therapeutic value. The bottom of the vessel was connected by wires to a battery. 'The liquid or beverage, while being imbibed, will constitute part of an electrode, which will conduct the electric current to the mucous membrane of the mouth, throat and stomach . . . as the current passes through the body of the drinker.'

(No Model.)

H. W. T. JENNER.
LIQUOR FLASK.

No. 330,709. Patented Nov. 17, 1885.

Fig. 1.

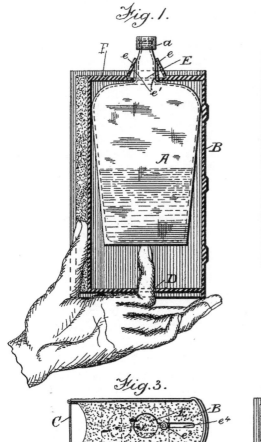

Fig. 2.

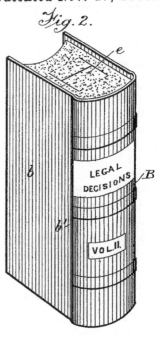

LEGAL DECISIONS

VOL. II.

Fig. 3.

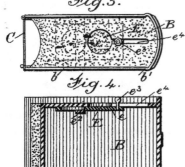

Fig. 4.

Fig. 5.

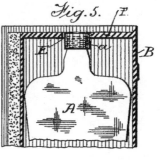

WITNESSES:

Paul M. Knobloch.

INVENTOR

Herbert W. T. Jenner.

Linotype®

The printing of books had changed little from the time of Gutenberg until the invention of Linotype®. The printer would have masses of pieces of type, with different (and many duplicate) pieces for each point size, typeface and capital letters. The pieces were assembled on a 'composing stick' and then inserted or 'locked' into the frame or 'chase', with empty spaces filled up by wooden quoins. The type was inked, a sheet of paper was put over it and the printing press was forced down on the paper by turning a screw. It was skilled, laborious work and a huge investment in pieces of type was needed. All the type used for a book had to be kept in reserve if reprints were required, or else the entire book had to be reset. Newspapers had been printed for decades by fast cylinder presses, but composing the type was still holding up the whole process.

Ottmar Mergenthaler was born in Hachtel, Württemberg, Germany in 1854, son of a schoolmaster. At the age of 14 he was apprenticed to a watchmaker cousin named Hahl. In 1872 to avoid conscription into the army he emigrated to the USA, where he joined a machine shop making signal equipment that was run by August Hahl, son of his former employer. In 1876 Charles Moore, an inventor, asked them if they could help improve a machine for printing words on stone (lithography). It had been invented to help James Clephane, the official reporter for the Senate, who became very active in encouraging and financing efforts to report speeches rapidly. Mergenthaler tried to improve the machine but his initial ideas were soon abandoned as unworkable. Instead he worked on a machine which impressed letters into papier-mâché so that type metal could be poured into the mould. This did not work either: strips of the papier-mâché stuck to the metal.

While on a train journey to Washington, DC, Mergenthaler thought of a machine which would combine the composing and casting. Characters would be entered at a keyboard and a set of matrices corresponding to them would be assembled in a line. Metal would be poured in to make the line. When it had hardened the metal was placed in a galley ready for the press, while the matrices were automatically put back in the right compartment by an endless belt arrangement. The next line was then keyed in the same way. The drawing only shows a small part of what was compared to an upright piano. It is a view from above with the middle segment, including most of the keyboard and cylinder, removed. It was first tried out at the *New York Tribune* on 3 July 1886. The editor and owner, Whitelaw Reid, cried out, 'Ottmar, you've done it! You've cast a line of type!' which provided the trademark for the product.

Numerous improvements such as justifying the ends of the lines were patented in the next few years and his machines were sold initially mostly to newspapers. A syndicate, mainly of newspaper publishers, bought a controlling interest in Mergenthaler's new company but forced him out in 1888 after a boardroom battle. Mergenthaler continued to work on improvements which he then sold to the syndicate. What he called in his autobiography (written in the third person) 'the mistake of his life' was agreeing to take $50 royalty per machine rather than the previous 10%: by 1890 they were selling for $1,200 each. For the last five years of his life he battled with tuberculosis before he died in Baltimore in 1899, aged only 45.

Ottmar Mergenthaler, Baltimore, Maryland
Filed 23 March 1884 and published as US 304272 and GB 11670/1884

O. MERGENTHALER.
MATRIX MAKING MACHINE.

No. 304,272. Patented Aug. 26, 1884.

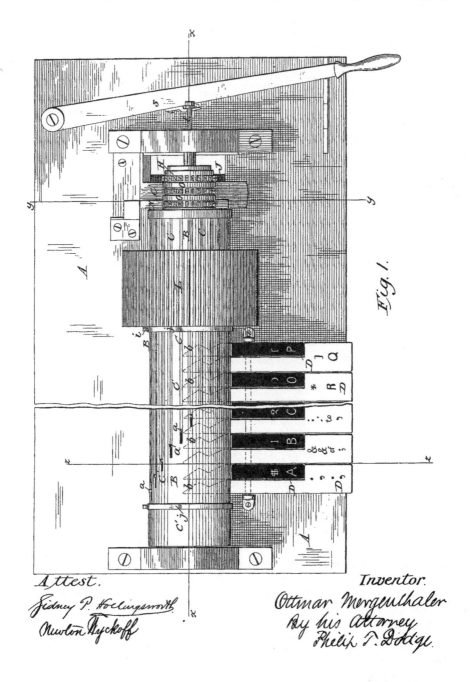

Fig. 1.

Attest.
Sidney P. Hollingsworth
Newton Wyckoff

Inventor.
Ottmar Mergenthaler
By his Attorney
Philip T. Dodge.

Locomotive apparatus for the air

There were numerous attempts to achieve heavier-than-air flight during the Victorian period. There were three main problems: achieving a favourable weight to power ratio (that is, light yet powerful engines), a useful wing structure, and working out the principles of controlling flight. These problems gradually became better understood and it was the Wright brothers who solved them with their US 821393, filed some 8 months before they actually flew in 1903. William Samuel Henson's is a vivid example of the hundreds of unworkable patents. Little is known of his life and inspiration, but he is believed to have been born in 1805 in Leicester, Leicestershire and while inventing lived mainly in Chard, Somerset. He took out patents in textiles and steam engines and became absorbed in the idea of his aircraft. He probably based his principles on the work of Sir George Cayley, who had worked out a number of important principles in flight such as a fixed wing structure (rather than flapping wings) and a rudder to act like a bird's tail.

Henson's patent has the title 'locomotive apparatus for the air, land, and water'. He dubbed his aircraft the 'Aerial Steamer' and it was also called the 'Bat' because of the fan-shaped tailplane, which was meant to control flight by going up or down. The pilot sat to the front of the tube in the middle which housed the 22.5 kilowatt steam engine (which was far too weak). The two propellers were behind the tube so that they 'pushed' the aircraft, unlike the normal 'pulling' of propellers. Some early aircraft did in fact fly using this principle. Sceptical of the ability of his aircraft to take off, he proposed gliding it down an incline on its wheels to gain momentum. Henson was aware of the problems of wind resistance, and the cambered wings were well designed for airflow over them. However he did not realise that controlling the wings and hence flight through, for example, flaps was vital. There was considerable interest in the press when the patent became known, some serious, some sarcastic. A prospectus was issued to raise funds for a company to build it. When a bill to incorporate such a company was read out in the House of Commons there was 'much laughter' from other members present. Like most early patented aircraft it was never actually built.

Henson then joined forces with John Stringfellow with an agreement in December 1843 jointly to share expenses and profits. Stringfellow had been born in Sheffield, Yorkshire in 1799 and worked in the textile industry before switching to designing powerful steam engines. They took 2 years building an aircraft with a wingspan of 7 m with a Stringfellow engine. Henson became discouraged, abandoned the work, and emigrated in 1849 to Philadelphia. The rumour that he had disappeared 'in the wilds of Texas from the ken of aeronautical science' was false, but he does seem to have stopped inventing. He died in 1888 in Newark, New Jersey.

Stringfellow finished his aircraft and had it moved by his workmen to a hill for testing. Tired of jeers from locals (who called him the 'flying man'), he first tried it out at night. The dew on the silk fabric made the wings droop, but he still could not get it to fly when he tried repeatedly by day. Then he built a second (unpiloted) aircraft. It had no tail fin, so any wind would make it veer. Hence he first tried it out inside a lace mill. It ran for 10 m down a guide wire but then stalled. A second flight was more successful: the aircraft flew for 10 m before putting a hole in the canvas wall at the end of the building. He worked on more and more elaborate models until he gave up just before his death in Chard in 1883. He did not patent his work.

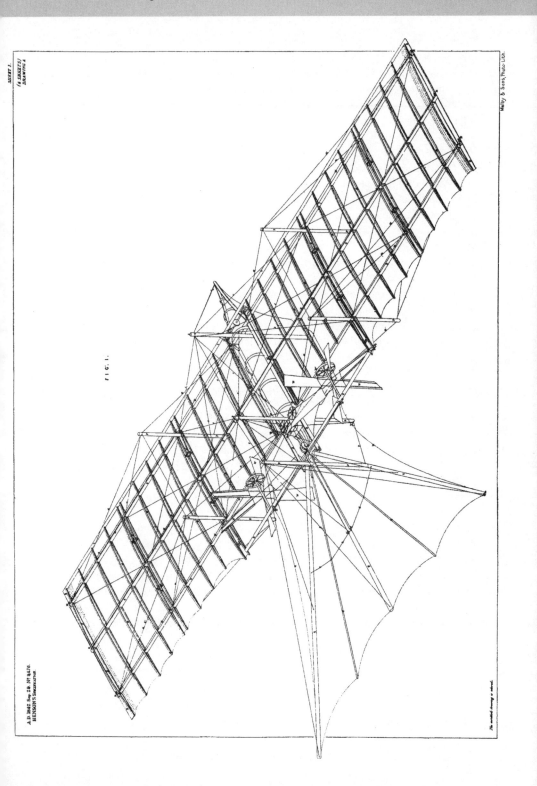

FIG. 1.

SHEET 1.

(4 SHEETS.)
DRAWING 4

Malby & Sons, Photo-Lith.

A.D. 1842. Sep. 29. No 9478.
HENSON'S Specification.

Machine for searching for gold

This is an example of a patent from one of the Australian colonies, which each had their own patent systems until they were unified in 1904 following the formation of the Commonwealth of Australia. Any book on Victorian patents should surely have one from the colony that was named after her when it was constituted in 1851. Half of the few patents from the colony in the 1850s were for gold mining. The patent's full title is 'The machine for searching in alluvial and other deposits to ascertain their auriferous qualities'.

Few outside Australia are aware that besides the Gold Rush, following its discovery in California in February 1848, Victoria had a similar influx in 1851—after a Californian had a lucky find. The gold was alluvial, that is, was found in the bottom of rivers or in old flood plains, and it is said to have been the richest such find in the world. Those who could not afford machinery 'panned' the silt hoping that the heavier gold would be left behind when the silt was washed away. Most inventions on the subject took advantage of the weight of gold and of the plentiful water where alluvial gold was found. Jacob Braché's invention was meant to bore into the earth and to bring up samples of 'auriferous', or gold-bearing, soil to see how rich the deposits were. The drawings show a machine, to be used by two to four men, which could be powered by hand, steam or horse.

Figure 1 shows a wooden carriage with shafts so that horses could take it from place to place. Jointed pipes which were graduated in feet and inches were provided with hollow bores of tempered steel. A crank turned a wheel which forced a screw within the pipe into the earth. At the same time water lubricated this action. The extracted material ascended to the basin (l) to be examined by the surveyor. This was then either discarded at (M) or retained for further examination at (N). Braché stated that if the soil changed colour the depth given on the pipe should be noted. Jacob Braché was a civil engineer who arrived from New York in 1853. He was well known in the community, and edited the *Transactions of the Mining Institute of Victoria* from 1859.

Many of the American patents on the subject, not surprisingly, came from the miners in California. An example is US 12453 in 1855 by 'Lewis Teese & Son' of San Francisco. This was for 'sluice-forks', pitchforks which were used to remove stones from sluice-boxes in which the soil from river beds was placed. They were designed to remove stones, and the point of the patent was to have the tops of the tines triangular rather than sharp to prevent pieces of gold from lodging there. Another patent on the subject was US 7678 by Arnold Buffum and Philip Thorp of New York City in 1850. Their 'double-acting rocker for washing gold' consisted of a trunk with two rockers at the bottom. A stake on the side on the trunk was used to operate the rockers. A pan in the lower section retrieved the gold while a screen in the upper section caught pebbles. There were 44 gold-washing patents alone among American patents in the period to 1873.

Jacob Braché, Melbourne, Australia
Filed 10 October 1854 and published as Victoria patent 12

Prospecting Machine

Vic. 12*/54

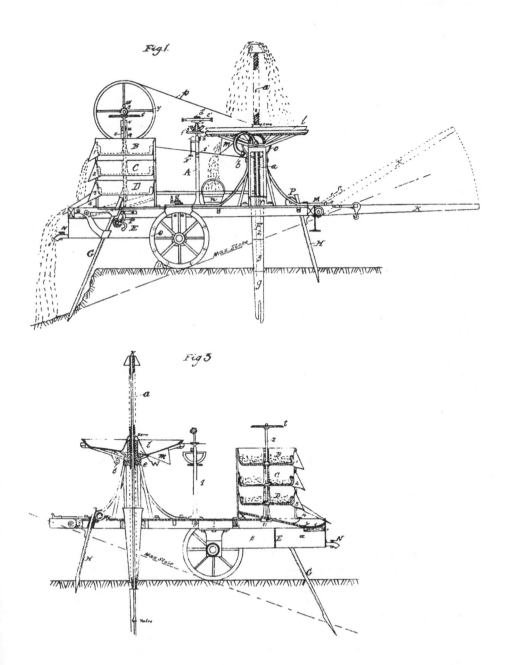

Fig.1

Fig 3

The mathematical divider

Sarah Marks was born in Portsmouth, Hampshire, in 1854, daughter of a watchmaker and jeweller. She went to live when aged nine with her Aunt Marion Hartog in London, who undertook to have Sarah educated with her cousins. In 1876 she went to Girton to study mathematics. This college, founded in 1869 in nearby Hitchin, was the first women's college at Cambridge University, and had only been established there for 3 years. Although taking final examinations she left without a degree, as Cambridge women were not allowed one until 1923. One day in February 1883 her cousin Ansel Leo brought her a drawing of a device for dividing a line into any number of equal parts. Sarah realised both the possibilities and the problems of the device. They worked together on an improvement and applied for a patent, but Sarah soon dropped the original idea and worked alone along a different path. She applied for a second patent before her successful GB 5443/1884, where she gave her occupation as 'spinster'. The line (g–h) is cut into say 17 equal parts by opening the mechanism so that (g) is at 8.5 on the graduated rule (each 0.5 inch [1.3 cm] representing $\frac{1}{17}$). The rule is slid down the holder (e–f) 1.3 cm at a time and the other arm moves in tandem so that each mark can be made on the line. This was not the first divider but just a very effective one for anyone wishing to carry out such work in art or mathematics.

In 1885 Sarah, who by now was calling herself Hertha, married a physics professor. William Ayrton was very unusual in encouraging her scientific work and treating her as an equal. *Who was who* states that Hertha Ayrton was the only woman member of the Institution of Electrical Engineers and that in 1902 she was legally refused membership of the Royal Society, presumably as she was not a man. Hertha Ayrton was a keen and active suffragette. A favourite argument against women's rights was that as they took no part in war they should not have a voice in deciding issues of war and peace. When World War I broke out she was anxious to help the Allied cause, but as women were at first given little scope to help, she was able to finish a lecture on pressure in water which she gave in May 1915 to the Royal Society. While returning from the lecture to her house in a taxi she thought of using the same idea to dispel poison gas from trenches. She had shown that waves made vortices: why could not vortices make waves, and waft the gas away? She gave instructions to her maid to be left alone in her laboratory all day and designed a fan hinged on a stick which, when beaten against something solid, dispelled gas.

It was apparently so simple that officials at first scoffed, although visitors to her laboratory called it 'magic'. A demonstration was held in Chatham, Kent in September and convinced the sceptical General in charge. Those who were armed with a fan did not need a gas mask. It was not until May 1916 that the first 5,000 of an eventual 104,000 'Ayrton fans' were sent out to the Western Front. Hertha Ayrton wanted millions to be sent out: 'You might as well try to sweep all the houses from Park Lane to Chancery Lane with one broom', she said. In any case instructions for the special technique of fanning that was needed were rarely given and so, as a Major in the Royal Engineers said in a letter to *The Times*, the fans were mainly welcomed by the soldiers as a source of firewood. The publication of her patent application GB 8541/1915 was delayed for security reasons until 1919; she later improved its design in three more patents. Hertha Ayrton died in 1923 in London.

A.D. 1884. MARCH 25. Nº 5443.
MARKS' COMPLETE SPECIFICATION.

(1 SHEET)

LONDON.—Printed by EYRE and SPOTTISWOODE.
Printers to the Queen's most Excellent Majesty. 1884

Malby &Sons, Photo-Litho.

Means for releasing draught animals

Sir Arthur Seymour Sullivan, 'Knight and Doctor of Music', was the famous composer of the Gilbert and Sullivan operas. He was born in London in 1842, son of an Irish military musician and an Italian mother. He collaborated with the lyricist Sir William Schwenk Gilbert on the operas between 1875 and 1896. The subject of Sullivan's invention was one that was close to many Victorians' hearts. At a time when the main way of getting around, at least for short journeys or in remote areas, was by horse it was important to have a safe, cheap and convenient way of releasing horses from their harness if they bolted or fell. The invention aimed to 'obviate the usual delay and danger, as at present experienced'.

Besides the usual bar connecting the pair of horses with the carriage there was a second 'splinter bar'. This was attached to the usual bar by rocking hooks held in place by a notched bar with a lever which, normally locked, was within reach of the driver. If an accident occurred the driver released the lever so that the horses were freed. This was not just with the horses' safety in mind: terrified horses galloping away could cause terrible damage to the carriage and its occupants. The lever was sizeable and was meant to help the driver in bringing the carriage to a safe halt if the brakes were inadequate. The details of the mechanism are shown in great detail on the other pages of the patent. The shafts are (a) which link with a frame (b). The lever (m) links with the mechanism to the notched bar (h). Many other patents were applied for in this area, and Sullivan's was only one of nine such British applications in 1898 which were subsequently published. These were listed in the British subject indexes under 'Runaway or fallen horses, releasing'.

Most inventions in this area worked along similar lines by using a release mechanism. A different approach was taken by Charles Moore and Richard Blair of Philadelphia with their US 129358 in 1872. The horse would have a tightly folded fan, secured to a vertical strap, between the eyes. This 'when not in use, will not be materially in his way and not occupy much space'. If the horse bolted the rider would suddenly or gradually open up the fan so that the horse, unable to see, would come to a stop.

Sullivan's invention was not his first encounter with the intellectual property system. He is thought to have been the first to fight those who stole copyrighted music. He fought British bootleggers, but was especially outraged by their American counterparts. These were publishers who took advantage of the fact that American copyright law denied protection to foreign authors. The irate Sullivan filed many lawsuits in American courts, but this hardly damaged the trade. To prevent the pirating of *The Pirates of Penzance* he refused for a long time to publish the score, and bouncers prowled every show to stop music thieves from writing down the melodies. Tired of what he regarded as 'guerrilla warfare', Sullivan paid American musicians to put their names on the scores of several operas, including *The Mikado,* and then to hand the rights back to him, thus satisfying the requirements of American copyright law. He sued American theatrical companies when the scores were pirated anyway—and lost. 'No Englishman possesses any rights which a true-born American is bound to respect', one judge supposedly said. Sullivan died in London in 1900.

A.D. 1898. Dec. 16. N.º 26,624.
SULLIVAN'S Complete Specification

(3 SHEETS)
SHEET 1.

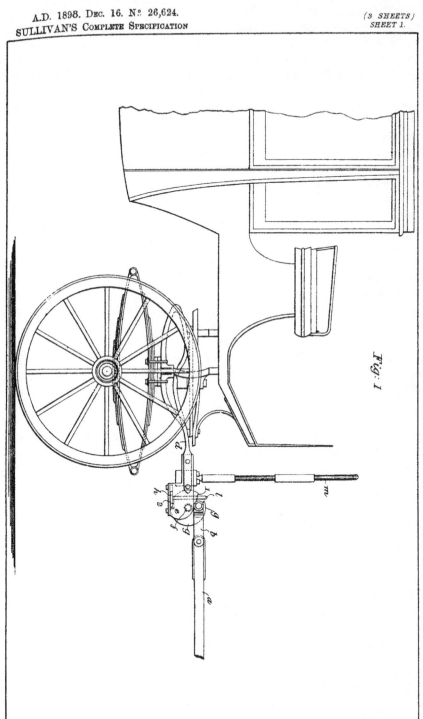

Fig. 1

[This Drawing is a reproduction of the Original on a reduced scale.]

Malby & Sons, Photo-Litho.

The mirror galvanometer

William Thomson was born in Belfast, Ireland, in 1824, son of a textbook writer and a Scottish mother. His father was a dominant figure and William was a submissive child. His father was teaching mathematics at Glasgow University when, at the age of 10, he was admitted as a student (along with his brother James, age 11). At 22 he became its professor of natural philosophy, aided by his father's campaign. He stayed there until he retired in 1899. Thomson was a scientist who wrote over 600 scientific papers. He believed that all phenomena that caused force—electricity, magnetism, heat and so on—were the result of invisible material in motion. He was the first to suggest mathematical relationships between different kinds of energy, now well accepted. He also opposed Darwin's theory of evolution. He began patenting with GB 2547/1854, on telegraphs, and many of his numerous inventions concerned the sea, where he kept a yacht. These included a compass that was adopted by the Admiralty; an analogue computer for measuring tides and for calculating tide-tables for any hour, past or future; and sounding equipment.

Much of his work was as a consultant in the planning and construction of submarine telegraph cables, and he grew wealthy in the process. Thomson was recruited when he wrote a letter to *The Athenaeum* in 1856. There were great, and expensive, plans to link Ireland with Newfoundland. Although the time taken to lay the cable was brief the risks were high, since if a cable broke when being 'laid out' from a ship, or if it broke for any other reason, the chances of retrieving the cable to repair it from the bottom of the sea were next to nil. The cables consisted of seven copper wires covered with three coats of gutta-percha wound with tarred hemp which was sheathed in 18 iron spiralling strands. In July 1858 one British and one American ship met in the middle of the Atlantic, spliced their cables, and set off in opposite directions. It took just a week, but after great celebrations the cable broke. In 1866 the work was completed, the equivalent of sending a man to the Moon, and all funded by private finance.

The illustration is from his most important invention, which enabled the very weak currents on long submarine cables to carry telegraph messages to be picked up at the other end. It was also used to check that the laid-out cable was still intact. It consisted of two main units: the mirror galvanometer, shown in Figure 5, and a calibrating apparatus and lamp. These faced each other. A beam of light was focussed from a lamp fixed below a calibrated scale onto a tiny mirror inside the galvanometer cover. When a current (the incoming signal) passed through the galvanometer coil it temporarily became an electromagnet. The magnetic field made the iron frame, to which the tiny mirror was fixed, move by a tiny amount. The beam of light was therefore deflected to the left or the right, depending on the polarity of the signal, which could be read off against the scale. Another important invention was his 'siphon recorder', with GB 2147/1867, which permanently recorded telegraph messages, including those received by a mirror galvanometer. Thomson was knighted in 1866 for his work on submarine cables and was made Lord Kelvin of Largs in 1892. He was given the honour of having absolute temperature measured in Kelvins, and it is said that he was entitled to more letters after his name than any other man in the British Empire, mostly from honorary degrees. He died in 1907 near Largs, Ayrshire, Scotland.

William Thomson, Glasgow, Lanarkshire, Scotland
Filed 28 February 1858 and published as GB 329/1858

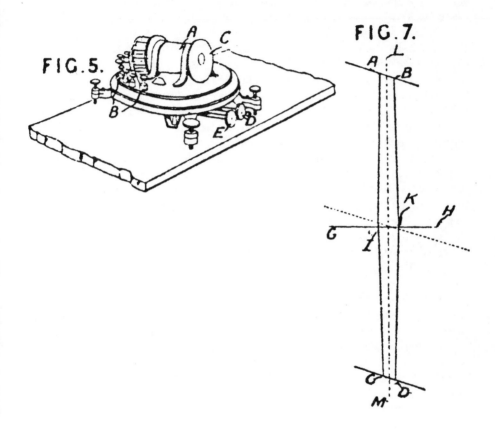

The motion picture camera

The question of who invented the first motion picture camera is controversial. Thomas Edison certainly improved and popularised it but the credit for its invention as a working model should go to a Frenchman, Augustin Le Prince. The idea is really an extension of photography by showing numerous images in quick succession to fool the eye into seeing motion, as with a child's flicker book.

Le Prince was an artist who was born in Metz, France in 1842. He migrated to Leeds, Yorkshire in 1866 and married a local girl in 1869. From 1875 he became interested in the concept of motion pictures. In 1881 he moved to New York to carry on his work. The patent drawings are of a 16 lens camera in Figure 1 and a view from above in Figure 2 of the mechanics behind the lenses. Many film historians dismiss his work because of his belief in 16 lenses but the American patent has only six 'claims' to his monopoly while the British patent had 11. The reason was that the US Patent Office said that they would remove any references to using a single lens on the grounds that a French engineer, Henry Du Mont, had done so with GB 1457/1861—although that was not for a motion picture camera. His patent agents did not tell Le Prince of this until it was too late and the alteration went through unchallenged. His British patent does contain references to both a single lens camera and a projector. In addition, his daughter recalled a single lens camera being used before they moved to England in 1887. In 1931 a Leeds woodworker swore an affidavit that he had helped Le Prince make a single lens camera in 1888, and its composition was described.

Above all, we have fragments of film, one of his father-in-law's garden in Leeds and one of traffic on Leeds Bridge, taken at 20 pictures a second. Both were taken with single lens cameras on sensitised paper about 54 mm wide. Le Prince switched to Eastman Kodak's new celluloid film when he was about to go to Paris to carry out demonstrations of his new projector. On 16 September 1890 Le Prince boarded a train at Dijon for Paris with his apparatus and films. He never arrived, and his disappearance has never been solved.

William Friese-Greene, photographer and Mortimer Evans, civil engineer, both of London, have also been put forward with their GB 10131/1889 as the inventors of the single lens camera. Friese-Greene was unsuccessful in his work and in 1921 at a meeting with top executives in the industry he collapsed and died while trying to claim the credit for motion pictures. By comparison with such claims the Lumière brothers with their FR 245032 of 1895 were latecomers. The difference was that from 28 December 1895 they actually made and showed short films for paying audiences in Paris on such themes as workers leaving a factory and a trick with a hose played on a gardener. And what of Thomas Edison? His contribution was certainly vital. He did not think the idea was very important and patented only in the USA (leaving the field open in Europe). These were his Kinetograph in 1893 with US 493426 for taking pictures and his Kinetoscope in 1897 with US 589168 for viewing them, though only one at a time: the original 'what the butler saw' peepshow. He used photosensitive emulsion on 35 mm wide flexible celluloid with holes at intervals along each side to govern the speed of projection; the same system is used today.

Augustin Le Prince, New York City, New York
Filed 2 November 1886 and published as US 376247 and GB 423/1888

(No Model.)   3 Sheets—Sheet 1.

A. LE PRINCE.
METHOD OF AND APPARATUS FOR PRODUCING ANIMATED PICTURES OF NATURAL SCENERY AND LIFE.

No. 376,247.   Patented Jan. 10, 1888.

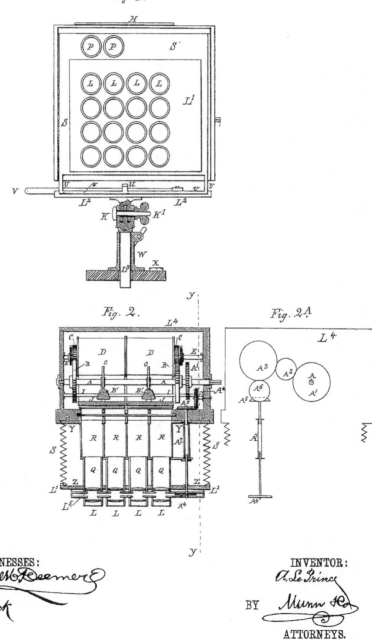

Fig. I.

Fig. 2.

Fig. 2ᴬ

The mousetrap

Traps for vermin were much in demand in Victorian times. This is the classic 'Little Nipper'. Born in Leeds in 1849, James Henry Atkinson initially described himself in his patents as an ironmonger but in this one he is a 'model maker'. He had dabbled with patents before, with his GB 14576/1886, a rack pulley for window blinds, and GB 667/1893, a cinder-sifter for fireplaces, as well as abandoned applications for window blind cords and for heating laundry irons in 1895 and 1897, but his true love turned out to be catching mice.

On 7 December 1898 he made an application for a mouse-trap but this was abandoned, perhaps in favour of his 'Improved treadle trap for mice, rats and the like', applied for on 30 December 1898, published as GB 27488/1898. This is almost the 'classic' mousetrap seen in cartoons and sold everywhere, but not quite. 'Treadle' means that, as he states in the patent, the mice are expected to set it off by running over it. He felt that in places with lots of food such as grocers there was no need for bait. Perhaps his customers complained that his mousetrap was not doing the job for he improved on it by providing a place for bait with the illustrated patent. He states in the patent that it is 'caused to "go off" by a pull at the bait'. It was made for ease of setting and handling 'with the minimum risk of the trap "going off" prematurely whilst being set and handled'. In the drawing (c) is the spring and (d) is the catch lever hinged on staple (e) so that the spring is held down while the trap is set. (fi) is the catch lever or bait staple hinged on (g). The bait is on (i) so that when it is tugged (d) comes loose from (e) and (c) is released.

Initially a manufacturer, Atkinson later sold the rights to Procter Brothers, a Welsh wire-working company. The first known advertisement for the trap was by Procter in the *Ironmonger* trade journal on 10 February 1900, which had one important change: the complicated means for holding down the bait was replaced by a pin sticking up, onto which the bait is pushed. This shows that an idea does not have to be complicated to work. This is the model that is common today and which is still made by the company at its factory in Bedwas near Newport, Gwent, Wales. Atkinson continued to work on the idea but this was his great achievement. His GB 2503/1900 was another treadle device, which was modified in GB 13993/1902 so that the plate was at an angle, with a second plate being hinged to it and flush with the floor. His GB 8317/1900 was surely not the first, and certainly not the last, to provide a box with a pool of water. The mice were expected to walk up a ladder and were tipped in to drown. His last word on the subject was a rodent trap, GB 465991, in 1938, when he was almost ninety years old. He died in Leeds in 1942.

A very similar invention was patented by William Hooker of Abingdon, Illinois with his US 528671, published in 1894. This model was successfully made in Lititz, Pennsylvania with the trade mark 'Out O' sight', with a mouse peering out of the middle O, printed on the base. Except for a hedge trimmer patent in 1865 all of Hooker's 27 patents between 1865 and 1908 were on either gates or animal traps. Atkinson's patent should probably have been rejected for lack of novelty because of the Hooker patent but it was not until 1905 that British patents were examined by the Patent Office to see if they were new. It is quite likely that Atkinson had seen the Hooker trap in the shops or in advertisements.

James Henry Atkinson, Leeds, Yorkshire, England
Filed 27 June 1899 and published as GB 13277/1899

A.D. 1899. June 27. Nᵒ. 13,277.
ATKINSON'S Complete Specification.

1 SHEET.

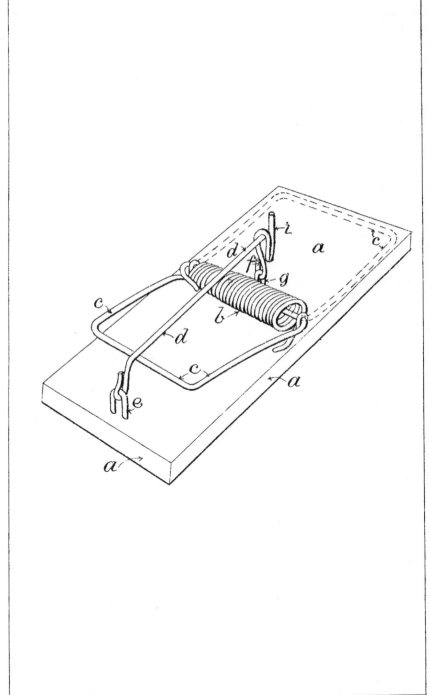

The moustache protector and trainer

The Victorian age was a time when great decorum was observed at middle-class dinner parties. Soup would have presented a problem for those wishing to preserve dry and unstained moustaches, and heat would melt any substance worked into the moustaches. This offering—by Harry Jones, an auctioneer—suggested a solution. In his own words 'This invention has for its special object the protection of the moustache during meals, and principally at the time of taking soup and other liquids, from which without some guard or protection the moustache becomes saturated and rendered unpleasant both to the wearer and those in his immediate company'.

The invention consisted of two pieces of soft leather (a), which were fixed upon a light steel spring (b) which ran through them and on which they could easily move. Two pieces of elastic (c) 'are fixed at the ends of the spring to fit readily on the ears'. The shields were curved at the mouth portion (d) and, thoughtfully, 'can be slid back on the spring to suit any particular conformation of the upper lip'. The 'trainer' part of the title of the patent quoted above consisted in enabling the hair to take any particular form or direction. It probably did not occur to the inventor that few would be likely to expose themselves to ridicule in the way that the gentleman wearing the product in Figure 2 was doing. It would have been much simpler to omit the soup course.

In the period to 1900 no fewer than 43 British patents on the subject were published. The first effort was GB 2213/1860 by Edward Field of London, hair dresser and perfumer, whose invention was made of shell, horn, ivory or metal and fastened with a comb into the hair at the back of the head. A different approach was to place the guard on the spoon, as in GB 2203/1876 by William Whitehead, consulting engineer and patent agent and James Bolt and William Weeder, all of Halifax, Yorkshire. The spoon had a guard which was fixed to the bowl or hinged on the handle. The guard if hinged would recede and not interfere with the filling of the spoon.

The USA trailed far behind with a mere five in the period to 1873, although numbers may have picked up thereafter. There the interest was more in placing the guard on a glass tumbler, as in US 91336 of 1869 by M.C. Hepstinstall of Enfield, North Carolina. Pauline Peck of the USA has researched the subject in detail and has even published a book with over 600 illustrations, *Mustache cups: timeless Victorian treasures*. She credits the invention of the moustache guard to Harvey Adams who in 1830 thought of a cup (but did not patent it) with a guard actually built in. As she points out it would have made the perfect gift. Moustache cups were made by such firms as Royal Crown Derby, Imari, Royal Bayreuth, Irish Belleek and Limoges. Although examples were also made in the USA, most of these have English names as British pottery had more prestige. Cups with guards made for left-handed users are apparently quite rare. Of course, such inventions would not have been popular until moustaches came into vogue. Except in army circles moustaches, and indeed beards, were uncommon (at least in the best circles) until the Crimean War of 1854–56 or, for the USA, until the Mexican-American War of 1846–47 and the Gold Rush of 1849–50. Perhaps illustrations in magazines inspired civilians to emulate the army.

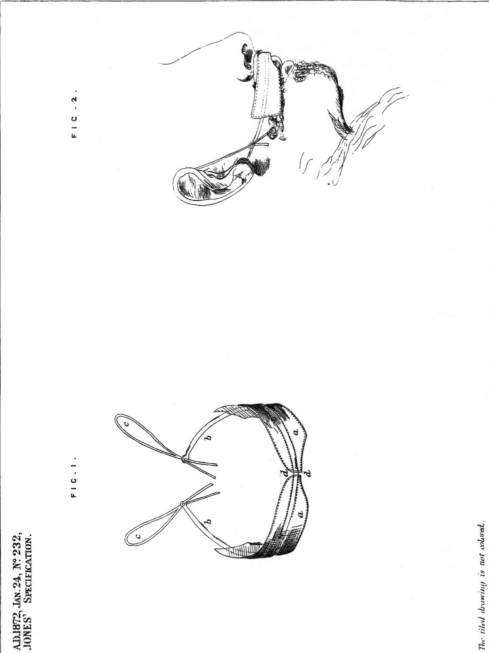

A.D.1872, JAN. 24, № 232,
JONES' SPECIFICATION.

FIG.1.

FIG.2.

The tiled drawing is not colored.

The multistage sugar evaporator

Norbert Rillieux was born in New Orleans in 1806, son of an engineer of French descent and one of his slaves, who was freed before Norbert's birth. His father had himself invented a steam-operated cotton baling press. Norbert showed promise and was sent to L'Ecole centrale in Paris, France to complete his education in engineering. He taught there for a while (as the youngest-ever teacher) and in 1830 thought of a method of improving sugar refining, but no French firms or individuals were interested. He then returned to New Orleans.

When white sugar is made the water used in the refining process has to be evaporated. The method used at the time was simply to pour the cane juice into open pans and to heat them over a fire so that the sugar condensed as the water evaporated. This was inefficient in fuel use, wasteful of water, and was exhausting and potentially hazardous to whoever was carrying out the heating—mostly slaves. Rillieux's concept was the first multistage evaporator. The original heat is used continuously at lower pressures in each vessel and as in a pressure cooker, where boiling occurs at relatively low temperatures, the process is carried out economically. It was also quicker than earlier methods and even made the sugar taste better. Rillieux with his US 3237 in 1843 proposed a double pan evaporator which carried out the process twice. US 4879 was for a still more effective triple effect evaporator.

The juice first went into a vessel which was heated by tubes which had themselves been heated by steam or hot water. The cooled and partly evaporated liquid passed through the 'Hall condenser' to make a partial vacuum in the next pan. The warm vapour from the evaporated juice heated the juice in the second pan and so on to the third pan. The third or 'striking' pan was the one from which the sugar was taken to be cooled. The drawings opposite show a series of evaporating pans, Figure 14; a side elevation, Figure 15; a 'plan thereof', Figure 16; and a horizontal section taken at line (x) in Figure 14, Figure 17.

The idea was enthusiastically taken up by the plantation owners in the USA, the West Indies and elsewhere. The savings were so large that the cost of the machinery was covered by the extra profit from the first year's sugar crop. The price of sugar also dropped, so that it became much less of a luxury item. Although Rillieux's engineering skills were in demand in Louisiana he was not allowed to stay overnight in the houses of the plantation owners because of his colour. Prejudice increased during the 1850s, especially for free Blacks, and Rillieux moved to France. There, however, there were problems as local engineers had misused his process and did not think much of it. He took out French patents on the same concept until as late as 1889. He did have other interests and in 1880 an American sugar planter, while on a visit to France, looked for Rillieux and found him in a library translating Egyptian hieroglyphics. He died in 1894 in Paris. In 1934 the International Sugar Cane Technologists raised a memorial to this remarkable engineer. Today Rillieux's evaporators are used for many purposes from the desalination of seawater to recycling processes in space.

N. Rillieux,

Evaporating Pan.

Sheet 4- 4 Sheets

Nº 4.879.

Patented Dec. 10, 1846.

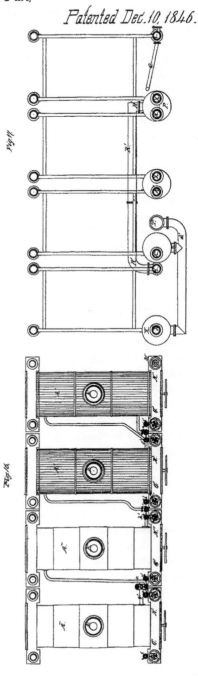

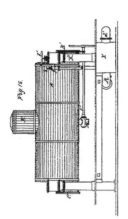

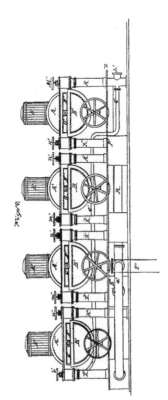

The Ouija® board

Modern spiritualism only dates back to 1848. Strange rapping noises had been heard in the house of sisters Margaretta and Kate Fox, aged 14 and 11, in Hydesville, New York. They challenged the perpetrator and claimed to have contacted the spirit of a pedlar who had been murdered 5 years before. This set off a craze for informal 'tea and table rapping parties' while the sisters took an act on tour with showman Phineas Barnum for the next 30 years. One of the sisters confessed in 1888 that she had faked the noises by using the bones in her foot, although she later retracted. By this time both sisters were, sadly, alcoholics.

The idea behind the concept of the Ouija® board itself has been attributed to a certain Planchette in France in 1853. A small, heart-shaped table was supported by two castors and a pencil as the third leg, which would 'write' messages. 'Planchette' actually means 'small board' in French, and no such person is known. The procedure often resulted in illegible writing. A number of different 'dial plates' were devised with a needle pointing to the letters of the alphabet. Finger-tips rested on the needle, which 'responded' in answer to spoken questions. The involuntary trembling of the hands is sufficient to generate the actual movement.

The Ouija® board only dates back to 1890, although there is some controversy about who contributed what. Some researchers say that a cabinet and coffin maker named Reiche devised the board and sold the rights to Charles Kennard, who formed the Kennard Novelty Company. The illustrated patent by Elijah Jefferson Bond—named as an attorney in the British patent—was certainly assigned to Kennard and shows the table on which the hands of the players would rest. Bond called it in the patent 'an Ouija or Egyptian luck-board'. Kennard was ousted in what would now be called a hostile takeover and the manager of Kennard's shop, William Fuld, began to run the renamed Ouija Novelty Company, claiming that it was all his idea. In March 1892 Fuld filed for what became US 479266, which was for a variation of the idea. The months were listed on each side of the board, the alphabet was in the shape of a horseshoe and there was a square table on stilts. He stated that in playing 'in this way much amusement and entertainment can be obtained at little expense'. The name itself can be taken from the French and German for 'yes', but it has also been said that Fuld was told (erroneously) that the name meant 'good luck' in Arabic, and another theory is that the name was taken from the Moroccan town of Oujda. The trade mark was not registered until 1950 but claimed prior use for a 'talking board' back to 7 January 1890.

William Fuld's brother Isaac initially helped out with the bookkeeping but was later fired for fraud. Fuld enthusiastically promoted the game although rivals appeared. An early advertisement read, 'Interesting and mysterious; surpasses in its results second sight, mind reading, clairvoyance; will give intelligent answer to any question. Proven at patent office before patent was allowed. Price $1.50. All first-class toy, dry goods, and stationery stores'. The claim about its being proven at the Patent Office raises odd thoughts about a demonstration of the product. Fuld died in 1927 when he accidentally fell off the top of a building. His family sold the rights to Parker Brothers (now Hasbro) in 1966, with Fuld's name still on the product until 1999. Fuld once said, 'It's only a game—isn't it?'

Elijah Jefferson Bond for Charles Kennard and William Maupin, all of Baltimore, Maryland
Filed 28 May 1890 and published as US 446054 and GB 2451/1891

(No Model.)

E. J. BOND.
TOY OR GAME.

No. 446,054.

Patented Feb. 10, 1891.

Fig. 1.

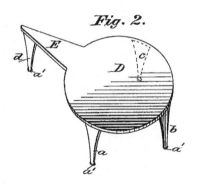

Fig. 2.

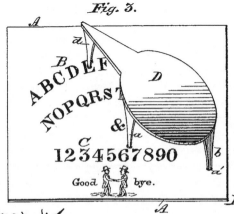

Fig. 3.

Witnesses:
Frank de W Benzinger
H. R. Walton.

Inventor:
Elijah J. Bond,
By T. C. Brecht
Attorney.

The parachute fire-escape

Benjamin Oppenheimer's superb patent is quite probably unique, but this is difficult to prove, as the American classification for the patent is merely for 'Safety lowering devices: parachutes', in which class it is the oldest patent. He states, 'A person may safely jump out of the window of a burning building from any height, and land, without injury and without the least damage, on the ground'. The patent is very short. The footwear consisted of thick elastic pads to absorb the impact of landing on the ground. The parachute was to be made of soft or waxed cloth with a suggested diameter of 1.2 to 1.5 m and was stiffened by a suitable frame. To us it may seem obvious now to have parachute straps underneath the arms, rather than on a headpiece, but somebody had to think of it first.

The basic concept of parachutes had been known since at least 1797, when a successful descent was made in Paris, France from a balloon at a height of some 700 m. The parachute had a diameter of 7 m. Other experiments were occasionally made, and the first fatality was as late as that of Robert Cocking in Greenwich, Kent in 1837, whose cone-shaped parachute disintegrated in a jump from 1,700 m. It is fortunate that Oppenheimer's idea was never used to add to the list of fatalities. Besides his optimism about the height at which it could be used, he was unaware of the impact on the limbs when landing rapidly, and did not think through the problem of getting his rigid parachute through a normal window.

There were of course numerous other devices for saving lives from fires. One of the 146 classes of British patents was entirely devoted to means of extinguishing or preventing fires and providing means of escape. These include GB 818/1866 by Ralph Jones and John Hedges of Aylesbury, Buckinghamshire. The escaping person was attached by straps to a drum round which a rope was wound which was then fastened to the wall. Use involved jumping out *while holding the drum*, which had a brake mechanism which was operated while in mid-air. A saner alternative, holding on to the rope while the drum was left behind, was also mentioned.

GB 1302/1888 by Stafford Campbell of Monkwearmouth, Durham, shipwright, had a method of saving people from the upper boxes of theatres. A sliding door in a corridor led to a descending endless belt with seating and footholds on it, with rollers underneath the belt. The seats meant an orderly departure without crowding. This was the Egress, and the Ingress, a parallel stairway, was separated from it by a low iron wall and provided access for firemen. It was also equipped with hosepipes. With typical nervous phrasing Campbell gives the 'Mode of operation' as 'Upon alarm of fire being made, all who are entrusted with key of escape to proceed to entrance with all speed, when opened Firemen, Policemen, or others who have practiced the operation of the escape, to ascend ingress steps unbolt and draw back hatch at top of escape. Officers must gain possession of entrance to escape from Gallery to prevent crowding. One officer will stand on top of ingress steps to regulate the speed of belt and assist to place the people on escape . . . a little practice will enable officers to perform this with quick despatch.' Campbell seems to have forgotten that power might fail when the fire broke out, and the fact that the entrances to his fire escape could only be unlocked from outside could scarcely have raised confidence among theatre-goers.

B. B. OPPENHEIMER.
Fire-Escape.

No. 221,855. Patented Nov. 18, 1879.

WITNESSES:
Henry N. Miller
C. Sedgwick

INVENTOR:
B. B. Oppenheimer
BY Munn & Co
ATTORNEYS.

Parlor base-ball

Many sports have at least one patented board game based on them. This is one of the first board games on the theme of baseball (there have been hundreds since). Edward Burgess Peirce's 'new and useful game' is dubbed by him 'Parlor Base-Ball' in his opening paragraph. Up to 18 persons could play, that number being determined by the total number of players on the baseball diamond, two teams of nine each. Therefore each person could be represented by one player. The circle (AA) lists the different events that could happen, with (B) the pointer spun to decide what happens. The baseball diamond is shown below with the batter at (H). Amusingly, the pitcher (bowler) is shown as just that at (P). The various fielders (D) are 'not absolutely essential' but 'make the game more interesting and lively'. On either side are cards for keeping score both for the individuals and the teams.

The circle for determining play is divided into four concentric portions starting from the outside and numbered at '10 o'clock'. The ring (0) is meant to determine the fate of the batter, (1) that of any player at first base, (2) at second base and (3) at third base, with that player not surprisingly either scoring or being got out. As the patent austerely states, when the spinner indicates a box 'the man is stationed in the miniature field accordingly'. The batter apparently always hits a 'base hit' to reach first base and never hits a double, home run and so on. He also cannot be struck out (bowled). The patent concludes, 'The utility of the game and the pleasure and amusement to be derived therefrom are readily perceived'. It is not known if Peirce's game were ever manufactured. The first board game based on baseball is probably US 67951 in 1867 by William Buckley of New York City. It was basically a pinball game. The next is US 74154 in 1868 by Francis Sebring of Hoboken, New Jersey. His game was played with a cent coin as the ball. One of the two players would pitch it at the other and hits would go to various areas on the field marked with what was supposed to happen.

Baseball was once attributed to Abner Doubleday of Cooperstown, New York thinking up the rules in 1839. It is now thought to be older and probably derives both from cricket, which was played by early Americans, and from the old, and informal, English game of 'Rounders', the rules of which vary. That too is (often) played on a diamond and players can only score if they hit what is in effect a home run. They are 'out' if hit by a (soft) ball. A reform led by Alexander Cartwright and others at the Knickerbocker Club in New York City in 1835 led to tagging being used instead of hitting the player. This meant that a smaller, harder ball and a larger diamond could be used. The first team to score 21 runs won. Daniel Lucius 'Doc' Adams of the club is thought to have later helped bring in rules closer to the modern game. At the time of the Civil War the troops for recreation played both cricket and baseball but the latter gained in popularity, perhaps because no wicket was needed, just sacks thrown down to mark the bases. The first primitive professional league was formed in 1871. The sport was well established by the end of the century and cricket was almost forgotten. The first patent for the manufacture of the actual baseball, and the first for the sport, seems to be US 72355 in 1867 by Henry Alden of Matteawan, New York. Significantly the patent was assigned to the New York Rubber Company, which suggests the business motive.

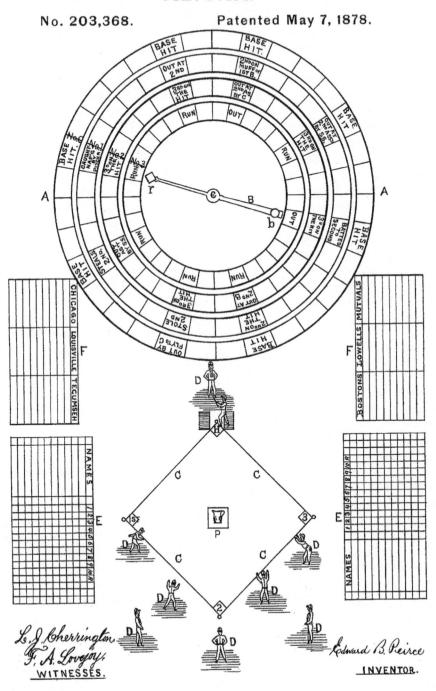

E. B. PEIRCE.
Game-Board.

No. 203,368.   Patented May 7, 1878.

The perpetual motion machine

It is difficult to make a choice among the rich vein of perpetual motion inventions, but this patent by a 'manufacturer' provides clear drawings of the pursuit for the holy grail of invention. Alexander Hirschberg called it in the patent a 'self generating power motor'. He did not obtain a German patent. There are numerous British patents on this topic as until 1905 patent applications were not examined for novelty or indeed utility. Even now inventions do not have to work, only to be new. The American Patent Office seems to have been more successful in avoiding granting perpetual motion inventions, if only by requiring from 1911 that a working model had to be submitted within one year. The British system granted over 500 patents during the Victorian period for what the patent indexes defined as 'self-driving motors'. Uniquely among all subjects, modern indexes to the patent classification used across the world now conceal the subject in the obscurity of Latin as 'Perpetua mobilia'.

Put simply, Figure 2 shows the tube tilting so that water washes down and depresses (H); (C) is then compressed, generating power. The balance (N) swings back so that the machine tilts back, then the same occurs with the other (H). The weight (N) and the float (E) are meant to assist this action. This cycle is supposed to recur endlessly. Tongue & Birkbeck, a patent agency based at 34 Southampton Buildings, a stone's throw from the then patent office, are given as having taken Mr Hirschberg for his money.

The reason why perpetual motion machines do not work is the principle of conservation of energy. A certain amount of work results in the same amount of energy, but only some of that results in a useful action such as lifting a weight. The rest is 'lost', or rather changed into something else, normally heat, as a result of friction. Perpetual motion does not even allow for this lost energy but means that more energy is created than was put in initially. There are numerous ways of 'demonstrating' perpetual motion, using hydraulics in the patent illustrated. A popular mechanical method was using numerous chains which chased each other in a circular motion. Other attempts used dynamos or magnetism. Brakes were often provided in case the machine ran too fast.

Henry Dircks, a London-based civil engineer, published in 1861 and 1870 in his *Perpetuum mobile* two volumes describing in great detail the futile attempts (including patents) to overcome the laws of physics. He normally gives the evidence from patents, magazines and newspapers without comment but for GB 942/1855 by George Huddart of Carnarvonshire, Wales he burst out with 'why attempt patenting such rubbish?' Dircks was also the co-inventor (with Professor John Pepper) of a once celebrated optical illusion which gives the impression of a ghost on a stage, 'Pepper's ghost', with GB 326/1853. Some of the inventors in the field were fraudsters, but many genuinely thought that they had solved a great problem, and were baffled by the lack of support from financial institutions. This account can be closed with a typical extract from Dircks. *The Times* in its 7 April 1862 issue quoted from the Halifax (Nova Scotia) *Sun* the death of a 'Mr Hart, of Wallace River, who was over 90 years of age, and had worked all his life at the problem of perpetual motion; but 90 years had not been long enough to solve it, and on the day before his death he had just "a few more wheels" to make to complete his work'.

Alexander Hirschberg, Luckenwalde, Germany

Filed 3 May 1889 and published as GB 7421/1889

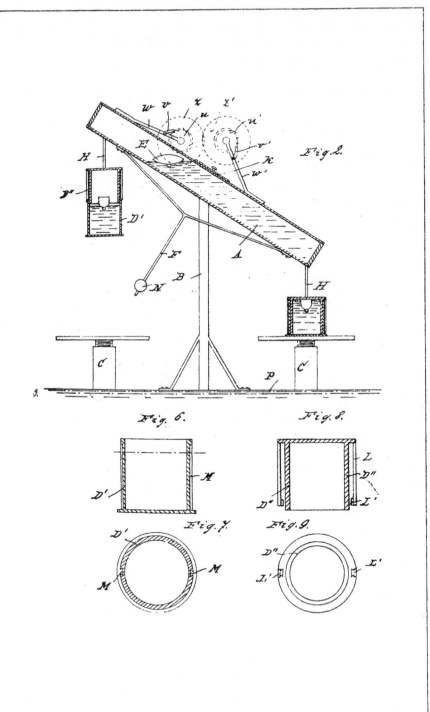

Fig. 2.

Fig. 6.

Fig. 8.

Fig. 7.

Fig. 9.

Malby & Sons, Photo-Litho.

The phonograph

Little work had been done on the concept of recording sound before Thomas Edison put his mind to it. There were some patents for the actual recording but, it seems, none for reproducing the sounds. One day Edison was working on a device to make a record of Morse Code messages sent by telegraph. The idea was that a rotating cylinder with paper wrapped round it would have indentations on it to mark the dots and dashes. The idea was not to provide a means of later reading off the messages but rather to 'play back' the dots and dashes at a speed faster than telegraph clerks could manage for rapid transmission, so that the line could be freed for another message. He noticed that when the cylinder was rapidly rotated a sound rather like speech came out.

At the same time he was working on a telephone diaphragm (or mouthpiece) with a sharp stylus on the rear side. As he spoke into the front of it the stylus was accidentally jabbed into his finger. He pondered the cylinder and the fact that the diaphragm was vibrating with the force of his voice. He brought them together, placed a piece of paraffin paper on the cylinder and tried shouting 'Hullo!' into the mouthpiece. He cranked again and very faintly, the word was heard. He drew a sketch and on 12 August 1877 handed it to John Kruesi, a Swiss watchmaker who was one of his assistants. The instructions on the paper were: 'Kruesi: Make this—Edison'. Kruesi had a budget of $18 for materials.

Kruesi made a brass cylinder covered with tinfoil that was mounted on a screw. On each side was a fixed diaphragm with a needle that could be manoeuvred close to the cylinder. The voice would, hopefully, make a grooved indentation in the tinfoil. Playing back a recording was done by another diaphragm with a rounded needle which could follow the groove. A handcrank needed to be turned for both recording and playback. The completed machine was handed over on 6 December. The staff gathered round as Edison turned the cylinder and screamed into the diaphragm (partly because there was no amplifier, and partly because he was somewhat deaf) the nursery rhyme 'Mary had a little lamb'. The needles were readjusted for the playback. To everyone's astonishment, including that of Edison, a recognisable sound was heard. His staff practised speaking into it for hours.

The patent was swiftly applied for and granted and the invention soon became popular, with an audience before the President, Rutherford Hayes. Sales soon dropped, though, because of the need to rotate the crank. There were also problems with sibilants: when practising with 'Mary had a little lamb' it was found that 'white as snow' kept on coming out as 'white as thnow'. Edison dropped the invention but others were working on improvements. German-born Emile Berliner of Washington, DC with US 372786 in 1887 came up with the flat disk concept, the gramophone. Edison then worked on a wax cylinder with a clock-spring mechanism. Berliner's concept eventually prevailed. It is interesting to note that Edison made a list of 10 possible uses of the gramophone. At the top was dictation by office managers. Music was not mentioned.

Thomas Edison, Menlo Park, New Jersey
Filed 24 December 1877 and published as US 200251 and GB 2909/1877

T A. EDISON.
Phonograph or Speaking Machine.

No. 200,521.   Patented Feb. 19, 1878.

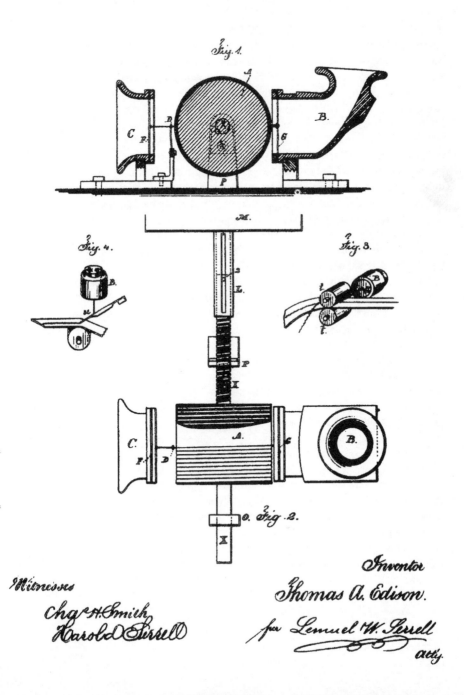

Inventor

Thomas A. Edison.

per Lemuel W. Serrell
atty.

Witnesses

Chas H. Smith
Harold Serrell

Photography

Joseph Nicéphore Niépce, a Frenchman, had been working on fixing the images seen through a camera obscura (a tiny hole through a card). In 1827 he obtained a photograph using a pewter plate with an 8-hour exposure. In 1829 Louis Jaques Maude Daguerre, a stage designer, entered into a 10-year partnership with him. Although Niépce died in 1833, Daguerre carried on the work with his son. One day in 1835 Daguerre put an exposed plate in his chemical cupboard and when he looked in several days later saw that an image had developed. He realised that vapour from one of the chemicals had done it and after testing each in turn saw that a broken mercury thermometer was probably responsible. He only learnt to fix an image permanently in 1837. He talked to French government officials, who were enthusiastic, and bought (but did not enforce) the rights to all countries except England. Details were announced on 19 August 1839. The illustrated page only mentions Berry but the next page explains that he had been instructed on 15 July by the (named) inventors to apply for the patent.

The technique was complicated and needed much skill. A copper plate was coated with a thin film of silver and cleaned and polished. It was sensitised in a box containing iodine so that the colour turned to a yellow rose tone. The plate was then placed in a light-proof holder and transferred to a camera. Light fell through the lens onto the plate which was then developed over hot mercury until an image appeared. To fix the image the plate was immersed in a solution of sodium thiosulphate, and from 1840 the tone was improved by adding gold chloride. The invention was a great success, and within a few years there were studios in every town. Daguerre sold the English rights to Richard Beard, an entrepreneur, who is shown from a court case to have licensed the rights for the city of Nottingham in 1841 to Alfred Barber for the then colossal sum of £1,200. Barber was charging 1 guinea (£1.05) a picture which became the normal price. The judge's summing up made an acid comment about the gold mountain that Barber expected to be reflected in the faces of the citizens of the city by the pictures he made.

The concept of 'Daguerrotypes' was in fact a scientific dead-end. Although they gave excellent detail, it was not possible to make more than one print from them. The exposures initially took from 3 to 15 minutes (hence the fixed stares in glass photographs, with unseen metal braces to keep the subjects rigid) although this was later improved to 1 minute. Their use was mostly limited to still-lives and studio work. Working independently, William Fox Talbot of Lacock Abbey, Wiltshire with his GB 8842/1841 and other patents used light-sensitive paper and patented the ideas of developing, fixing and printing an image. Some have suggested that between them Daguerre and Talbot hindered the spread of photography in England for a decade. In 1852 Talbot was persuaded not to enforce his patents on amateurs and artists, but he took those who charged fees to court, such as a hapless 'photographic artist' named Henderson who was practising on London's Regent Street in 1854. Frederick Scott Archer of London worked out the wet collodion process in 1851 which doomed daguerrotypes to extinction by allowing more than one print. He did not patent his idea (which was itself superseded by 1880) and died in poverty in 1857. The British government granted an annual pension to his wife and family.

A.D. 1839 . . . . Nº 8194.

Obtaining Daguerreotype Portraits, &c.

BERRY'S SPECIFICATION.

TO ALL TO WHOM THESE PRESENTS SHALL COME, I, Miles Berry, of the Office for Patents, 66, Chancery Lane, in the County of Middlesex, Patent Agent, send greeting.

WHEREAS Her present most Excellent Majesty Queen Victoria, by Her
5 Royal Letters Patent, under the Great Seal of Great Britain, bearing date at Westminster, the Fourteenth day of August, in the third year of Her reign, and in the year of our Lord One thousand eight hundred and thirty-nine, did, for Herself, Her heirs and successors, give and grant unto me, the Miles Berry, Her especial license, full power, sole privilege and autho-
10 rity, that I, the said Miles Berry, my executors, administrators, and assigns, and such others as I, the said Miles Berry, my executors, administrators, or assigns, should at any time agree with, and no others, from time to time and at all times during the term of years therein mentioned, should and lawfully might make, use, exercise, and vend, within England, Wales, and the Town
15 of Berwick-upon-Tweed, and in all Her Majesty's Colonies and Plantations abroad, an Invention of "A New or Improved Method of Obtaining the Spontaneous Reproduction of all the Images received in the Focus of the Camera Obscura," being a communication from a foreigner residing abroad; in which said Letters Patent is contained a proviso, obliging me, the said
20 Miles Berry, by an instrument in writing under my hand and seal, particularly to describe and ascertain the nature of the said Invention, and in what manner the same is to be performed, and to cause the same to be inrolled in Her

A

The pneumatic railway

An underground railway was first built in London in 1863. The 6 km long track, known as the Metropolitan Railway, was built by using the 'cut and cover' technique. The line was popular, despite the soot from the steam driven locomotive and the gas lighting. There were no windows in the carriages, since of course there was nothing to look at. London also had, in 1869–70, the first 'tube', which involved a shaft being dug and then workmen behind a tunnelling shield digging a horizontal tunnel. The underground railways are represented here by the work of Alfred Ely Beach, a little-known hero of American enterprise. He was born in 1826 in Springfield, Massachusetts. His father acquired a newspaper, the New York *Sun*, and Alfred soon became involved in journalism. In 1846 he joined with others to form Munn & Company, which took over a new periodical, *Scientific American*. He greatly increased its sales by promoting inventions. The company itself ran a patent agency to help inventors obtain patents.

Beach's patents included a typewriter that made embossed letters for the blind. He specialised in work on pneumatic tubes. These are sometimes still seen in shops, and work by either removing the air before, or compressing the air after, introducing a small parcel. One of Beach's patents is the delightful US 59739 of 1866 where a drawing shows a man posting a letter in a pillar box; the letter then descended a chute, was dropped into a vehicle when it passed, and in turn as the vehicle passed a chute the mail was dropped into a sorting office, where a man busily sorted the mail. For some time the principle of pneumatic tubes was used in sending mail around New York and other cities. However, Beach had bigger ambitions. At an 1867 fair he demonstrated a tube in which a 10-passenger carriage was moved back and forth by a powerful fan. He decided to build an experimental underground line in New York City. 'Boss' William Tweed was hostile but Beach obtained a charter in 1868 for a 1.2 m wide tube to demonstrate mail delivery, a condition being that there could not be any digging in the streets. A shaft was dug down to a 2.4 m wide tunnel 100 m deep—opposite Boss Tweed's headquarters.

The drawings opposite show the idea. The 'car' fitted snugly into the tube and was propelled by air behind it. At the 'landing place' or stop the width of the tube was increased, as shown at (C), so that there was less pressure and hence the car could more easily slow down or (slowly) speed up when leaving the stop. The car used normal brakes, and starting was simply by releasing the brakes. At each stop there was a sliding door (B[1]) so that the tube could normally be kept sealed, as well as a door within the car. Figure 2 shows the car at the stop, with the unexplained front door presumably being for the driver at the end of the line. The car ran along tracks (g) upon the support (E). The recess (F) was for an enclosed light. After a year of secret work the one-block long tunnel was suddenly unveiled. Crowds flocked to the bright and clean railway and 400,000 paid 25¢ for a ride back and forth. A 75 kwatt blower either pulled or pushed the car along the tunnel. An extension was blocked first by Tweed and then, fatally, by the financial panic of 1873. Beach died in 1896 in New York City. New York finally got its first subway, or underground, in 1904. In 1912 workmen building more of the system came across the abandoned tunnel, which is now City Hall station on the BMT line.

Alfred Ely Beach, Stratford, Connecticut
Published 5 November 1867 as US 70504

A.E.Beach,

Pneumatic Railway,

No. 70,504,

Patented Nov. 5, 1867.

Fig. 1.

Fig. 3.   Fig. 2.   Fig. 4.

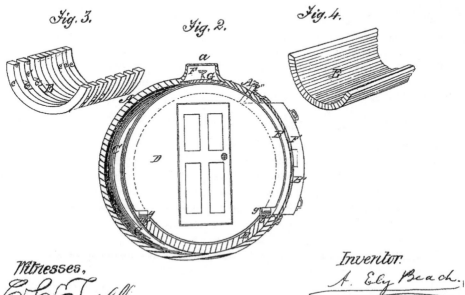

Witnesses,
C.L. Topliff
Wm. Trewin

Inventor.
A. Ely Beach.

The pneumatic tyre

The usefulness of bicycles was distinctly limited as long as the wheels were made entirely of metal or wood. They were not called 'boneshakers' for nothing, particularly if cyclists were taking a rough ride on unmetalled roads. John Boyd Dunlop was born on a farm in Ayrshire, Scotland in 1840. He qualified as a veterinary surgeon and 10 years later moved to Belfast. One day he watched his 10-year old son, Johnnie, riding a tricycle round the garden, leaving deep tracks. He took some garden hose and filled it with water, proposing to wrap it round the wheels. The family doctor, Sir John Fagan, happened to be present and, being familiar with the problems of patients who needed cushions or mattresses, suggested using air rather than water. This time Dunlop used sheet rubber which was wrapped round the wheel and inflated with a football pump.

The invention was fitted to the rear tyres of Johnnie's tricycle and the boy tried it out that evening. Dunlop later purchased a bicycle from Edlin & Company and fitted it with his new tyres, covered with sailcloth. He had never actually been on a bicycle at this time. Edlin made an agreement with Dunlop to manufacture bicycles using his new tyre, and on 19 December 1888 there appeared in the *Irish Cyclist* the first advertisement: 'Look out for the new Pneumatic Safety. Vibration impossible. Sole makers— W. Edlin and Co., Garfield St, Belfast'. The front forks had to be widened to allow the wider wheel to fit, and the entire bicycle had to be purchased rather than tyres alone as the tyres were stuck onto the rim of the wheels. Early sales were slow but they soon picked up.

In fact Robert William Thomson of London (but originally from Stonehaven, Kincardineshire, Scotland), a civil engineer, had already patented the idea with his GB 10990/1845. It described the idea of bolting an outer casing of india rubber round a wheel. It had some success at the time but was very expensive as 70 bolts had to be fitted by hand. This patent was long out of protection, and so Dunlop could not be sued for infringing it. Before 1905 there was no procedure at the Patent Office of looking through the old, 'prior art' literature which was why the Patent Office had not refused his patent. Dunlop got to hear about Thomson's work during 1890 and kept quiet, hoping no one would notice. Sadly for him, *Sport and Play* magazine published details of Thomson's work in September. Dunlop asked if he could amend his patent and the illustration is of this amended version in July 1892. It is dated 31 October 1888 as that was the date of the 'complete' specification which followed the original July application. The italics show the added wording.

Inspired by the usefulness of the pneumatic tyre, a craze was set off for cycling. The British Patent Office annual report noted that in 1897 there were 6,000 applications for patents in cycling, out of a total of nearly 31,000. Women inventors made 106 of those cycling applications. Cycling gave many women freedom of movement, and many of their inventions were for preventing skirts and dresses from being caught in the mechanism. Dunlop founded the Pneumatic Tyre Company and Booth's Cycle Agency in 1889, which were to become the Dunlop Rubber Company Ltd. Production at its Fort Dunlop, Birmingham site carried on for many years and the company was famous as a tyre producer. Dunlop retired to Dublin where he died in 1921.

Dunlop's Improvement in Tyres of Wheels for Bicycles, Tricycles, or other Road Cars.

COMPLETE SPECIFICATION (AMENDED).

An Improvement in Tyres of Wheels for Bicycles, Tricycles, or other Road Cars.

I JOHN BOYD DUNLOP of 50 Gloucester Street, Belfast, Veterinary Surgeon do hereby declare the nature of this invention and in what manner the same is to be performed, to be particularly described and ascertained in and by the following statement :—

My improvements are devised with a view to afford increased facilities for the 5 passage of wheeled vehicles—chiefly of the lighter class such for instance as velocipedes, invalid chairs, ambulances—over roadways and paths, especially when these latter are of rough or uneven character, as also to avoid the sinking of the wheels of vehicles into the ground when travelling over boggy soil or land ; and likewise for the tyreing of wheeled vehicles generally, in all cases where elasticity is requisite and immunity 10 from vibration is desired to be secured, and at the same time ensuring increased speed in travelling owing to the resilient properties of wheel tyres according to my Invention.

In carrying out my Invention, I employ a hollow tube tyre of india rubber, sur-rounded with cloth canvas or other suitable material adapted to withstand the pressure of the air introduced and contained within the tube tyre as hereunder mentioned. 15 The canvas or cloth being covered with rubber or other suitable material to protect it from wear on the road. Said hollow tube tyre is secured to the wheel felloes—say by a suitable cement or by other efficient means—and is inflated with air or gas under pressure. I may use, for the purpose of inflation, any ordinary forcing pump or like device ; the air or gas (as the case may be) under pressure being introduced to the 20 interior of the hollow tube tyre through a small duct formed in the rim of the wheel and provided with a non return valve.

Having now particularly described and ascertained the nature of my said Invention and in what manner the same is to be performed, *I would have it known that I make no claim to the construction or use of any tyres which are not in accordance with the* 25 *description set forth in the last preceding paragraph of this my Specification commencing with the words " In carrying out my invention " and ending with the words " with air or gas under pressure "* but *subject to this disclaiming note.* I declare, that what I claim is :

For wheel tyres, the employment of a hollow tube or of hollow tubes of india rubber 30 inflated with air or gas under pressure substantially as herein set forth.

Dated this 31st day of October 1888.

                                     JAMES STEVENSON,
                                     Gray's Inn Chambers,
                    20, High Holborn, London, W.C.   35

London : Printed for Her Majesty's Stationery Office, by Darling & Son, Ltd.—1892

The pocket protector

There was a great deal of crime in Victorian London, and it has been said that the reason why so many thieves looked famished was that it was an overcrowded profession. The poorer sort looked for their prey at railway stations and street markets while the 'swell mob' were well-dressed and would endeavour to rob those middle-class folk whom they intentionally jostled in the smarter districts, or would steal while crammed together on the seats of horse-drawn omnibuses. A successful street thief needed to be young and sober as acute responses were needed to avoid quick detection and arrest.

'Tailing' was the business of stealing handkerchiefs from back pockets. Pickpockets were dubbed 'buzzers' or 'dippers' while those who helped by obstructing pursuit were the 'stalls'. Those who specialised in stealing purses were 'finewirers' or 'maltoolers', a reference to their fondness for using (unpatented) devices to steal purses. The devices included slender blades to rip pockets, or tools which had a three-way gripping hold that could be inserted into pockets, and which cost 10 shillings (50p) a time from disreputable shopkeepers. In defence many inventors such as Leon de Landfort patented methods of preventing theft, and the drawings shown by a 'gentleman' are of 'An apparatus for protecting the contents of the pockets of wearing apparel from theft and loss'. The device was a frame of sheet metal which would be inserted in the actual pocket. Figure 1 shows a spring to hold the pocket shut (with a watch inside) which was held by a trigger attached to a cord. Figure 2 is a side view while Figure 3 shows the pocket closed (the bend in the middle allows for a watch chain) and Figure 4 shows it open.

Another patent, GB 1464/1855 by James Clements, a tailor of Birmingham, Warwickshire is somewhat similar. It had two elliptical pieces of steel secured by a spring catch round the top of the pocket. In this case the pocket was strengthened by wires to hinder those slashing the pocket. There were many patents for protecting watches alone as wrist watches did not exist and watches were carried in pockets and examined as required for the time. Devices to prevent their theft were called, not surprisingly, watch protectors. A normal method was to use a chain or the beloved's hair to fasten the watch. GB 415/1875 by Joseph Maclaren of Edinburgh, Scotland showed a guard passed through a ring secured to a button in the watch pocket. The button had a pointed screwed pin which was passed through the vest and screwed to a button inside the vest. Fashion in clothes could make theft easy or difficult. A gradual move from coat-tails in men's clothes to buttoned-up jackets made it more difficult to avoid detection while reduced use of snuff made both snuff boxes themselves (prized by thieves) and handkerchiefs (for subsequent sneezing) less common. Most spectacular of all was the passing of the crinoline in the 1870s. This meant that great, billowing dresses were replaced by clothes much closer to the lady's body, and hence pockets were less easy to reach into by both the wearer and thieves. Women thieves also looked more conspicuous if they continued to wear crinolines, with their deep pockets sewn in to hide any booty.

Leon de Landfort, Higher Broughton, Lancashire, England
Filed 31 October 1857 and published as GB 2770/1857

A.D. 1857. Oct. 31. N° 2770.
DE LANDFORT'S Specification.

FIG. 1.

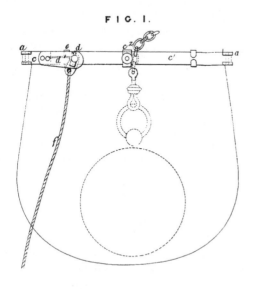

FIG. 2.

FIG. 3.

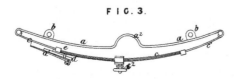

FIG. 5.

FIG. 4.

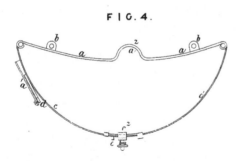

The Pullman sleeping car

George Pullman was born in Brocton, New York State in 1831. Originally a cabinet-maker, he moved to Illinois in 1855 and began to work as a contractor for the railways, accumulating some capital so that he could work on his idea of providing sleeping accommodation on railway carriages. Figure 1 shows the car with day-time arrangements on the left and night-time on the right. The upper berth (A) is hinged at (B) and pivots on (C). In the day it is raised to the roof and pinned there by using weights (D) running on rods (L) as a counterbalance so that it can be moved with a hand. The seats (G) provide the lower berth by being supported on bar (H). The sliding head board (I) rises up from the seats to block off the space between berths. This was the original 'Pioneer' carriage. A Pullman carriage was used to convey President Lincoln's corpse to Illinois in 1865 and this gave the concept much publicity. The Pullman Palace Car Company (the use of 'palace' is significant) was formed in 1867 to manufacture the carriages and to operate them under contract for the railway companies. During 1880–84 a planned community was built for the workers, Pullman, which still stands today just south of Chicago. It was complete with its own shops and schools. All premises had to earn a 6% return—including the church, which was hired out to any interested denominations.

Pullman and Field were also responsible for two 1869 patents, US 89537 for a dining-car and US 89538 for a hotel-car. The dining-car featured a kitchen in the middle and dining areas at each end, the idea being that the cooking odours would be wafted away from half the diners, and that passengers would not have to pass the kitchen as they arrived from either end. The hotel-car contained connecting small rooms that could be used by families, or opened up into the corridor if strangers were using the rooms. US 89539 was published at the same time by Aaron Longstreet on behalf of Pullman and involved a lighting system for carriages. After the financial panic of 1893 the company temporarily got into difficulties, and Pullman cut the already low wages of the hourly-paid staff by 25%. No cuts were made in the rents (which were deducted from wages) or in food prices in his planned community. A delegation went to speak to senior management and the next day three of the delegates were sacked. A strike by the factory workers broke out, which was supported by the Socialist leader Eugene Debs's American Railway Union. No trains that included Pullman cars were worked by union men. The railway companies supported Pullman, and insisted that Pullman cars were attached to mail trains, so when these were also not operated the dispute became a Federal matter. Over the protests of the State Governor 12,000 army troops were sent in and the strike was suppressed.

Pullman died in 1897 in Chicago. It was feared by his heirs that his body might be stolen and held for ransom, so his coffin was covered by asphalt, and sealed in a huge block of cement, the size of a large room, reinforced by railway ties, and buried in Graceland Cemetery. The satirist Ambrose Bierce commented, 'It is clear the family in their bereavement was making sure the sonofabitch wasn't going to get up and come back'.

George Pullman, Chicago, Illinois and Ben Field, Albion, New York
Issued 19 September 1865 as US 49992

FIELD & PULLMAN.

Sleeping Car.

No. 49,992.   Patented Sept. 19, 1865.

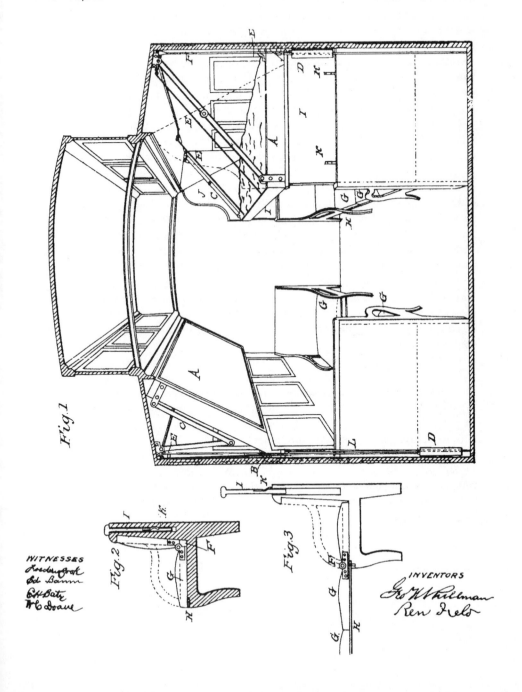

WITNESSES

INVENTORS

Punched card tabulation

Herman Hollerith was born in 1860 in Buffalo, New York State, the son of German immigrants. Trained as a mechanical engineer, he joined the census office in 1879. The census was required by the Constitution and had been compiled every decade since 1790. An increasing population and more and more questions to help decide government policies meant hundreds of clerks counting from the forms, with numerous errors creeping in. Any attempt to combine data such as the number of literate native-born women in Kentucky meant much work going through the forms. Some data from the 1880 census did not emerge until 1888, when it had lost much of its usefulness. An attempt to solve the problem had been made by Charles Seaton, head of the bureau, with his US 127435 in 1872, where a box with rollers at the top and the bottom meant that paper could be fed in so that the same lines of information appeared at the top as the paper was threaded through for easy tabulation.

This invention originates with physician John Shaw Billings, who was working with Hollerith on health statistics, saying as they watched hundreds of clerks toiling away at collecting information, 'There ought to be a mechanical way of doing this job, something on the principle of the Jacquard loom, whereby holes in a card regulate the pattern to be woven'. This was a reference to FR 658 from 1805 by Joseph-Marie Jacquard of Lyons. Another story is that Hollerith observed ticket collectors on the railways punching tickets. The illustration shows the general concept. A single form held numerous fields and was punched to indicate which fields were valid for that person, such as being female, between 30 and 40 and so on. The table holds a tray with such a form (A) on it. The flat platen (B) holds the form and (P) swings down the nails (C) which were designed only to go through the punched holes. An electrical circuit was established and the clock faces on the walls were advanced for whichever fields were relevant. In this way facts about people in a particular district or group of people could be established. The presence or absence of electric charges are what makes computers work.

The patents did not come out until 1889 and improvements continued to be made. By trying out the system in a trial in Baltimore, Hollerith realised that punching 12,000 holes was exhausting and he temporarily lost most of the feeling in his hand. He modified the puncher so that little force was needed. His machine was used in the 1890 census and from an initial 500 cards being handled daily by an average operator 8,000 became normal. The idea was subsequently widely adopted in Europe. Hollerith also patented a number of (unsuccessful) railway brakes in the 1880s while living in St Louis, Missouri and for a while taught engineering at MIT. He founded the Tabulating Machine Company in 1896 which from mergers evolved into International Business Machines, or IBM, in 1924. Herman Hollerith died in 1924 in Washington, DC.

Herman Hollerith, New York City, New York

Filed 23 September 1884 and published as US 395781-783 and GB 327/1889

(No Model.)

H. HOLLERITH.

ART OF COMPILING STATISTICS.

No. 395,781.

Patented Jan. 8, 1889.

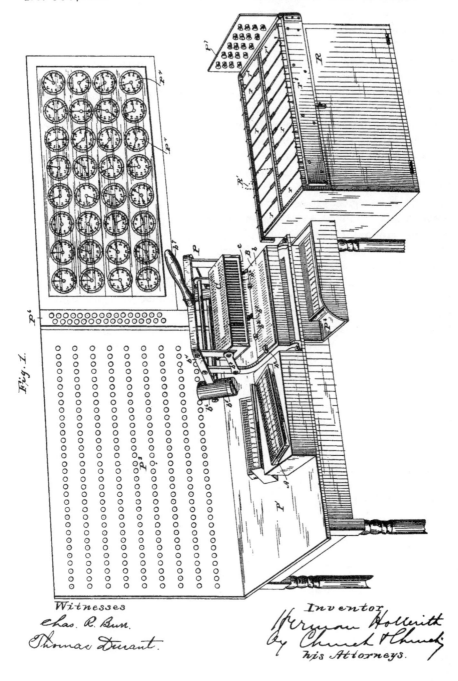

Fig. I.

Witnesses

Chas. R. Burr.

Thomas Durant.

Inventor

Herman Hollerith

by Church & Church

his Attorneys.

The push-up player piano

Edwin Scott Votey is thought to have been born in 1853 and to have moved to Detroit in his late twenties. He both built and sold reed organs. Votey patented numerous musical inventions including the first usable 'self-play piano attachment of practical and economical construction which can be quickly applied to or removed from any piano'. Sing-songs around the piano were popular in Victorian times, but there was a problem if a skilled player were not available. Previous attempts to reproduce music involved mechanical barrels where turning a handle played a tune. The trouble was that only one tune could ever be played. Votey's push-up enabled anyone to 'play' different tunes on a piano. All that was needed was a roll of perforated paper for each tune.

The mechanism was powered by suction, which was generated by pressing two foot pedals. The 'tracker bar', a pneumatic reading device over which the roll travelled, had a row of equally spaced holes, one for each note. A perforation passing over a hole caused a valve to open, which triggered a pneumatic 'motor'; this operated a felt-covered wooden finger to press the appropriate key. The drawing shows keystrikers (10) and (11) and the actual keyboard (9). The prototype is now in the Smithsonian. The paper rolls were cheap, compact and easy to produce. The trade mark Pianola® was registered in 1905 and is still active.

The idea was a great success and the Aeolian Corporation acquired the rights and produced large numbers. A vast quantity of music was produced on rolls. There were problems, however. There was a limited musical range on the push-up piano. Votey's model could only play 58 notes (later 65) while pianos had 85 or 88. Music sounded odd—a disgruntled listener pointed out that Mendelsohn's 'Spring song' shot out like bullets—and some classical compositions were specially rewritten so that they would suit the limitations. The push-up itself was heavy and cumbersome; it was awkward to adjust it exactly to fit the piano; and the wooden fingers were vulnerable to damage. In many places no pianist was ever available to play the piano itself. After 1900 Melville Clark of Chicago, a prolific patentee, devised the 'Apollo' which was the next logical step, an all in one player piano which did not require an actual piano, at first for 65 and then for 88 notes. By 1910 production of the push-up had stopped. Sales were helped by the fact that the player pianos were designed to look just like ordinary pianos.

The various manufacturers caused problems when using the music rolls. Apart from the different numbers of notes a player piano would play, rolls could be of different sizes and would often fit only one model. In 1908 one of the first ever conventions to discuss standardisation was held. It was decided to adopt 65 or 88 note player pianos and a uniform size for the rolls. The concept stayed popular into the 1920s, but radio and records had killed it off by World War II, by which time about 2.5 million player pianos had been sold in the USA alone.

No. 650,285.

Patented May 22, 1900.

E. S. VOTEY.
PNEUMATIC PIANO ATTACHMENT.
(Application filed Jan. 25, 1897. Renewed Feb. 5, 1900.)

(No Model.)

2 Sheets—Sheet 1.

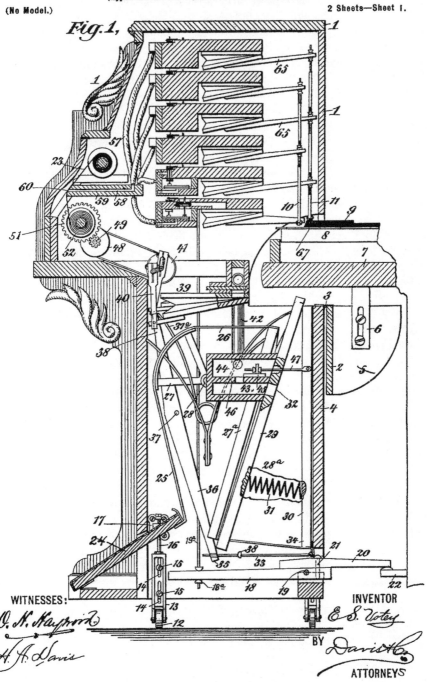

Fig. 1,

The radio

Guglielmo Marconi was born in Bologna, Italy in 1874, son of an Italian estate owner and an Irish mother. He received a science education and then, not having to worry about making a living, carried out experiments on his father's estate after reading in 1894 about Heinrich Hertz's work on electromagnetic waves travelling at the speed of light. He dreamt of making telegraph signals travel without wires. At first he could only send Morse Code signals a distanced of 10 m, but this soon improved to over 1 km. His older brother Alonso helped by signalling when the messages were received, initially by using a white flag and then by a rifle shot when off in the hills. In 1896, his idea having been turned down by the Italian postal authority, he went to England with his mother, who had great faith in him. Suspicious custom officials, thinking they had an anarchist on their hands, ruined his equipment by roughly searching it on his arrival. He soon applied for GB 12039/1896 covering the principle of sending radio messages. He also met the chief engineer of the General Post Office, William Preece, who actively helped him, and James Kemp, an engineer who became a life-long associate. A company was formed in 1897 and by the end of 1900 they were able to send signals 50 km. Experts had predicted that radio messages would not be able to travel beyond the horizon, but they had not realised that radio waves will bounce off the ionosphere.

On 12 December 1901 signals were sent for the first time across the Atlantic, from Cornwall to St John's, Newfoundland, where Marconi and Kemp were based: three dots, the letter S. Oliver Lodge, a Liverpool physics professor, disputed Marconi's patent, claiming that his GB 11575/1897 covered the technology. Using a different device (soon superseded) he had been able to detect Morse messages at ranges of 50 m in 1894. However he did not try longer distances because he assumed that they would not work. A sympathetic court nevertheless extended the term of his patent in 1911 for 7 years on the grounds that he had not been able to make money from it as he had been refused a licence to operate under the Wireless Telegraphy Act of 1904.

The drawing is from a patent which had a different purpose than merely sending a message in Morse Code. It enabled several stations to operate on different wavelengths without electrical interference by using 'tuning' across the entire radio frequency spectrum. This meant that many stations rather than just one could operate at the same time—the basis of how radio stations work. The aerial is represented by (A) with the transmitter in Figure 1 and the 'receiver' (or radio set) in Figure 2. The first experimental radio station sent out a few broadcasts in 1906 from Massachusetts but regular broadcasting did not begin until 1920 in Detroit, Michigan. Marconi went on to receive the Nobel Prize for Physics in 1909 jointly with Carl Braun of Germany, another pioneer, for 'their contributions to the development of wireless telegraphy'. Marconi died in Rome in 1937 and radio stations around the world ceased broadcasting for 2 minutes in tribute. In 1943 the American Supreme Court ruled that there were forerunners to Marconi's patent such as Nikola Tesla with work from 1893 and from his US 645576, and from Lodge's American patent. Nevertheless it is clear that it was Marconi who publicised and marketed the use of 'tuning'.

Guglielmo Marconi and Marconi's Wireless Telegraph Company, London, England
Filed 26 April 1900 and published as GB 7777/1900 and US 763772

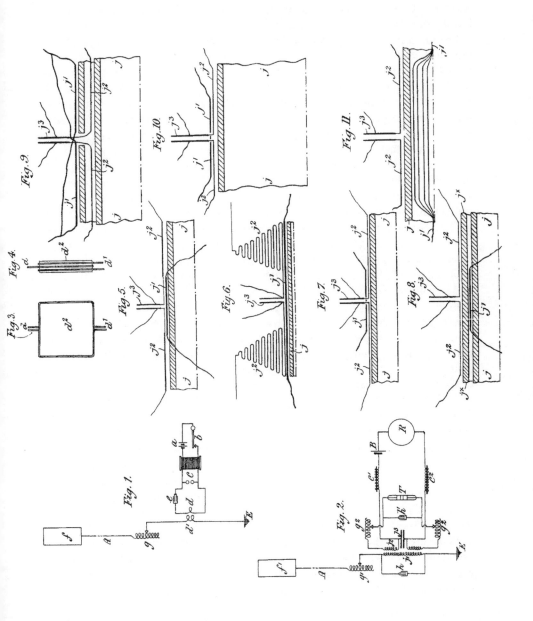

The 'Resurgam' submarine

In June 1877, in the Russo-Turkish War, a Russian spar torpedo vessel made two abortive attempts at Sulina in the Black Sea to destroy the Turkish warship *Idjilacic*, but was thwarted by the presence of defensive chain netting around the hull.

The Reverend George William Garrett, a Manchester clergyman, thought of a solution. He had been born in Lambeth, Surrey in 1852, son of an Irish clergyman. He suggested not trying to penetrate the torpedo nets but rather diving beneath the nets to plant a mine under the hull. The illustrated submarine was an experimental model. The patent's title was 'Improvements in and appertaining to submarine or subaqueous boats or vessels for removing, destroying, laying, or placing torpedoes in channels and other situations, and for other purposes'. Torpedo was the word at the time for what we now call a mine. The submarine was 5 m long and had hand-cranked propellers (although he does mention a hydrocarbon gas engine). Trimming was achieved by pulling or pushing on a piston of a cylinder (S) open to the sea—much the same idea as blowing tanks on modern submarines. The hand shown at the top was meant to be thrust through a greased leather gauntlet to place a mine on a hull. (P^1) was the hatch while (G) was the seat. The crew of one was meant to swing an electric lamp before portholes (Q) and to use a toolkit to cut wires and so on, both of which were kept outside. Telegraphic or telephonic contact with an ironclad was suggested to 'report progress or issue orders'. The hull was preferably to be made of wood, or else thin steel. It was built and actually worked in trials.

In 1879 Garrett produced the *Resurgam*. This was about 15 m long and 3 m in diameter and was professionally built at Birkenhead, Cheshire. It had a steam plant which shut down when underwater and used latent heat to generate steam to drive the connecting rod cylinder engine for up to 4 hours. There was an air purification plant of his own design to extract carbon monoxide with potash. The Admiralty requested that Garrett bring his boat to the Portsmouth naval base for evaluation. *Resurgam* was launched into the Wallasey Dock at Liverpool on 26 November 1879 and after a period of dock trials Garrett was satisfied. The ship's builder begged Garrett to transport the submarine to Portsmouth by rail, but Garrett insisted on sailing her there personally with two crew members. She set sail on 10 December but problems meant that the propeller had to be replaced, under great secrecy, at a foundry at the resort of Rhyl.

The second attempt was made from Rhyl on 10 February 1880 at 10 pm. This time they used a steam yacht, the *Elphin*, to tow the boat. The *Elphin* had problems feeding her boilers and the *Resurgam* crew were asked to join her to help out. There was no latch to secure the hatch from outside, and hence increasing amounts of water came in, until the tow rope broke under the strain. *Resurgam* eventually sank in 18 m of water. Her location was soon forgotten until in 1985 a trawler's nets became snagged on the craft. The wreck has been explored and there are plans to raise her, hence justifying her Latin name which means 'I shall rise again'. Garrett continued to design submarines for Sweden, Greece, Turkey and Russia, some of which were actually built in partnership with Thorsten Nordenfeldt of Sweden, until 1887. His only other patent was GB 6489/1888 for a 'vapour engine'. He emigrated to the USA in 1890, served as a corporal in the Spanish-American War and died penniless in New York City in 1902.

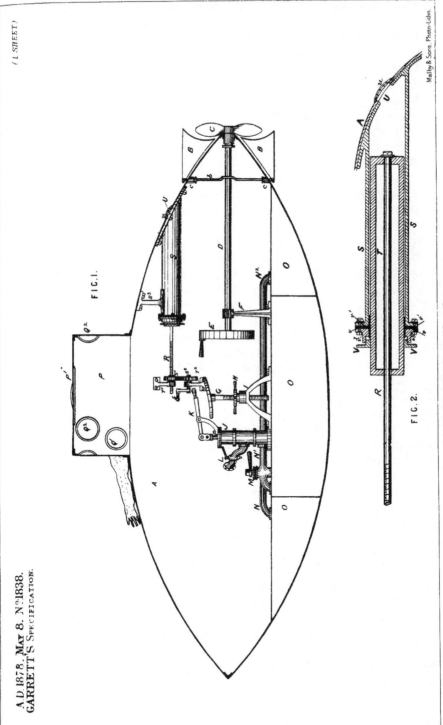

(1 SHEET)

A.D. 1878. May 8. Nº 1838.
GARRETT'S SPECIFICATION.

FIG. 1.

FIG. 2.

Malby & Sons, Photo-Litho.

LONDON. Printed by GEORGE EDWARD EYRE and WILLIAM SPOTTISWOODE,
Printers to the Queen's most Excellent Majesty. 1878.

The roll-film camera

George Eastman was born in 1854 in Waterville in upstate New York. His family moved to Rochester in 1860 where after his father's death the family went through hard times. Eastman worked as a bookkeeper at a local bank and became an enthusiastic photographer. He found taking his 'pack-horse load' of tripod, chemicals and a dark-tent when photographing a strain, and wondered if there were an easier way. He read all the literature he could find and began experimenting with photographic plates in his mother's kitchen, using her stove to cook plates, sometimes sleeping there in his enthusiasm.

Collodion wet-plates were employed at the time but these were very awkward to use. Eastman began to work on ideas published in English photographic journals about dry-plate processes. Using pre-coated plates meant that chemicals would not be needed when photographing. He obtained his first patent for such film, US 226503, in 1880. This improved film was ordered in large quantities by Anthony, the leading American photographic supplies company, and Eastman quit the bank and opened a factory in Rochester. He came to realise that the way to grow was to expand the market by cutting prices and simplifying photography.

He and camera designer William Walker patented a roll holder that could be attached to an existing camera with US 316952. Another improvement resulted in the invention shown. Eastman used extensive magazine and newspaper advertising under the slogan, 'You press the button, we do the rest'. Each camera had a paper roll containing 100 pictures. There was no viewfinder and hence no focusing. A string was lifted to open the shutter and a button was pressed to take a picture. The key at the top of the camera wound on the film. Figure 2 shows the shutter (S) and the lens (L). When the film was completed the entire camera was mailed to the company at Rochester or Harrow, England and a month later the reloaded camera came back with the pictures stripped from the film and mounted on glass plates. Eastman explained why he chose his famous trademark. It had to be short, vigorous and would mean nothing. He liked the letter K and eventually chose Kodak®. It also sounded like a camera shutter closing. The camera cost $25, a lot for the time, as developing the films still cost a great deal. The camera was bulky and did not show how many exposures had been taken, but it still caused a sensation.

To bring down costs Eastman hired Henry Reichenbach to develop a flexible and transparent nitrocellulose film which could easily be developed. This was published in 1889 as US 417202. However Hannibal Goodwin, a clergyman from Newark, New Jersey had filed for a celluloid film in 1887 and an 'interference' was called to decide who had invented it first. Goodwin received his US 610861 only in 1898 but the court case dragged on and was only settled in 1914, long after Goodwin's death in 1900, with Eastman having to pay out millions of dollars. In 1892 the company became Eastman Kodak and the famous yellow packaging was adopted. Other developments followed such as the Brownie, the first snapshot camera, which sold for just $1. Eastman became a multimillionaire and gave away $125 million during his lifetime, mainly to universities, medicine and music. He was also a generous employer, with a bonus scheme and a pension fund. In 1932, suffering from a degenerative spinal disorder, he shot himself. His suicide note read, 'To my Friends. My work is done, why wait? GE'.

George Eastman, Rochester, New York
Filed 30 March 1888 and published as US 388850 and GB 6950/1888

(No Model.) 3 Sheets—Sheet 1.

G. EASTMAN.

CAMERA.

No. 388,850. Patented Sept. 4, 1888.

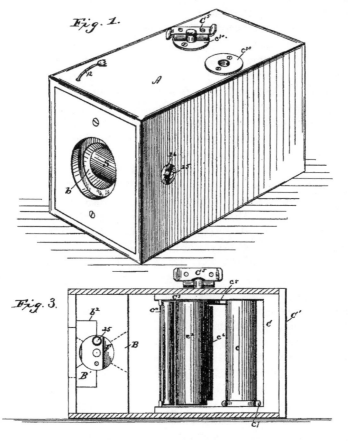

Fig. 1.
Fig. 3.
Fig. 2.

Witnesses.
Chas. R. Burr.
A. J. Stewart.

Inventor.
George Eastman.
by Church & Church
his Attorneys.

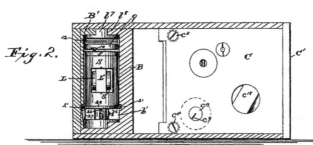

Roller skates

Ice skates go back a long time in history, but the summer variant of roller skates are thought to date to 1759. Joseph Merlin, a Belgian, put wooden spools on skates and made an entrance at a London masquerade while playing a violin. Unfortunately as there was no way of controlling his direction, or braking, he collided with a mirror worth £500, smashing it and the violin to pieces, and badly injuring himself. Despite this inauspicious beginning there were other experiments. In 1840 a Berlin beer hall tried out roller-skating barmaids. Skates even appeared in opera, when Jakob Meyerbeer's 1849 opera *The prophet* required ice skating in the third act, and roller skates were used as converting the stage to an ice rink was unfeasible. The main problems were working out the number and arrangement of the wheels, and, especially, controlling the direction. In 1823 Robert Tyers of Piccadilly, London filed GB 4782/1823. This patent copied ice skates by placing five small wheels in a single line, hence inventing in-line roller skating, but still with no way of controlling direction.

James Leonard Plimpton solved these problems with the illustrated patent. He had already had US 34590, for (ice) skate fastenings, issued to him. He called his invention 'parlor skates' as he envisaged their use indoors on a prepared rink or room, as there were no good surfaces outside that could be used. He introduced the now conventional four wheel arrangement (the wheels being of boxwood) with the direction changing with the user leaning that way. The pivoting that occurred would be dampened by a rubber cushion above the wheels. He described it thus: 'The rollers or runners are made to turn or cramp like the wheels of a wagon by the rocking or canting of the stock or footstand to facilitate the turning of a skate with a wide bearing upon the floor or ice'. The fastenings were as given in his earlier patent. His US 55901 in 1866 improved the mechanism for turning.

In 1866 Plimpton opened the first roller rink at the Atlantic House resort hotel in Newport, Rhode Island for 'educated and refined classes'. A craze took off, initially among adults, that carried on in the USA for decades. The next roller skate patent was however not until 1869 when A. J. Gibson of Cincinnati, Ohio with US 97075 suggested circular plates on which the wheels would rotate when changing direction. Micajah Henley of Richmond, Indiana made the next big advance with patents from 1884 onwards. He introduced brake pads and a key to adjust the tightness of the shoe in the skate. With his nephew Robert Henley he also introduced ball bearings to facilitate turning, which meant that more sophisticated tricks could be done. Soon he was producing 15,000 of his 'Chicago skate' a *week*. Speed skating came in with the 1890s, and later there were roller derbies on banked tracks before spectators as enthusiasm for the sport continued, with thousands of rinks opening.

England too played its part. The first rink was only built in 1875 with the Belgravia Skating Rink in London but 'roller polo' or roller hockey was first introduced at the Denmark rink, also in London, in 1878. The growth of interest is vividly shown by the number of British patents on skates (including some on ice skating). From a few each year in the 1860s, and 8 in 1874, there were 64 in 1875 and over 200 in 1876, only to sink back to 18 in 1877. British patents were not examined for novelty until 1905, so that some of these would have been deliberate or accidental copies of each other.

James Leonard Plimpton, New York City, New York
Published 6 January 1863 as US 37305 and GB 2190/1865

J. L. Plimpton.

Parlor Skate,

No. 37,305. Patented Jan. 6, 1863.

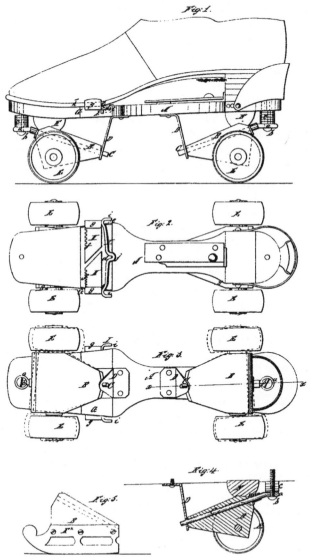

Fig: 1.
Fig: 2.
Fig: 3.
Fig: 4.
Fig: 5.

Witnesses:

W. S. Partridge
Saul Robertson

Inventor:

James Leo Plimpton

Safety-apparatus for sea-bathers

This delightful invention, patented by Lorenzo Dow Smith and John Bruster Smith, was designed to 'provide a new and improved apparatus for preventing sea-bathers from being drowned or carried out by the waves, tide, or under-tow'. The frame (A), which was preferably in the shape of a cross, was secured by an anchor attached to chain (B). A balancing weight (C) was suspended from each end of the frame (A) to hold it steady. 'Carriers' (L) could slide along the cable. Each was designed for three bathers. By winding the rope (P) on the windlass drum (Q) the carrier was drawn to the shore. 'The ropes (T) are hooked on the belts of the bathing-dresses. . . . The ropes (T) are to be of sufficient length to permit the bathers to move about. The bathers are thus held by these ropes (T), and need not hold onto the ropes or cable, and always have their hands disengaged. If an accident happens to a bather, he can hold himself above water by grasping the cable (D), and at any time that the bathers wish to go to the shore the carrier (L) can be moved towards the shore; or the bathers can disengage themselves and swim or wade to the shore.' Perhaps the swimmers would strangle themselves on the cables, or sink to the bottom while still secured by their ropes.

Louis Dusens of Paris, France with US 45368 in 1864 suggested an unusual approach. The bather lay in a bathtub-sized and shaped network of ropes with floats. This was connected to the shore by an endless chain. The bather's feet were pressed against a mechanism which operated a screw propeller so that, depending on the direction the feet turned, the bather would either go out further or return to shore. The bather was confined to the small space and so did not actually swim. A variation provided for a sail in a swan-like craft. This was his 'new and useful Bath or Bathing Machine Adapted for Deep Water'. The older bathing machines which allowed someone to change and then descend directly into the water (perhaps while still in the machine) do not, sadly, seem to have been patented. Another invention using a screw propeller was patented by Josef Tichy of Vienna, Austria with GB 11093/1895. He proposed a 'Swimming Appliance or Water Velocipede'. The swimmer clutched a buoyant pad which had a screw propeller underneath it. This was driven by hand while the legs were kept free.

Few bathing costumes seem to have been patented, perhaps because ungainly outfits were taken for granted. One of the few was by Ozias Morse of Concord, Massachusetts with US 87107 in 1869. The decorative effects he adds make the drawing look like a costume for a Ruritanian opera. It consisted of pantaloons and a sleeveless shirt with buttons down the front, with elaborate decoration. It was made as a single item of dress 'to protect the person of the wearer'. He commented that it avoided the problems with bathing-dresses as usually made. 'The water gathers in the folds when the upper and lower garments are fastened together at the waist. A larger amount of material is required and used, and the strain is unequal, and impedes the motion of the wearer, by binding, etc.' Therefore his 'compact and cheap' dress was slipped into and buttoned up. The bottom half was like drawers and he suggested omitting the elastic belt (mentioned by the Smiths above) round the waist. He mentioned the possibility of placing the buttons on the back 'but I esteem the front opening the most convenient', with which most people would agree.

(No Model.)

L. D. & J. B. SMITH.
SAFETY APPARATUS FOR SEA BATHERS.

No. 262,843.   Patented Aug. 15, 1882.

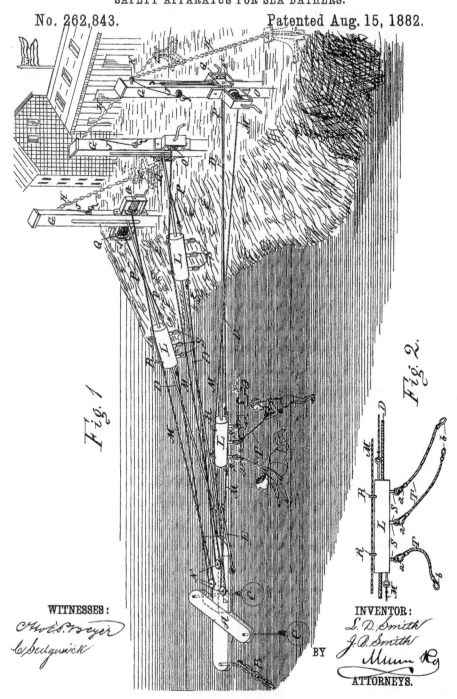

Fig. 1

Fig. 2

WITNESSES: INVENTOR:
Chas. S. Dwyer   _L. D. Smith_
C. Sedgwick   _J. B. Smith_

                                        BY _Munn & Co._
                                            ATTORNEYS.

The safety lift

Otis did not invent the lift but rather the safety lift, and without safe lifts skyscrapers would not have been built. The lift itself may be attributed to William Horner of Howick, Northumberland with his GB 4312/1818, who installed it in his Coliseum building in Regent's Park in 1829, where for sixpence (2.5p) visitors could ascend in a 'moving apartment' for six to eight persons to arrive in a room surrounded by a panorama of London. This worked for many years, but does not seem to have led to other installations. By 1850 some (non-safety) lifts had been installed in the USA.

Elisha Graves Otis was born on a farm near Halifax, Vermont in 1811. Although plagued by ill health he worked at a variety of occupations in New York State until in 1845 he began work in a bedstead factory in Albany as a master mechanic. When working for another bedstead company in Yonkers he was asked to supervise the hoisting of machinery to an upper floor. He realised how dangerous it would be if the cables broke and devised a toughened steel wagon spring which meshed with a ratchet. If the rope broke, the spring would catch and hold it. He was persuaded partly by his son Charles and partly by interest from manufacturers to leave his job and to set up a shop in Yonkers to make his new lifts. Otis decided on a *coup de théâtre* for the public unveiling of his idea. It was the Crystal Palace Exposition in New York in 1854. Before a crowd he ascended a platform suspended by a rope in an open-sided shaft. Suddenly an axe swung and the rope broke, and the platform began to fall. There were cries of horror, but it only fell a few centimetres before the safety mechanism caught it. A clamping mechanism gripped the guide rails when the rope was no longer in tension.

Despite the interest in the new lift, the first installation was not until 1857, at the Haughwout department store in New York. The steam-powered lift could climb the five floors in less than a minute and was considered a great success. Even by the relaxed standards of his time it seems odd that he did not receive a patent for his invention until 1861. It may have been to keep money coming in that he patented a steam plough, US 18468, in 1857 and a bake oven, US 21271, in 1858. The drawings show the principle of his lift. Figure 2 has the cage (D) suspended by a rope. The complicated mechanism ensures that the cage can be hoisted or lowered but also that if the rope broke, the metal springs would catch on the upwards-pointing teeth (C) of the walls (B). The weight of the cage itself would ensure that the springs securely held the cage.

Otis himself died a few months after the patent was issued, when about 10 men worked for the business, and the value of the equipment was $5,000. His sons Charles and Norton carried on the business, and patented a number of improvements. By 1873, 2,000 Otis lifts had been installed in buildings across the USA. From the late 1880s electric lifts began to take over from either steam or hydraulic lifts. Push button controls came in in 1894. From 1895 instead of a winding drum with ropes or wires there was the modern principle of hoisting apparatus applying power to pulleys at the top of the shaft. There was a counterweight on each lift car.

Elisha Graves Otis, Yonkers, New York
Published 15 January 1861 as US 31128 and reissued as Re 4269-71

E. G. OTIS.
HOISTING APPARATUS.

No. 31,128.

Patented Jan. 15, 1861.

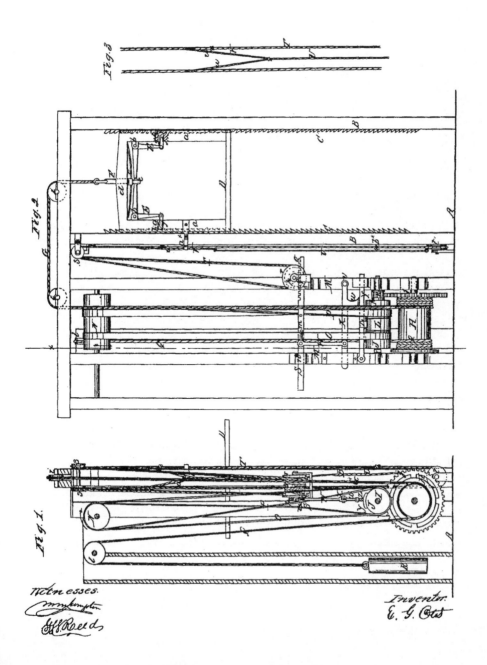

Witnesses:

Inventor:
E. G. Otis

The safety pin

The original paper drawing for this patent looks quite ragged, which is probably because it was much handled by those looking for evidence of prior research on this little, but very important, subject before it was microfilmed by the Patent Office. Walter Hunt was born in 1796 in Watertown in upstate New York. He was a mechanic who was responsible for a variety of patented inventions, beginning with an 1827 patent for an alarm for coaches, and including a stove, a spring for belts, a saw, a castor globe for the feet of furniture and a knife sharpener. He also invented and built the first proper sewing machine in 1834, with an eye-pointed needle, but deliberately did not patent it as he thought that it would destroy many jobs. One day he owed $15 to, apparently, one or both of the Richardsons. They were probably the draughtsmen for his patent drawings. The creditor offered him a long piece of wire and told Hunt that he would receive $400 in exchange for the rights to a useful invention from the wire. Hunt spent 3 hours twisting the wire and came up with the safety pin. He was $385 in profit after paying the debt, but the Richardsons, who were named as 'assignees' at the beginning of the patent, made a fortune from the invention.

The idea seems so simple, but someone had to think of it in the first place. By providing a means of protecting the sharp end the finger is not punctured whether the pin is secured or is not in use. Hunt called it a 'dress pin' and in a half page description states, 'The distinguishing features of this invention consist in the construction of a pin made of one piece of wire or metal combining a spring, a clasp or catch, in which catch, the point of said pin is forced and by its own spring securely retained'. He wrote of the 'perfect convenience' of inserting it into clothes without damage to the fabric or 'wounding the fingers'. It does in fact leave tiny holes in fabrics. Figure 1 shows the ideal configuration with the others being possible variants, Figures 7 and 8 being decorative variants.

The only major changes since have been that the sharp end of the pin is normally more securely held within a cup of metal, and a piece of metal helps hold it there. Pins had existed since Roman times but this was the first drastic change, facilitated by the use of wire. A forerunner was Thomas Woodward of Brooklyn's 1842 patent US 2609 for a 'Victorian shielded shawl and diaper pin'. This was somewhat similar but lacked the springy circle or oval at the other end from the pin which makes its use easier. Woodward also suggested that the pin should be of 'silver, or other metal' which would not be easy to manipulate. By a strange coincidence, the day following the American publication of Hunt's patent, an English patent was applied for that included a safety pin. GB 12796/1849 by Charles Rowley of Birmingham, Warwickshire covered several ideas including weaving, buttons and slides for garters but included as Figures 8 and 8a was a pin which could be secured by a loose cap which was jointed. This would have been distinctly clumsy to use and would easily have been broken off. Hunt's last patent was US 24517 in 1859 for a heel for boots or shoes. He died the same year and was buried underneath a majestic tomb in Greenwood Cemetery, New York City. A wit joked, 'His name would be obscured but without him we would be undone'.

Walter Hunt, New York City, New York for William Richardson and John Richardson
Issued 10 April 1849 as US 6281

W. Hunt.

Pin.

Nº 6281.　　　*Patented Apr. 10. 1849.*

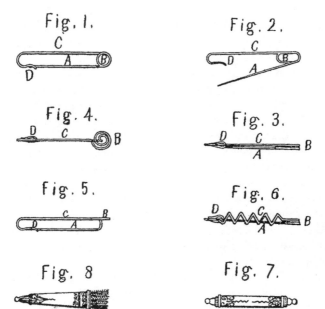

Fig. 1.

Fig. 2.

Fig. 4.

Fig. 3.

Fig. 5.

Fig. 6.

Fig. 8

Fig. 7.

The saluting device

'This invention relates to a novel device for automatically effecting polite salutations by the elevation and rotation of the hat on the head of the saluting party when said person bows to the person or persons saluted, the actuation of the hat being produced by mechanism therein and without the use of the hands in any manner.' James Boyle's interesting idea reflects both the importance of hats in an age when workman and 'swell' alike wore them, and of politeness to others. Presumably the wearer was either too lazy to tip his hat or had his arms heavily laden and was unable conveniently to do so. The idea was that by nodding the head the mechanism would 'raise the hat, completely rotate it, and deposit it correctly on the head of the wearer every time said person bows his head and then assumes an erect posture'. Any accidental bowing to tie shoelaces and the like would provide an odd effect for anyone watching. Besides the page shown, a further seven 'figures' or drawings are provided and three dense pages of description of how the mechanism works. A bow-piece was attached to the hat with strings to pull the hat's sweatband at the front and back and in turn was attached to the controlling mechanism which in turn was perched on the head.

Boyle seems to be at least partly aware how bizarre his invention was as he concludes, 'There may be a sign or placard placed on the hat having the improvements within it, and the saluting device be used to attract attention of the public on a crowded thoroughfare to the advertisement on the hat, the novelty of its apparent self-movement calling attention to the hat and its placard'. One half of the rights were assigned to John Neill so he too was a firm believer in the success of the invention, perhaps paying the patent fees. The Patent Office classifies this invention under 2/209.13, 'Head coverings: combined with diverse article'.

This invention is believed to be unique. Among the numerous British patents on the subject of hats are many concerned with hat ironing (in their manufacture) and many with ventilation. These include GB 2181/1855, a 'communication' taken out by a London patent agent on behalf of an anonymous person (probably a foreigner), which is for a moveable crown which could be closed or opened 'at pleasure'. The crown was in two parts joined by a strip of perforated material. Rods lifted the crown when ventilation was required so that the perforated strip was revealed. Then there was GB 763/1870 by Paul de Ferrari of Paris, France, architect. It was for a topper with a double brim and was meant 'for protecting the brain of the wearer from solar heat'. A lifting mechanism lifted the brim so that ventilation holes appeared in the inner brim. Stranger still is GB 762/1859 by William Redgrave of London, tailor. This, says the Patent Office's summary, is for a cap for deadening the effect of blows, and its use was suggested for travellers, women, children—and lunatics. It consisted of a circular tube of airtight material. Its particular use by lunatics becomes clearer when it is added that it can cushion the impact of falling over.

James Boyle, Spokane, Washington State
Filed 18 September 1895 and published as US 556248

(No Model.)　　　　　　　　　　　　　　　　2 Sheets—Sheet 1.

J. C. BOYLE.
SALUTING DEVICE.

No. 556,248.　　　　　　　　Patented Mar. 10, 1896.

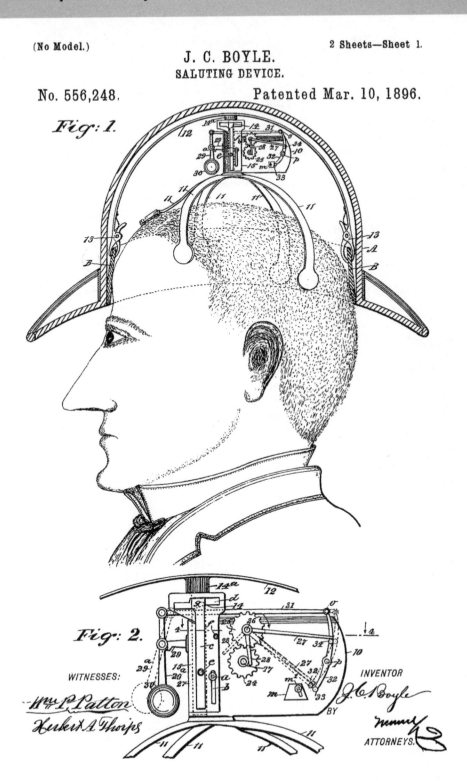

Fig: 1.

Fig: 2.

WITNESSES:

Wm P. Patton

Hubert A. Thorps

INVENTOR

J. C. Boyle

BY

ATTORNEYS.

The school desk and chair combined

This invention looks distinctly odd because the school desk with its liftable top and inkwell, all too familiar to some, is placed *behind* the chair. The reason is simple: the desk was meant for the 'scholar' sitting behind the desk, not in front. In a sense the position of the desk is incidental as what George Buchanan really meant to do was to promote a healthy posture. Figure 2 shows that the seat was pivoted so that the back could be moved forward. 'By this arrangement of seat, scholars will be compelled, by reason of their own weight, when it is deemed advantageous, to sit in a posture which will cause their chests to be thrown forward in a manner to insure a free action and healthful condition of their lungs, instead of being allowed to throw their chests inward in a manner to contract and impair their lungs, as is the case with ordinary school desk seats which allow their scholars to lean forward and rest their arms upon the desk.' Buchanan failed to think his invention through. His arrangement would mean that the scholars in the front row would have nothing to write on, while those using the desks in the back row would have nothing to sit on.

There were numerous Victorian patents for designs for school desks and for teaching aids, but few for the actual design of a school. One such is rather spooky. George Stevens of London, England, 'Bachelor of Arts and Laws', suggested with GB 854/1880 an octagonal school. Each side formed the outer wall of a classroom with in the middle a small, elevated space with sight holes looking into each of the eight rooms. It was designed 'to enable the classes under tuition in a number of different rooms to be constantly supervised by a single inspector, who, without quitting the same post and without being seen by anyone in the rooms under inspection can overlook all the class rooms in the structure'. The narrower end of each room was for the 'instructor's platform and appliances'. The idea was that while the teaching was going on the inspector could be keeping an eye on everyone. Teachers were unlikely to have been enthusiastic about being watched and there was the problem of what to do if a pupil misbehaved. Was the inspector supposed to rush in and collar the offender? It is more likely that Buchanan intended a note to be made. A second objective of the patent was more modern: to enable two of the rooms to be temporarily merged into one for teaching purposes.

In the USA there were many patents for what were called 'scholar's companions'. They would nowadays be called pencil cases. Mary Spencer of Brooklyn, New York with her US 291415 in 1884 made an eminently sensible invention. Metal pencil cases made a noise if they fell to the ground. Her flexible case, which was made of cloth or leather, could be rolled up if not in use. It had a buttoned flap which fitted over the openings for separate pouches for pencils, pens, and also for a sponge for wiping slates clean.

George Buchanan, Hickory, Pennsylvania
Published 11 January 1859 as US 22545

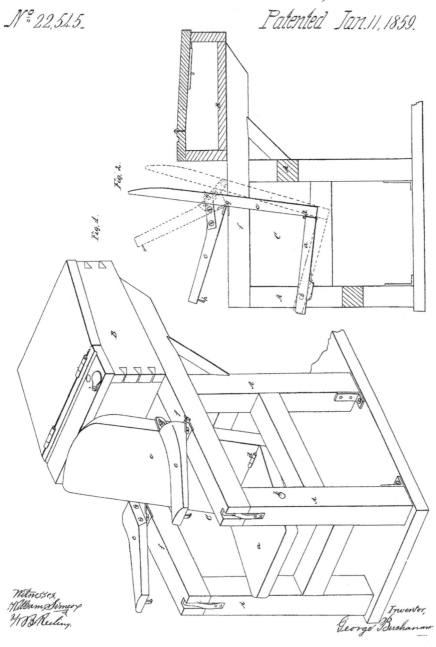

G. Buchanan,

School Desk and Chair,

Nº 22,545.

Patented Jan. 11, 1859.

Witnesses,
William Simcox
W. B. Reeling.

Inventor,
George Buchanan

The sewing machine

There were forerunners of the sewing machine, but this account can only give an idea of the extraordinary 'Sewing machine wars'. Elias Howe Jr was born in Spencer, Massachusetts in 1819. Lame from birth, he worked as a machinist in a cotton machinery factory. Someone told him that the first to invent a practicable sewing machine would make a fortune. He watched his wife sewing for hours, studying each movement, and spent 5 years working on the idea, patenting the illustrated invention. Power was provided by turning the winch (E) to rotate the flywheel (D). The bobbin (F) supplied thread to the curved needle (a) (at the bottom right of Figure 2) with the cloth on the point below it. A stitch was inserted each time the shuttle went back and forth, rather like a loom. It was awkward to use, and involved frequent halts to re-pin the cloth onto wires. Nevertheless, when he personally demonstrated it against the fastest hand sewer it won every time. Yet nobody would buy one. Hoping for sales in England, Howe sent his brother Amasa there. Only William Thomas, a corsetmaker from Cheapside, London, was interested. Thomas paid £250 for the British rights and applied for the English patent. Howe came over with his wife and three children, hoping to cash in on this success, but was merely hired to spend a year altering the machine so that it could sew corsets. When he succeeded, Thomas refused to pay up. Howe sent his family back to America and later, destitute, returned himself only to find his wife dying. He had to borrow a suit to attend his wife's funeral.

He now found that many were making and selling copies of his machine, but none were paying royalties. One of the most successful was New Yorker Isaac Singer, another machinist (and inventor). Singer had been asked to repair a copycat machine and decided that he could improve it. In 11 days of work he came up with the familiar idea of a long arm holding the needle bar over an integral surface so that any part of the fabric could be worked on, and stitching was continuous: the basic method used today. It also included Howe's eye-pointed needle and lock stitch. This was patented as US 8294 in 1851. Howe, in despair, offered to sell all rights to Singer for $2,000, but as Singer too had no money, he angrily ordered Howe out of the office.

A complicated court battle ensued until in 1854 the American courts decided for Howe. It is pleasant to record that royalties then streamed in until his patent expired, and he died wealthy in 1867 in Brooklyn, New York. Singer too did well as sales gradually climbed with his superior model. He initially tried selling to professional garment workers, but switched to housewives, offering credit terms and delivering direct to the house. These were both novelties. After patenting 19 improvements up until 1867, he retired to England in that year and died in 1875 at Torquay, Devon. He is said to have fathered at least 24 children by four women. Meanwhile William Thomas back in Cheapside had won two English court cases in 1857 against infringers. He had had to modify the patent with a 'disclaimer' in 1855 to exclude aspects covered by GB 10424/1844 by John Fisher and James Gibbons for sewing lace. Until its 1860 expiry his patent stifled the British market. Over 1,000 improvements in sewing machines were patented in the USA by the early 1870s. One was US 118537-8 by Solomon Jones of New Orleans, Louisiana, which was the first electric model. 700,000 machines were being produced annually by 1871, mainly by Singer's company.

3 Sheets—Sheet 2.

E. HOWE, Jr.

Sewing Machine.

No. 4,750.

Patented Sept. 10, 1846.

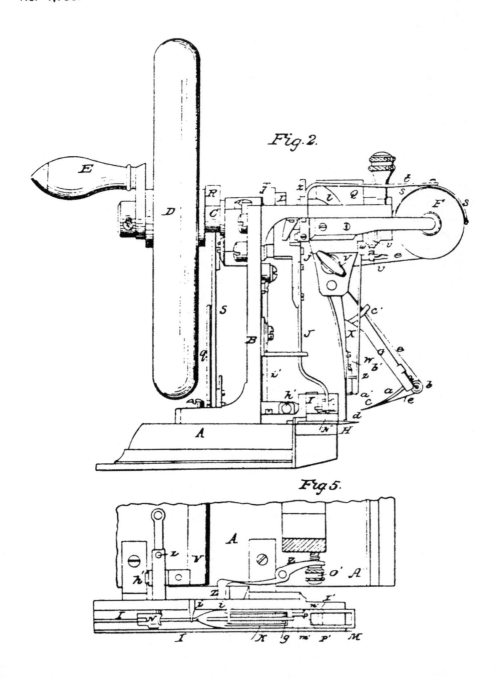

Fig. 2.

Fig. 5.

The silent valveless water waste preventer

This particular invention, by a 'gentleman', was sold as Crapper's Silent Valveless Water Waste Preventer. Everyone expects Thomas Crapper to be in this book, and this is perhaps the most significant of all the inventions sold by his prospering company. Albert Giblin probably sold the rights to Crapper who was born at Thorne, near Doncaster, Yorkshire in 1836. When he was 11 years old he walked to London, over 300 km, and got a job with a master plumber in Chelsea, a locality which was his professional base for the rest of his life. He set up his own business in 1861 at the Marlboro' Works. He had a number of patents himself, such as GB 3964/1891 which enabled a lavatory to flush at intervals and is often used today. Many aspects of the modern lavatory had already been worked out, with the first water closet dating back to Sir John Harington in 1589. Following a Parliamentary act it was required that lavatories save water. The usual valves leaked water and some people tried letting the lavatory flush perpetually to keep the bowl clean. The invention shown is a valveless system whereby the cistern need only be half full and would still work. It is commonly used in Britain today. A different solution was devised in the USA with the flapper valve which is also still used today.

Figure 1 shows the (high-level) cistern holding a water supply and Figure 2 is a view cut through the length. The flush lever is (q) on the left of Figure 1 with chamber (b), open to the water at the bottom, and a syphon (a) next to it. Through the top of (b) runs a spindle (c) of the displacement plate which is shown in Figures 3 and 4 as (d) resting near the top of chamber (b). The lever (q) is attached to the spindle so that when pulled the plate (d) rises and causes some water to flow uphill and then down the syphon (which is (h) in Figure 2). Air is present at the top of (h) (as it is above the top level of water in the cistern) and by a natural syphonic action more water is pulled up and then down the syphon, with 'considerable velocity' as the sales literature said. When emptied the cistern refills until the copper float (unlabelled but shown at the right of Figure 1) rises to a level which blocks the inlet and the flow ceases. Until the lever was pulled again no water could escape. This was sold as the 'pull and let go' model. Painted or galvanised models were available, with the 2 gallons (9 litres) painted variant selling for 20 shillings and 6 pence (£1.025), with a lid being an extra.

Crapper received a royal warrant as a manufacturing sanitary engineer to royalty. This was proudly referred to in his copious trade literature where the many designs, all with their own names (mostly named after streets near the Works) were displayed. His Works included a heavily used area where cisterns could be temporarily installed for repair or, if new models, tested. Apples and paper were used to check the efficiency of the flushes. Thomas Crapper retired in 1904 and sold up to his two partners, who carried on the business under his name until 1966. He died in 1910 in Bromley, Kent after an illness during which it is said that, hearing his niece struggle to flush the toilet, he crept out when no one was looking and fixed the problem with his practised hands. An affectionate biography, *Flushed with pride*, by Wallace Reyburn, was published in 1969.

A.D. 1898. March 1. N°. 4990.
GIBLIN'S Complete Specification.
(1 SHEET)

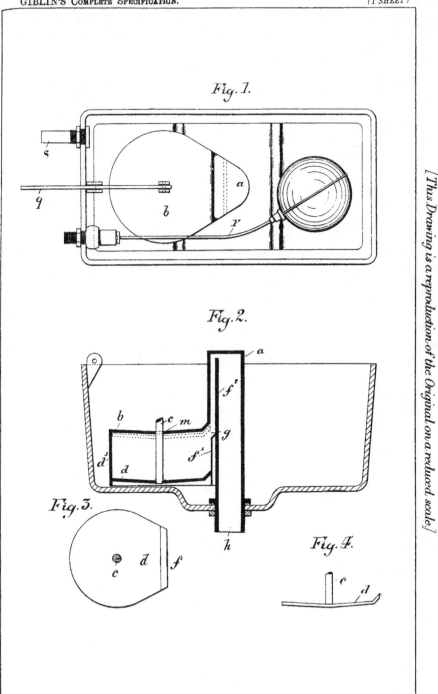

Fig. 1.

Fig. 2.

Fig. 3.

Fig. 4.

[This Drawing is a reproduction of the Original on a reduced scale]

The square-bottomed paper bag

Luther Childs Crowell was born in 1840 in West Dennis, on the Cape Cod peninsula, Massachusetts. The son of a sea-captain, he spent several years in the merchant marine but abandoned that career. His real interest was in tinkering with ideas. Paper in particular fascinated him. His neighbours would watch him spend hours with a piece of paper, folding it again and again into unique shapes. His first patent however was for an 'aerial machine' in 1862, US 35437, a strange contraption.

His second patent was more successful. US 65176 of 1867 is still widely used today. The idea was that thin strips of iron or tin were placed round the neck of a bag and this stiffening would both keep the bag open for filling and then seal the bag. After patenting a stove-polishing brush his next patents were more successful still. The drawing is of his idea for a square-bottomed paper bag with the familiar corrugated top—familiar, at least, to everyone in the USA when taking groceries out to the car, as in Europe plastic bags are much more common. He describes his idea as 'so folding and cementing a strip of paper that when cut into sections of suitable length, one end being closed by one fold, the bottom of the bag or case thus formed when opened or filled will assume a quadrangular shape'. The paper was cemented into a tube with a fold on each side as shown in Figure 1. It was then cut from (b) to (c). The protruding lip (d) was then cemented so that it would fold over as shown in Figure 3. Figure 4 was the finished product with Figures 5 and 6 showing the inside and outside appearance of the bottom.

The result was a strong bag which easily stays open so that it can be filled with groceries. The patent indicates that one quarter of the rights went to Luther Crane of Cambridge and one quarter to Galen Coffin of Boston, who presumably were backers. At the same time US 123812 was granted to Crowell for complicated machinery to assist in the production of the bags. Square-bottomed bags may sound very simple but the fact that they are convenient, and used to this day, show how an unperceived need was satisfied. Crowell had to take infringers to court and subsequently sold partial rights in his bag inventions to the infringers. He went on to patent with US 188779 in 1877 a machine to deliver folded newspapers, which was first used when incorporated with new machinery by the *Boston Herald*.

A Brooklyn printing company named R. Hoe realised that they were infringing Crowell's patents. They offered to pay him for their use and to hire him to invent more solutions in their trade. From 1879 he spent the rest of his life working for the company. He invented mostly in the area of wrapping newspapers and paper feeding or folding mechanisms. He also patented methods of preventing fraud by newspaper sellers. His US 480423 of 1892 explains that the return of unsold newspapers by sellers could be open to fraud. Some dealers would collect discarded newspapers in good condition and sell them back. His solution was to have a seal on an interesting part of the paper which the purchaser would have to remove. One of his last inventions was US 787876, a method for labelling bottles. A forthright and proud Yankee, Crowell died back in West Dennis in 1906 with nearly 300 patents to his name.

L. C. CROWELL.
Paper Bag.

No. 123,811.

Patented Feb. 20, 1872.

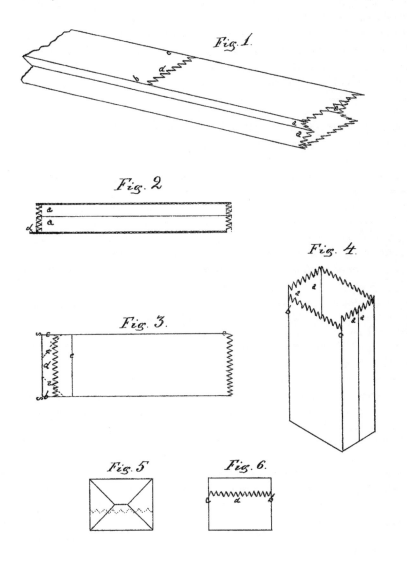

Fig. 1.

Fig. 2

Fig. 3.

Fig. 4.

Fig. 5

Fig. 6.

Witnesses:

Alban Andrén.

Burton Caswell

Inventor:

Luther C. Crowell

The steam locomotive

Ross Winans certainly did not invent the locomotive, which predates the Victorian age. He was, however, an important and interesting pioneer. He was born in 1793 on a Sussex County, New Jersey farm. He obtained patents in 1821 for fulling cloth and another in 1824 for an iron plough. Stories of how he became involved with the railways vary. One is that he was trying to sell horses to the first American railway, the Baltimore and Ohio Railroad, which had begun building its track in 1828. Another was that he showed model trains and track to its chairman. Baltimore was envious of New York City's success in 1825 in enlarging its hinterland with the Erie Canal which led from the Hudson River to Lake Erie. They hoped to match that success by linking up with the growing population along the Ohio river. Some hoped to do this with the Chesapeake and Ohio Canal, while others put their trust in the new railway.

Winans took to the new profession with enthusiasm, and rapidly became knowledgeable. He devised a model 'rail wagon' which was the first to have pivoting rather than fixed wheels, so that it could go round curves. The new railway car was demonstrated by placing the 90 year old Charles Carroll, last surviving signatory of the Declaration of Independence, in it and towing him along tracks by a pulley operating under a small weight. This was in front of a crowd of Baltimore's most distinguished citizens. In 1829 Winans joined others on a tour of England's railways to learn of developments there since the first railway between Stockton and Darlington in 1825. On his return he worked with Peter Cooper and his Tom Thumb engine and until 1860 he worked on improving machinery used by the Baltimore & Ohio Company.

In his patents he often makes interesting comments on others working in the field and in his US 308 of 1837 comments on the horizontal 'English' boiler and compares it with a splendidly illustrated vertical 'Baltimore' boiler. In the drawing shown here he seems to have reverted to the idea of a horizontal boiler. He states that it is an improvement on the work of Hopkins Thomas of the Beaver Meadow Railroad in Pennsylvania. Thomas used six wheels in all for the locomotive 'but his engine was found to be objectionable on account of its too great tendency to run off the road'. He thought that eight wheels would mean more contact with the rails and less of a tendency to leave the track. The connecting rods (C) conveyed power from the steam cylinders to driving wheels (B). The connecting rods (D) allowed the other four wheels also to be driving wheels in an early model of the familiar rhythmically moving locomotives.

With the outbreak of the Civil War, Winans, a Southern sympathiser in a slave state that the Union had to hold to keep in contact with Washington, DC, was asked by the State of Maryland to devise a steam-operated cannon. Gunpowder was something that the South was short of, so such a cannon would have been very useful. The shipment of the cannon was intercepted on its way to Virginia and Winans was put in jail. His release may have come about because the cannon did not work. Later he built a small fort with six fake cannon on his son's estate to 'protect' it from roaming Union troops. Winans's sons were hired by the Russian Czar in 1837 to build the first Russian railways and they did not finish their contracts there until 1851. All but one stayed on in Europe. Ross Winans died in 1877 in Baltimore, a multi-millionaire.

Ross Winans, Baltimore, Maryland
Published 11 October 1846 as US 4812

R. WINANS.

Locomotive.

No. 4,812.

Patented Oct. 14, 1846.

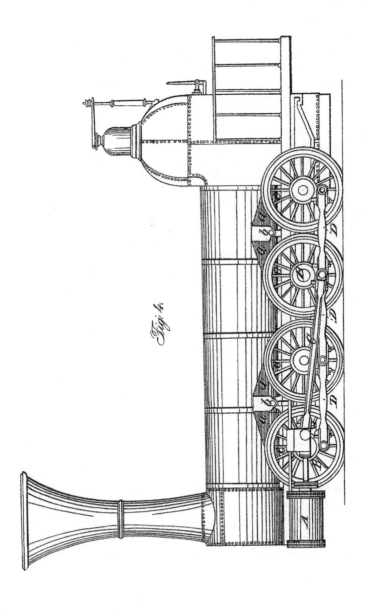

Fig. 4.

The steam turbine

Charles Algernon Parsons was born in London in 1854, son to the 3rd Earl of Rosse, a noted amateur astronomer. He was educated by tutors at home in Birr, Offaly, Ireland and after a university education in mathematics spent much time studying the problem of obtaining power from turbines. This involves converting a stream of fluid to mechanical energy by passing it through fan-like blades, rather like a windmill and the wind. The Swedish inventor Gustav De Laval had the idea of an 'impulse' turbine where a fast stationary jet was fired at a rotor containing blades. Huge centrifugal forces on the materials available at the time meant failure. Parsons grasped why it did not work: to avoid stress a succession of rotors was needed so that the stream would be accelerated at each one. Small, strong blades would cope with the initial stream and then larger, more vulnerable blades. Steam would expand as it drove the blades which would lower both the pressure and the temperature. Each successive set of blades would be designed to cope with this to extract the maximum heat energy.

In 1877 Parsons joined the Armstrong Works at Newcastle-upon-Tyne, Northumberland as a 'premium' engineering apprentice, which meant that he was destined for management. For someone of his background it was very unusual. He worked on his 'epicycloidal' engine and rocket powered torpedoes and later became a junior partner with Clarke Chapman & Co. at Gateshead. He designed a turbine with a power rating of 4 kwatts. The schematic drawing is taken from the American patent. It involves 15 stages of expansion for steam moving through sets of blades off a single shaft. He sold early turbine patents to partners, then bought them back in 1894. By 1892 he was able to generate 100 kwatts and he had an experimental vessel, the *Turbinia*, launched in 1894. It was 30 m long by 2.7 m wide and could move at 60 km/hour, much faster than any ship of the time. Three rotors were linked. Parsons had to deal with many problems with such advanced technology, including cavitation, where a vacuum formed behind the propellers.

In an effort to get noticed, *Turbinia* arrived uninvited at the Navy Review for Queen Victoria's Diamond Jubilee at Spithead, off the Isle of Wight, on 26 June 1897. The Prince of Wales was representing the Queen and there were numerous British and foreign dignitaries. When the bands began to play *God save the Queen* Parsons boldly rushed at high speed between two lines of large ships. Patrol boats were unable to catch the *Turbinia*, and one nearly sank in her wash. *Turbinia* nearly collided with a French yacht, the line on a small boat being towed by *Turbinia* having parted and the boat hitting the side of the French vessel. *Turbinia* had made her presence felt as the fastest boat in the world. Charles Parsons had made his point, not only to the Admiralty, which had already shown interest in his work, but also to the foreign naval representatives present at the review. In 1897 Parsons asked for an extra patent term because he was unable to exploit his invention properly. The Privy Council decided in his favour and this gave much information about Parsons's financial affairs. In 1899 the Royal Navy launched two ships using the new turbines. After many more inventions, including a helicopter, Parsons was knighted in 1911. He died in 1931 in Kingston, Jamaica while on a cruise. The principle continues to be much used to generate electricity as well as in ships and in aviation.

Charles Algernon Parsons, Gateshead, Durham, England
Filed 23 April 1884 and published as GB 6735/1884 and US 328710

(No Model.) 5 Sheets—Sheet 1.

C. A. PARSONS.

ROTARY MOTOR.

No. 328,710. Patented Oct. 20, 1885.

Fig. 1.

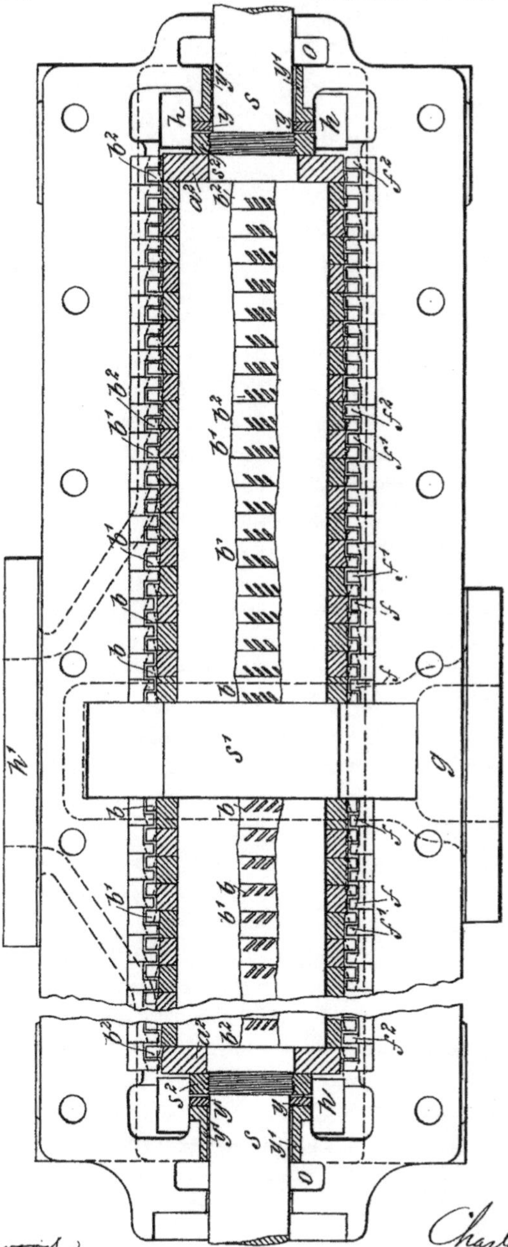

Witnesses
J. A. Blackwood
F. S. Chapman

Inventor:
Charles A. Parsons
by W. H. Doolittle
attorney

Sulphuric ether

The early history of anaesthetics research is truly bizarre. William Morton did not discover ether but he established the use of anaesthetics in medicine. This is despite the fact that Horace Wells of Hartford, Connecticut, a shy man who only wanted humanity to benefit from his work, had used nitrous oxide ('laughing gas') from 1844. One of his dentistry students was Morton himself, who was born in 1819 in Charlton, Massachusetts, son of a farmer. Like other dentists Morton found removing teeth was agonising for the patients, and few accepted the treatment. He tried giving the patients alcohol or opium, or hypnotising them to deaden the pain, but nothing worked.

Charles Jackson, a chemistry professor, suggested that Morton try ether in drops as a local anaesthetic. Jackson had already demonstrated before classes that inhalation caused a loss of consciousness but like others had not reasoned that it would be helpful in medicine. During the summer of 1846 Morton tried it on a goldfish, a hen and his pet spaniel. All recovered. Then he tried ether on himself. On 30 September 1846 a man named Eben Frost came to Morton with a toothache. Morton without explaining got him to breathe the ether and the tooth was quickly and painlessly extracted. Morton got Frost to sign an affidavit that he had been without pain and a vague account appeared the next day in the *Boston Daily Journal*. Word spread and, 2 weeks later at the invitation of Massachusetts General Hospital, Morton successfully administered ether to patients undergoing operations at a hospital. But there were doubts, as Morton was not a doctor and would not say what he was using.

Much happened within a few weeks. Morton began to spend his time and money publicising ether. On the advice of the son of a patent commissioner (and also a friend of Jackson) Morton applied for a patent, although ether was already known. Legal advisers urged him to mention Jackson as an inventor. He tried to disguise his agent as 'letheon', from the Greek for oblivion, but the patent clearly says that it is sulphuric ether. An enthusiastic, and famous, article written by Henry Bigelow appeared in the *Boston Medical and Surgical Journal* on 18 November only for a long counterblast by Josiah Flagg to appear 5 days later with language like 'But we are still told that it is patented. What is patented? A power? A principle? A natural effect? The operation of a well-known medicinal agent? I doubt the validity of such letters patent. It would seem to me like patent sun-light or patent moon-shine.'

Morton expressed his willingness to license his patent, but on a doctor's advice said that he was willing to repay all such fees should the government pay compensation to him. Until 1864 efforts were made by sympathisers in Congress to have sums of $100,000 awarded to him, but the bills never passed the Senate. He eventually went bankrupt. Horace Wells meanwhile had while experimenting with chloroform become an addict and committed suicide in 1848. Jackson and Crawford Long, a Georgia physician who claimed that he had used ether in 1842, both fought their cases. Morton died in New York City's Central Park in 1868, while in a carriage, of apoplexy. At the time he was reading yet another attack on himself, made on behalf of Jackson, which was meant to prejudice a testimonial subscription for Morton. Jackson himself, on seeing Morton given the credit for anaesthetics on his tombstone, went mad and had to be placed in an asylum.

Charles Jackson and William Morton, both of Boston, Massachusetts
Published 12 November 1846 as US 4848

United States Patent Office.

C. T. JACKSON AND WM. T. G. MORTON, OF BOSTON, MASSACHUSETTS; SAID C. T. JACKSON ASSIGNOR TO WM. T. G. MORTON.

IMPROVEMENT IN SURGICAL OPERATIONS.

Specification forming part of Letters Patent No. **4,848,** dated November 12, 1846.

To all whom it may concern:

Be it known that we, CHARLES T. JACKSON and WILLIAM T. G. MORTON, of Boston, in the county of Suffolk and State of Massachusetts, have invented or discovered a new and useful Improvement in Surgical Operations on Animals, whereby we are enabled to accomplish many, if not all, operations, such as are usually attended with more or less pain and suffering, without any or with very little pain to or muscular action of persons who undergo the same; and we do hereby declare that the following is a full and exact description of our said invention or discovery.

It is well known to chemists that when alcohol is submitted to distillation with certain acids peculiar compounds, termed "ethers," are formed, each of which is usually distinguished by the name of the acid employed in its preparation. It has also been known that the vapors of some, if not all, of these chemical distillations, particularly those of sulphuric ether, when breathed or introduced into the lungs of an animal have produced a peculiar effect on its nervous system, one which has been supposed to be analogous to what is usually termed "intoxication." It has never to our knowledge been known until our discovery that the inhalation of such vapors (particularly those of sulphuric ether) would produce insensibility to pain, or such a state of quiet of nervous action as to render a person or animal incapable to a great extent, if not entirely, of experiencing pain while under the action of the knife or other instrument of operation of a surgeon calculated to produce pain. This is our discovery, and the combining it with or applying it to any operation of surgery for the purpose of alleviating animal suffering, as well as of enabling a surgeon to conduct his operation with little or no struggling or muscular action of the patient and with more certainty of success, constitutes our invention. The nervous quiet and insensibility to pain produced on a person is generally of short duration. The degree or extent of it or time which it lasts depends on the amount of ethereal vapor received into the system and the constitutional character of the person to whom it is administered. Practice will soon acquaint an experienced sur-

geon with the amount of ethereal vapor to be administered to persons for the accomplishment of the surgical operation or operations required in their respective cases. For the extraction of a tooth the individual may be thrown into the insensible state, generally speaking, only a few minutes. For the removal of a tumor or the performance of the amputation of a limb it is necessary to regulate the amount of vapor inhaled to the time required to complete the operation.

Various modes may be adopted for conveying the ethereal vapor into the lungs. A very simple one is to saturate a piece of cloth or sponge with sulphuric ether, and place it to the nostrils or mouth, so that the person may inhale the vapors. A more effective one is to take a glass or other proper vessel, like a common bottle or flask, and place in it a sponge saturated with sulphuric ether. Let there be a hole made through the side of the vessel for the admission of atmospheric air, which hole may or may not be provided with a valve opening downward, or so as to allow air to pass into the vessel, a valve on the outside of the neck opening upward, and another valve in the neck and between that last mentioned and the body of the vessel or flask, which latter valve in the neck should open toward the mouth of the neck or bottle. The extremity of the neck is to be placed in the mouth of the patient, and his nostrils stopped or closed in such manner as to cause him to inhale air through the bottle, and to exhale it through the neck and out of the valve on the outside of the neck. The air thus breathed, by passing in contact with the sponge, will be charged with the ethereal vapors, which will be conveyed by it into the lungs of the patient. This will soon produce the state of insensibility or nervous quiet required.

In order to render the ether agreeable to various persons, we often combine it with one or more essential oils having pleasant perfumes. This may be effected by mixing the ether and essential oil and washing the mixture in water. The impurities will subside, and the ether, impregnated with the perfume, will rise to the top of the water. We sometimes combine a narcotic preparation—such as opium or mor-

Synthetic dyes

Most people do not know what aniline dye is, yet it paved the way for the synthetic dye industry. William Henry Perkin was born in 1838 in London and became a student at the Royal College of Chemistry. He was an excellent student and became the assistant of the German-born professor Augustus William von Hofman. Von Hofman had himself been a student of Justus Liebig, who was the leader in the new interest in making synthetic substances, such as artificial fertilisers and meat extracts. Von Hofman suggested that Perkin try to synthesise quinine from coal tar. Quinine was a valuable antimalarial agent that would be valuable in the Empire. Coal tar was the messy residue left after lighting gas from coal or after deriving coke (for making iron) from coal. Perkin worked on the problem in his laboratory at home during the Easter break and attempted to oxidise allyl toluidine with potassium dichromate. He then tried replacing the toluidine with aniline. Some toluidine impurities remained in the aniline and, when washing out glass beakers holding the resulting black sludge, noticed glints of purple. He was able to refine this to a deep purple colour. It was the first synthetic dye. He called it Tyrian purple (later it was called mauve).

Perkin, only 18, was clearly a born entrepreneur (although apparently rather shy). He spent two years working out how to make his new colour, and how to use it to dye cloth properly. Together with his builder father and his brother Thomas (and against his professor's wishes) he set up a chemical factory making the dye in Harrow, just outside London. Others tried to compete, but his method was always the cheapest. Within a few years he was wealthy and in 1873 he sold up and retired to work in chemistry full-time. He bought the house next to his own and altered the old one to be his laboratory. Soon after he synthesised commarin, the first synthetic perfume (it smelt like newly mown grass), and continued to do valuable work. He died in 1907 of pneumonia after the excitement of celebrations by the British and the Americans in his honour on the 50th anniversary of his discovery, and being awarded a knighthood.

It was, though, Germany and not Britain which became the centre of the new industry. Its universities taught industrial chemistry to a high level, and much research and investment was made in the new industry. There was plenty of coal, which was very suitable for chemical work as it is a polymer, with long chains of atoms, providing many possibilities. Increasingly it was German discoveries that dominated the field, with synthetic versions of indigo and madder driving out the natural colours. Whole families of colours were worked out. By World War I German companies such as Brüning and Bayer had 75% of the world's dye industry, and from its profits they were able to branch out into pharmaceuticals and explosives. The World War I blockades meant that Germany had to rely more than ever on its synthetic industries, but also meant that the price of dyes climbed many-fold in other countries. Patent offices licensed out German-owned patents to British or American companies for the duration of hostilities. Britain then banned chemical product patents from 1919 until 1949, so scared were they of German competition. Another example of the anxiety aroused is from a letter from a patent agent published in an American patent journal in November 1918 claiming that German dye patents were unworkable or dangerous. He cited one from 1880 (I won't say which one) which would explode if you tried it out. American equivalents of these patents were said to be as bad. He asked that these patents not be cited as prior art against new applications.

A.D. 1856 . . . . Nº 1984.

Dyeing Fabrics.

LETTERS PATENT to William Henry Perkin, of King David Fort, in the Parish of Saint George in the East, in the County of Middlesex, Chemist, for the Invention of " PRODUCING A NEW COLORING MATTER FOR DYEING WITH A LILAC OR PURPLE COLOR STUFFS OF SILK, COTTON, WOOL, OR OTHER MATERIALS."

Sealed the 20th February 1857, and dated the 26th August 1856.

PROVISIONAL SPECIFICATION left by the said William Henry Perkin at the Office of the Commissioners of Patents, with his Petition, on the 26th August 1856.

I, WILLIAM HENRY PERKIN, do hereby declare the nature of the said
5 Invention for " PRODUCING A NEW COLORING MATTER FOR DYEING WITH A LILAC OR PURPLE COLOR STUFFS OF SILK, COTTON, WOOL, OR OTHER MATERIALS," to be as follows :—

Equivalent proportions of sulphate of aniline and bichromate of potassa are to be dissolved in separate portions of hot water, and, when dissolved, they are
10 to be mixed and stirred, which causes a black precipitate to form. After this mixture has stood for a few hours it is to be thrown on a filter, and the precipitate to be well washed with water, to free it from sulphate of potassa, and then dried. When dry it is to be boiled in coal-tar naptha, to extract a brown

The telephone

Alexander Graham Bell was born in Edinburgh, Scotland in 1847, son of an elocution and speech teacher and, significantly, a deaf mother. He was largely self-taught and became interested in sound when, aged 13, he realised that a struck key in a piano in one room made a piano in the next room faintly respond in the same pitch. The family emigrated to near Brantford, Ontario in 1870 and Bell went on to teach speech in Boston, where he was particularly interested in the problems of the deaf. He wanted to work on the idea of transmitting sounds by electricity, and the fathers of two of his deaf pupils supported this work. (Bell later married one of those two pupils, Mabel Hubbard.)

Bell was not good with his hands, and Thomas Watson, a machinist, was employed to help him with the work. One day in June 1875 a transmitter spring on a 'harmonic telegraph' (a method of sending more than one message at a time over a telegraph) stuck and was plucked to release it. This set off a current and both a tone and overtones were heard. Bell realised that just as the steel spring was heard a voice too could be heard. Briefly, his patent involved using the vibration of magnets to transmit 'by undulatory currents of electricity' the voice, using sound waves and hence an analogue method rather than a digital one. This is why the Internet has to change data from digital to analogue and back again over telephone lines. The top and bottom of the voice range is cut off which is why some people's voices sound odd on the telephone. Bell filed for his patent on 14 February 1876. On the same day Elisha Gray, an Ohio inventor, filed a caveat for a telephone. The way the caveat system worked was that you could file a document that briefly stated an idea that you were working on. This would gain for you 'priority' over later applicants provided that you filed a patent within 3 months. Bell was then still a British subject and therefore not entitled to file a caveat, and had to rely on the actual application. The records showed that Bell filed 2 hours before Gray and therefore it was Bell who received the patent, despite the fact that Gray's idea was workable and Bell's was not.

It was not until 10 March that, after making an adjustment to the apparatus, and accidentally spilling acid on his clothes, Bell cried out 'Mr Watson, come here, I need you' and Watson heard him over the telephone: the first ever telephone call. Bell's apparatus was good at receiving but not at transmitting sound. Thomas Edison's US 203011-19 of 1878 later improved the transmitter. There was a sensation when Bell displayed his telephone at the Centennial Exposition in Philadelphia in June 1876. The Emperor of Brazil, Don Pedro, cried out 'My God, it talks!' and dropped it in his surprise. Bell's company offered to sell all rights in the invention for $100,000 in late 1876 to the Western Union Telegraph Company but this was rejected. His company decided to sell a service and not the telephones, which were leased to customers. There were 50,000 customers within 3 years. Bell resigned from the company in 1880, rich already, to pursue other interests, such as working for the deaf and building giant hydroplanes. He took out 30 patents in all including US 747012 in 1904 for a 'compound cellular aerial vehicle'. He also founded the National Geographic Society in 1888. Bell spent his final illness in 1922 at his summer house in Nova Scotia. Too ill to write, he dictated entries for his journal. In his last dictation he was told, 'Don't hurry' only to reply, 'I have to'.

2 Sheets—Sheet 2.

A. G. BELL.

TELEGRAPHY.

No. 174,465.

Patented March 7, 1876.

Fig 6.

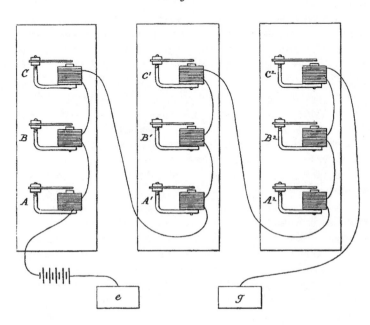

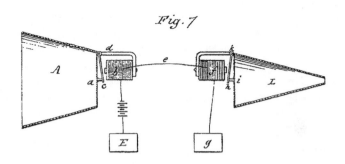

Fig. 7

The tell-tale

A 'tell-tale' was a device which ensured that workmen were alert in their work, and was popular in the 19th century. The British Patent Office's subject indexes defined it as 'Tell-tales for checking watchmen, workmen, servants, and the like' and index several annually for much of the Victorian period. When Thomas Edison was a junior telegraph operator he was supposed to tap a key at intervals to show that he was being attentive. Instead he improvised an automatic device to do this for him while he read technical books (he was sacked when this was discovered). Typically, tell-tale apparatus involved a clockwork mechanism which governed the speed of a piece of paper passing an aperture and being perforated, written on or marked at set intervals. Paper sufficient for a week was usually supplied. The patent illustrated is taken from the British patent as FR 167827, 'Contrôlent du ronde', was not published since the first year's renewal fees were not paid. The inventors Laurent Stanislaus Naudin and Florentin Naudin were machinists. Their title was 'New and improved watchman's indicator or tell-tale'. They first explained that current tell-tales could easily be falsified and were in the hands of those 'interested in hiding their own negligence or absence from duty'. Their solution was to end the idea of the watchman himself physically marking the paper, with the recording apparatus being safely kept in the manager's office.

The watchman pressed a button which completed the circuit in the electromagnet (B), causing wire (C) to withdraw from (D) so that it fell on cam (H). (H) was on the end of axis (h) which received a rotary motion from a spiral spring. Through (I) and (J) the motion moved pencil (L) to mark the paper, shown in more detail in Figure 2. As the spindle rotated because of the clockwork mechanism cam (H) lifted (D) again to be ready for another signal from the watchman. An electric bell to indicate that a mark had been made was an optional extra. 'The night watchman, for example, may have instructions to press the button every quarter of an hour. Every time he does so the fact is registered in the apparatus, and the next morning the manager will be able to verify, with certainty, whether his orders have been carried out faithfully or not.' A different approach was taken by Armand Collin of Paris, France with his GB 1431/1862. The watchman had a portable clock with a handle. The handle was inserted into a box at each designated place on his rounds. A letter would be printed and the time he was there would be known. A variant on the basic idea of checking on diligence was GB 3169/1868 by Walter Church of Derby, engineer. A steam boiler had a low and high water alarm for the water level. If either were exceeded, a glass broke and could not be repaired or replaced by the 'attendant' so that the guilty evidence could be seen. How the workmen themselves felt about all these devices to keep watch on them is not, however, recorded.

A.D. 1886. MARCH 15. № 3655.

BECK'S COMPLETE SPECIFICATION.

(1 SHEET)

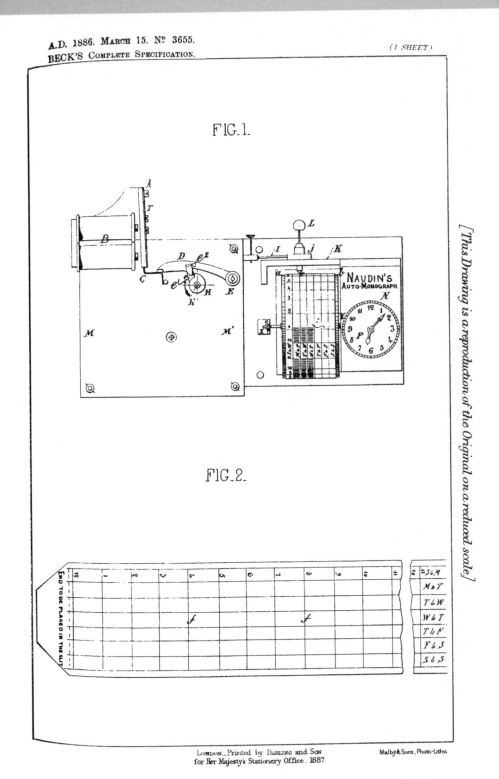

FIG. 1.

NAUDIN'S
AUTO-MONOGRAPH

FIG. 2.

[This Drawing is a reproduction of the Original on a reduced scale]

LONDON. Printed by DARLING and SON
for Her Majesty's Stationery Office. 1887.

Malby & Sons, Photo-Litho.

Tiddlywinks

This is one of the shortest and simplest patents ever, with less than a page describing how to play a game, yet it provoked a craze among adults that went on for years. The game is described as 'A new and improved game played with two sets of counters of different sizes and a bowl made of China . . .', the object being 'the larger counters . . . to press the edge of the smaller counters and cause them to jump into the bowl'. Joseph Assheton Fincher gives his occupation as 'gentleman' on the patent.

A flurry of patents on variations soon emerged. This began with George Scott of Birkenhead, Cheshire with his GB 9387/1889, for golf played on a board, who was ambitious enough to secure an American patent as well. In 1890 there was US 441099 by Charles Hoyt of Brooklyn, where counters received more points for getting close to the centre of a board; US 442438 by Edward Horsman Jr, also of Brooklyn, for the delightful idea of playing the game on a miniature tennis court; and Hoyt again with US 453480 where the counters had to be put through a vertically mounted ring. Charles Zimmerling of Philadelphia with his US 477287 suggested cups held on a vertically mounted board. Invention was not quite exhausted as Johannes Klauder of Dessau, Germany with his US 611915 in 1898 proposed using hooks instead of cups on such a board. Meanwhile back in Britain there was GB 11033/1890 by L. Bennett of Wimbledon, Surrey with his game where players were either 'cats' or 'mice' and the mice tried to reach a tent-like refuge, and John Peasgood, 'games manufacturer' of Upper Norwood, Surrey with GB 13768/1890 which also featured a horizontal board with scores marked on it.

The craze must have spread quickly, for the British journal *Notes and Queries* in its 18 January 1890 issue had a query about the name by a correspondent from remote British Guiana, now Guyana. A somewhat unrestrained account of the game was given by Lady Emily Lytton, writing on 24 April 1892, aged 17, to the Rev. Whitwell Elwin: 'After dinner we all played the most exciting game that ever was invented, called Tiddleywinks. It consists in flipping counters into a bowl, and being a good number we played at two tables, one table against another, and the excitement was tremendous. I assure you everyone's character changes at Tiddleywinks in the most marvellous way. To begin with, everyone begins to scream at the top of their voices and to accuse everyone else of cheating. Even I forgot my shyness and howled with excitement. Con darted around the room snatching at counters, screaming and trembling with excitement. Lord Wolmer flicked all the counters off the table and cheated in every possible way. George was very distressed at this and conscientiously picked every counter up again. Even Gerald got fearfully excited and was quite furious because someone at his table knocked over the bowl just as all the counters were in. . . . I assure you no words can picture either the intense excitement or the noise. I almost scream in describing it.'

Numerous editions and variants of the game were issued with little credit, apparently, being given to Fincher, though he did receive a British trade mark for 'Tiddledywinks' in 1889. He also received GB 3238/1890 for cuff links and GB 14931/1897 for candlesticks.

A.D. 1888. Nov. 8. № 16,215.

FINCHER'S COMPLETE SPECIFICATION.

(1 SHEET)

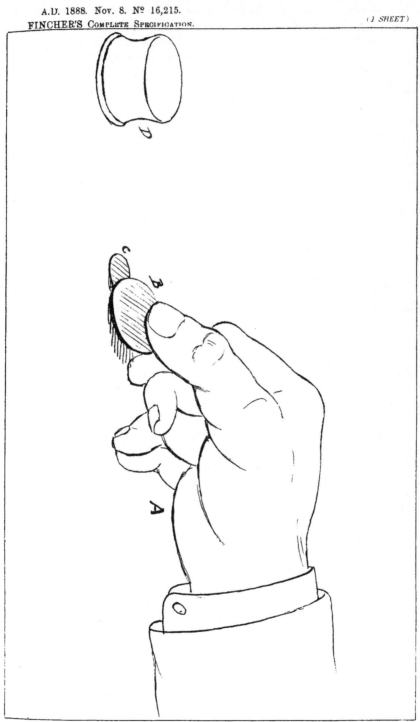

[This Drawing is a full-size reproduction of the Original.]

LONDON....Printed by DARLING and SON Ld.
for Her Majesty's Stationery Office . 1889.

Malby & Sons, Photo-Litho.

The traveling thrasher and separator

Thrashing or threshing removes the grain from the husk in crops while separating keeps them apart. The drawing shows how engines were beginning to take over from horses in agriculture. However, many thrashers were too expensive for most farmers to afford so there was a lively trade in hiring out equipment and men to thrash crops for farmers. There were over 200 previous American patents for thrashers before this one. In most designs the grain was brought to the thrasher rather than, as in this model, where everything was done in one machine.

The steam engine on the left powered drive belts connected to the actual 'separator' and was also supported by a truck or carriage at ground level. A set of wheels by the engine and a set in front of the separator meant that the truck and everything support-ed by it was moved along by the two horses in front. The truck formed a 'goose's neck' rising up and then down to the axle of the front wheels to allow them to make sharp turns. This, really, was the new invention, a thrasher which 'traveled' as the actual sep-arator was 'of any approved construction'. More horses moved the reaping apparatus and had wheels in front and behind them. The 'steam-motor' was something that Winthrop Norton would have taken for granted. It was to be a boiler and engine 'of the ordinary portable type'. What cannot be seen is the actual mechanism for thrashing and separating. The crop was cut and passed up carrier-belts to the separator. Cylinders then pressed the crop to separate the grain from the husk, 'the rollers receiving their motion through the medium of any convenient gearing receiving its motion from the running-gear of the separator'. It is not clear how the husks go one way and the grain another but the patent seems to expect a spout to take the grain away, probably relying on the lightness of the husks to keep them separated.

It was this very quality of husks—their lightness—which accounted for the fact that there were few patents for separators. It simply was not worth it. Farmers soon realised that beating or 'flailing' crops with some sort of stick would separate the grain from the husk, and this was the common method used until mid-Victorian times. Separating the husks was done by 'winnowing', when everything was thrown into the air on a windy day and the husks were blown away. There was even some grading, as the heavier grain would land nearest the farm worker and the lighter grains would fall further away. Bigger equipment such as Norton's was only likely to work on large, flat fields. The patent very exactly states that 49.03% of rights had been assigned to Charles John Russell Ballard, also of Orland, and to Hiram Mizner of Colusa County. Both places are in flat country to the north of Sacramento in the Central Valley. Britain, too, had many patents for thrashing machines. A hint of the dangers of such machines was the passing of a Parliamentary Act in 1878 for the 'prevention of accidents by threshing machines'. It provided for secure fencing at the feeding mouth of steam-powered thrashing machines. Oddly, the Act only applied to England and Wales.

Winthrop Norton, Orland, California
Filed 21 October 1884 and published as US 315651

(No Model.)

W. NORTON.
TRAVELING THRASHER AND SEPARATOR.

No. 315,651.   Patented Apr. 14, 1885.

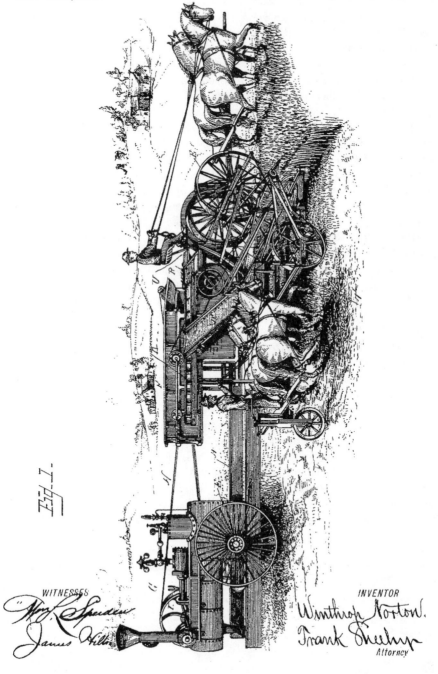

Fig. 1.

WITNESSES

INVENTOR

Winthrop Norton.

Frank Sheehy.
Attorney

The treadmill

The treadmill as used in British prisons was invented (but not patented) by William Cubitt in about 1817. Treadmills vary, but the general idea was that a cylinder was kept revolving by the weight of persons on boards who then had to keep stepping forward. It was meant for grinding corn but was swiftly adopted as a means of prison discipline in Brixton Prison, Surrey. It was used when someone was sentenced to 'hard labour', while prison warders who might turn a crank to make the work harder were promptly nicknamed by the inmates 'screws'. The British Patent Office indexed treadmills under 'Animal-power engines'.

The system illustrated here was designed by an architect. His explanation of the invention shows how particularly grim prison was meant to be. The idea was that 'prisoners or others having to labour at the treadwheels or cranks may pass to and from their places at the treadwheels or cranks without seeing each other, and without leaving vacant places at the treadwheel or crank'. The prisoners were divided into three groups, with at any time two groups working and one resting. The drawing shows a building designed for 42 prisoners divided into four identical 'compartments', each with seven treadmills or treadwheels under roof (m). Doors were represented by (k) and (l) with (k) hinged on wall (h) and (l) hinged on wall (i). Suppose the prisoners were in groups (a), (b) or (c). The prisoners in group (a) might be resting while those in (b) and (c) were working. When it was time for a changeover the 'officer in charge' would open or authorise the opening of alternate doors (l) from his watching place in an upper gallery so that prisoners in group (b) could move to a seat to rest. Those doors would then be closed and doors (k) would open so that prisoners in group (a) could work. And so on, with each prisoner resting and working successively in different places. William Martin did not explain why he wanted to treat the prisoners in this way, and it is not known if his invention were adopted.

Similarly, GB 9262/1885 by Robert Boyle of London was for a prison designed 'to prevent transmission of sound from one cell to another'—not so that prisoners could get a good night's sleep but to increase their isolation. The walls were double with a layer of insulation between while there were no windows but rather thin, oblique passages allowing air to circulate through baffles to an adjacent passage. This suggests that the cells would be very dark as well as quiet. However Enoch Jacob of Cincinnati, Ohio filed US 24307 in 1859 to achieve the opposite effect. He had a 'secret guard chamber' built round a jail made of iron plates, which he believed would transmit sound. 'A person moving carefully along the chamber may hear distinctly any sound in the cells.' Meanwhile James Cook and James Heath of Memphis, Tennessee had a number of patents for prisons including US 168455 which appeared in 1875. They state that one of them used the plan to build the local county jail in 1860. 'The entire prison consists of a jail within a jail', with a cell block supported on pillars within an outer shell. This basement area was used for exercise and led by stairs up to the block. The pillars contained water and sewage pipes, which were at least an improvement on 'slopping out' buckets. Each cell door was placed at an angle to the wall so that the entire cell could be viewed by a warder through a 'perforated jamb'. The only way out of the block was by an upper drawbridge which crossed the outer portion of the exercise area.

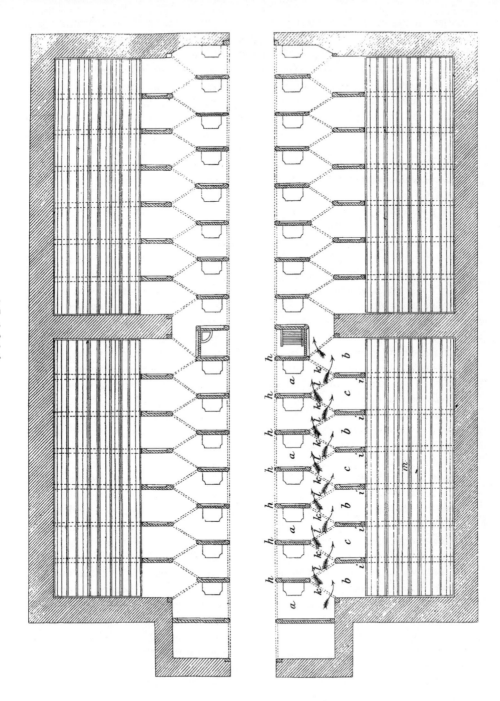

FIC.2.

The typewriter

Christopher Latham Sholes was born in 1819 on a Pennsylvania farm and moved on to Wisconsin, where he worked as a newspaper editor and later Collector of the Port of Milwaukee. He enjoyed seeing his friends at Kleinsteuber's Machine Shop where they tinkered with machinery. He and his friend Samuel Soule, an engineer, both patented page-numbering inventions in the 1860s. Carlos Glidden, also working in the shop (on a steam-driven plough) showed them an article in an 1867 issue of *Scientific American* about John Pratt's GB 3163/1866: a new idea called 'typewriting'. Sholes thought of a flat glass plate with underneath it carbon paper sandwiched between sheets of paper. By tapping down on an old telegraph instrument, printer's type on a long rod would strike upwards to leave ink from the carbon on the paper. The sentence used to test the machine was one they invented: 'Now is the time for all good men to come to the aid of the party'.

Originally the keys gave the alphabet in order but if adjacent rods were swiftly used one after the other they often jammed. To prevent this Sholes deliberately spread out common pairings such as 'ed' and came up with the famous 'qwerty' keyboard. Only 5,000 typewriters were sold in the first 5 years. Improvements were patented with US 79868, 182511 and 207559. An investor, James Densmore, suggested changes but also upset Soule and Glidden who left the partnership. Fifty models were tried out until Remington, gunsmiths who were diversifying, became interested and made typewriters from 1873. They offered Sholes and Densmore either $12,000 or a royalty for the rights. Sholes took the cash but it was Densmore, who took the royalty option, who grew rich. The early models looked like old sewing machines with fancy gold lettering on black metal, and a foot treadle to enable the carriage return and line spacing. This was not surprising as the engineer delegated to oversee production had been transferred from the sewing machine division. The Remington No. 2 in 1878 looked more modern and even allowed lower case as well as capitals. It was still a 'blind' typewriter, meaning that the text typed could not be seen. Franz Wagner of Germany in 1893 made the first model enabling the text to be viewed as it was typed.

Typing might have been seen as a boon to the (male) clerks, but there was resistance, as they could no longer hide their spelling mistakes with fancy writing. Women turned out to be faster and more accurate at typing so they began to enter the office market for the first time. The first manuscript of a novel to be typed is thought to be Mark Twain's *Life on the Mississippi* in 1883. Twain told the following (probably tall) tale about how he got interested in typewriters. He and a friend were in Boston when they saw a machine in a shop window. Wondering what it was, they went in, and examined samples of typed pages. The salesman said that the machine could do 57 words a minute. Twain refused to believe it and the 'type-girl' was put to work. He timed her and she indeed typed at exactly 57 words a minute. As she typed away Twain and his friend kept on stuffing the completed sheets into their pockets to show friends later on. The price was a hefty $125 but Twain bought one on the spot. Back at the hotel they took the sheets out of their pockets and realised that she had simply typed the same lines over and over again. He began to practise by typing out repeatedly Felicia Heman's poem *Casabianca*, which begins with the once famous line, 'The boy stood on the burning deck'. Sholes died after years of bad health in 1890.

Christopher Latham Sholes, Carlos Glidden and Samuel Soule, all of Milwaukee, Wisconsin
Published 23 June 1868 as US 79265

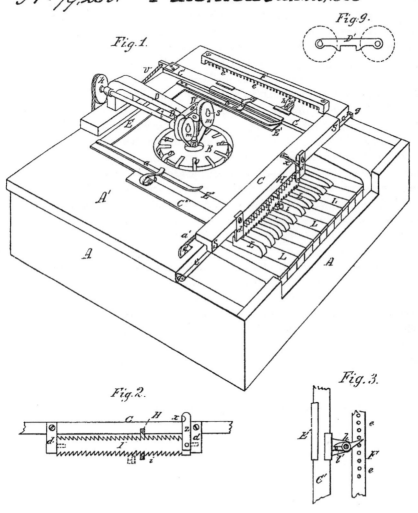

Sheet 1. 2 Sheets.

Sholes, Glidden & Soule.
Type Writing Mach.
Nº 79,265.   Patented Jun. 23, 1868.

Fig. 9.

Fig. 1.

Fig. 2.

Fig. 3.

INVENTORS.
C. Latham Sholes
Carlos Glidden
S. W. Soule
by Sodge & Munn
attys.

WITNESSES.
James Densmore.
L. Wailer.

The veil that brings a blush to the cheek

Veils were worn extensively during the Victorian period, particularly in the *mantilla* fashion down the back of the head. Veils were worn across the face at society weddings (white, and drawn back after the wedding) and at funerals. Mourning lasted for 2½ years by convention and deep mourning, featuring black veils, was for the first 18 months. Queen Victoria defied convention by staying in black for some four decades after the death of her husband, Prince Albert, in 1861.

Veils were sometimes worn across the face on other less formal occasions. The illustration opposite shows an ingenious attempt to make money out of bringing a blush to the cheek. In Richard Paulson's own words, 'The object of this invention is to so construct these improved veils, that they impart to the face of the wearer a greatly improved appearance as of a healthy bloom or heightened colour and which is confined principally to the cheeks'. Elsewhere he talks of a 'healthy or ruddy glow'. The veil was made of lace or silk and the part labelled (B) was tinged with pink. The whole veil could be a lighter shade of pink if desired. The veil consisted of two layers with the pink being confined to the bottom layer. The little detail of the butterfly is, of course, charming on such an awkward-looking sketch. It shows how little was typically revealed of the body in fashionable society. A tanned complexion was definitely not desirable in Victorian society as it suggested manual labour, hence the need for the patent.

Paulson describes himself in the patent as an 'engineer and inventor'. He had a number of other patents with a distinctly military tone such as GB 63/1884, a torpedo; GB 14015/1884, a breach-loading fire-arm; and GB 14130/1886, a revolver. His GB 7633/1889, unfortunately abandoned and therefore not published, was on gloves and button fasteners and is the only other one known by him on fashion. It is intriguing to wonder why he developed this little side-line. It is not known if Paulson made any money out of the veil invention, but it seems doubtful, particularly as he stopped paying fees to keep it in force in 1894. By coincidence one of the few other patents for veils in Britain was from the town of Nottingham itself. Joseph White and William Farmer applied for GB 12067/1891 which was for a lace veil wherein the upper part was thicker, with eye holes, so as to act as a mask. Meanwhile in the United States John Tuttle of Watertown, Massachusetts was responsible for US 145977 in 1873. This was for 'Combined nubias and veils', a nubia being a knit scarf. A veil was worn like a hood and a scarf came down from it on both sides of the head, crossing over at the neck, and was draped across the shoulders, with a tassle hanging down from each shoulder.

A.D. 1890. Oct. 7. Nº 15,845.

PAULSON'S COMPLETE SPECIFICATION.

1 SHEET

Figᵀ I.

A

London Printed by Darling and Son Ld
for Her Majesty Stationery Office 1891.

Malby & Son. Photo-Litho.

The vending machine

This invention is usually given the credit for the vending machine, or at least popularising it. Simeon Denham of Wakefield, Yorkshire with GB 706/1857 applied for a vending machine for selling stamps but he only sent in an extended abstract which was not granted. Perhaps it would not have worked. Percival Everitt is described as an engineer on his patent. John Glas Sandeman, 'gentleman', was born in 1836 in Hayling Island, Hampshire, and was a cavalry officer. He wrote prolifically to *The Times* on a variety of subjects and died in 1921. It is possible that he was merely the financial backer as Everitt was solely responsible for many other patents on the subject. The patent is illustrated here by a drawing from the American patent. The invention was reputedly first used on the platform of Mansion House underground station in London in April 1883. If so, this was an astonishingly rapid introduction to commerce. The inventors' keenness is shown by a preamble to the American patent which quotes patent numbers from 17 countries or colonies. The number is high since each present-day Australian state such as Victoria had its own system at the time.

'The main object of this invention is to facilitate the automatic delivery of Post Cards and Stamped Envelopes with a blank enclosure for persons depositing say a penny or two pence in a slit or slits prepared for the reception of a coin.' Figure 1 shows the machine from the front, with a useful 'Empty' sign for those who refilled the machine. Figure 2 shows in detail what would be in the portion marked (A). The slide (C) with the postcard is shown extended. Figure 3 is a side view showing the slide pulled out and featuring a slanted top for writing on. The cards within the machine were above a spring which, if the pile were low and therefore light, would allow them to rise to the top. The coin mechanism (not shown here) involved a penny knocking a lever and then several other pieces so that the slide mechanism was released. A smaller coin than a penny would slide past the mechanism.

GB 10406/1885 was an improvement to overcome vandalism. 'It has been found in practice that although the apparatus is perfectly successful when not designedly misused, articles such as pieces of paper, orange peel, and other rubbish have been maliciously placed in the slit provided for the admission of the coin.' Vending machines soon became popular and the USA dominated the world market. By the turn of the century a vast number of products or services could be obtained from a vending machine. These included the familiar 'lollipop' weighing machines (the most popular single use), peanuts, cigarettes, eggs, quinine, biscuits, condensed milk, hot and cold drinks, handkerchiefs, towels, cough lozenges, insurance papers and even (in Corinne, Utah) divorce papers. Everitt continued to patent in the field until 1891. His later patents included adapting vending machines to tell fortunes, sell opera glasses, spray perfume, and test strength (with a hand-grip tester). Most of his patents were for weighing machines although like others he was working on means to prevent fraud. He also, with GB 31581/1887, patented an alarming 'Improvements in machinery for giving currents of electricity on the insertion of a coin, token, or the like'.

John Glas Sandeman and Percival Everitt, London, England
Filed 21 April 1883 and published as GB 2033/1883 and US 323213

(No Model.)   3 Sheets—Sheet 1.

J. G. SANDEMAN & P. EVERITT.

APPARATUS FOR AUTOMATICALLY DELIVERING PREPAID GOODS TO ACCORD WITH THE PRICE PAID THEREFOR.

No. 323,213.   Patented July 28, 1885.

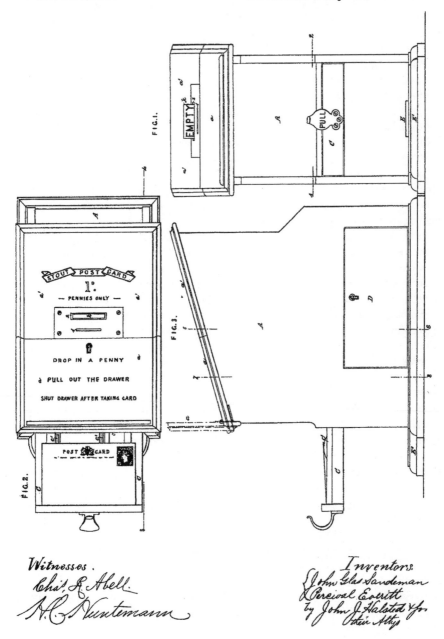

Witnesses.
Chas. R. Abell.
H. C. Nuntemann

Inventors
John Glas Sandeman
Percival Everitt
by John J. Halsted & Son
their Attys

Vulcanised rubber

Charles Goodyear was born in New Haven, Connecticut in 1800. He opened a hardware business in Philadelphia and in 1834 visited a rubber company in Roxbury, Massachusetts to offer his invented valve for rubber life preservers. The manager explained that the entire rubber industry was in danger because of problems with the material. Rubber had been known as a method of waterproofing from, for example, Charles MacIntosh of Lanarkshire, Scotland with GB 4804/1823 for a waterproof cloth with a coat of rubber between layers of cloth. A fad had started for importing it from Brazil and making products from it. However, exposed rubber softened in hot weather, and became hard and brittle in winter, and this both limited its uses and meant angry customers returning ruined goods (which were buried at night).

Goodyear spent several years experimenting with rubber, using his kitchen to mix rubber with many different materials. Sometimes the work was carried on in his 'hotel', a jail where he was sent for debt (he would then ask his wife for a rolling pin and raw rubber). He moved to New York to avoid neighbours annoyed by the smell, where his brother-in-law lectured him on his duties to his family. Rubber was dead. 'I am the man to bring it back', he replied. One day he happened to remove gilt from rubber with some nitric acid and realised that there were better properties in rubber treated in this way. He received US 240 for this in 1837. He found financial backing and made his improved product in an abandoned rubber factory on Staten Island, the family camping in the factory and fishing for food. Sales were poor.

In 1838 Goodyear visited Roxbury again and talked to Nathaniel Hayward, the former manager of a closed rubber factory. Hayward had found that sulphur that was dissolved in turpentine, mixed with rubber and exposed to sunlight would lose its stickiness. A little later Goodyear was showing off this product in a general store and accidentally flung it onto a hot stove. It charred but did not melt. This was the answer: rubber was mixed with sulphur and then heated. For 5 years Goodyear worked to give the product the right properties. By the time he got the patent shown for the process he was in debt again, having borrowed $50,000 for his experiments. He licensed the process cheaply so that relatively little money came in, yet had to fight 32 cases over infringement of his patents.

Before applying for the patent he tried to sell the 'British' rights to Charles MacIntosh, but this was unsuccessful as he did not have the money to secure a patent (and hence a monopoly for sale) in Britain. Thomas Hancock, a London waterproofing manufacturer who had been working on the problem for many years, examined a sample left with MacIntosh and realised from the yellow tinge that sulphur had been used to treat it. He experimented and discovered vulcanisation for himself and obtained GB 9952/1843 for the idea. Goodyear took Hancock to court but lost both the case and his own application for an English patent. His attempt to get a French patent also failed because he had earlier sent some rubber shoes to France and the idea was no longer novel. Goodyear spent 1851 to 1858 in Britain and France trying to market his invention, and spent a great deal of money displaying products at the Great Exhibition of 1851 in London, as well as spending time in jail for debt. He took out many patents for different rubber products and suggested hundreds of uses, but omitted the potentially most valuable: tyres. He died in New York in 1860 leaving debts of nearly $200,000. He once said, 'A man has cause for regret only when he sows and no man reaps'.

UNITED STATES PATENT OFFICE.

CHARLES GOODYEAR, OF NEW YORK, N.Y.

IMPROVEMENT IN INDIA-RUBBER FABRICS.

Specification forming part of Letters Patent No. 3,633, dated June 15, 1844.

To all whom it may concern:

Be it known that I, CHARLES GOODYEAR, of the city of New York, in the State of New York, have invented certain new and useful Improvements in the Manner of Preparing Fabrics of Caoutchouc or India-Rubber; and I do hereby declare that the following is a full and exact description thereof.

My principal improvement consists in the combining of sulphur and white lead with the india-rubber, and in the submitting of the compound thus formed to the action of heat at a regulated temperature, by which combination and exposure to heat it will be so far altered in its qualities as not to become softened by the action of the solar ray or of artificial heat at a temperature below that to which it was submitted in its preparation—say to a heat of 270° of Fahrenheit's scale—nor will it be injuriously affected by exposure to cold. It will also resist the action of the expressed oils, and that likewise of spirits of turpentine, or of the other essential oils at common temperatures, which oils are its usual solvents.

The articles which I combine with the india-rubber in forming my improved fabric are sulphur and white lead, which materials may be employed in varying proportions; but that which I have found to answer best, and to which it is desirable to approximate in forming the compound, is the following: I take twenty-five parts of india-rubber, five parts of sulphur, and seven parts of white lead. The india-rubber I usually dissolve in spirits of turpentine or other essential oil, and the white lead and sulphur also I grind in spirits of turpentine in the ordinary way of grinding paint. These three articles thus prepared may, when it is intended to form a sheet by itself, be evenly spread upon any smooth surface or upon glazed cloth, from which it may be readily separated; but I prefer to use for this purpose the cloth made according to the present specification, as the compound spread upon this article separates therefrom more cleanly than from any other.

Instead of dissolving the india-rubber in the manner above set forth, the sulphur and white lead, prepared by grinding as above directed, may be incorporated with the substance of the india-rubber by the aid of heated cylinders or calender-rollers, by which it may be brought into sheets of any required thickness; or it may be applied so as to adhere to the surface of cloth or of leather of various kinds. This mode of producing and of applying the sheet caoutchouc by means of rollers is well known to manufacturers. To destroy the odor of the sulphur in fabrics thus prepared, I wash the surface with a solution of potash, or with vinegar, or with a small portion of essential oil or other solvent of sulphur.

When the india-rubber is spread upon the firmer kinds of cloth or of leather it is subject to peel therefrom by a moderate degree of force, the gum letting go the fiber by which the two are held together. I have therefore devised another improvement in this manufacture by which this tendency is in a great measure corrected, and by which, also, the sheet-gum, when not attached to cloth or leather, is better adapted to a variety of purposes than when not prepared by this improved mode, which is as follows: After laying a coat of the gum, compounded as above set forth, on any suitable fabric I cover it with a bat of cotton-wool as it is delivered from the doffer of a carding-machine, and this bat I cover with another coat of the gum—a process which may be repeated two or three times, according to the required thickness of the goods. A very thin and strong fabric may be thus produced, which may be used in lieu of paper for the covering of boxes, books, or other articles.

When this compound of india-rubber, sulphur, and white lead, whether to be used alone in the state of sheets or applied to the surface of any other fabric has been fully dried, either in a heated room or by exposure to the sun and air, the goods are to be subjected to the action of a high degree of temperature, which will admit of considerable variation—say from 212° to 350° of Fahrenheit's thermometer, but for the best effect approaching as nearly as may be to 270°. This heating may be effected by running the fabrics over a heated cylinder; but I prefer to expose them to an atmosphere of the proper temperature, which may be best done by the aid of an oven properly constructed with openings through which the sheet or web may be passed by means of suitable rollers. When this process is performed upon a

The Winchester repeating rifle

Oliver Winchester was born in Boston, Massachusetts in 1810. He ran a business making and selling shirts in Baltimore, Maryland. His US 5421 in 1848 was for a method of cutting shirts which increased business so much that he opened a factory with his partner John Davies in New Haven in 1850. Winchester also began to buy shares in a local company called the Volcanic Repeating Arms Company. At the time it was normal to load a firearm at the muzzle. This was slow and awkward, and a rifle which repeatedly fired without reloading would have been a great improvement. The Volcanic rifle was a repeater but it had underpowered ammunition. By 1856 Winchester was the principal shareholder of the company and in 1857 it was reorganised.

Winchester's flair was not in inventing but in recognising opportunities and talent and encouraging invention. He also realised that a variety of firearms were needed. For example, some preferred a shorter gun barrel. His company inherited inventions from a number of men including Benjamin Tyler Henry, who had been the Superintendent. Winchester asked Henry to work on the ammunition side of development. He first developed a cartridge and then the illustrated Henry rifle, the first useful repeating rifle. It was actually meant for sportsmen. It worked by loading 15 cartridges from the muzzle end of a long tube directly underneath the barrel (as shown in Figure 4) besides one in the chamber. Getting it ready for action was clumsy by later standards and it was heavy as it was made from a single piece of steel. Still, as one bullet was fired another cartridge was ready. Winchester boasted, 'A resolute man, armed with one of these rifles, particularly if on horseback, cannot be taken!' Production did not begin until 1862, after the start of the Civil War. The War Department was not interested, preferring the Springfield rifle, and most of the 11,000 rifles that were sold to Union soldiers were purchased (for a hefty $42) out of their own money by the soldiers themselves. The Confederate soldiers called the Henry rifle 'the damned Yankee rifle you could load on Sunday and shoot all week'. The Indians, too, were amazed at the speed and accuracy of the firearm and called it the 'Spirit Gun of many shots'.

In 1866 the Henry rifle was replaced by the Winchester 66, based on US 55012 and US 57636 by Nelson King. This was the first of the series that made Winchester a household name. It loaded by a lever action using a gate in the frame and avoided the fouling to which the Henry rifle could be prone. That year Winchester sold his remaining shirt interests and launched the Winchester Repeating Arms Company. It was the Winchester 73's improved lever action that earned it the title 'the gun that won the West'. A feature film was even made in 1950 about fights for ownership of one, *Winchester 73*, starring James Stewart. Both lawmen and outlaws used this firearm freely and over 700,000 were manufactured until production ceased in 1919. Oliver Winchester died in 1880 in New Haven. His daughter-in-law Sarah's husband William died aged 41 in 1881 leaving her grieving despite a $20 million fortune. A medium told her that she would die unless she continuously enlarged a house to avoid the curses of those killed by Winchester rifles. A house in Santa Clara, California was hence extended to about 160 rooms (tallies varied at each counting, as the design was so rambling) until her death in 1922. It can be visited.

B. T. HENRY,

Magazine Fire Arm.

No. 30,446.

Patented Oct. 16, 1860.

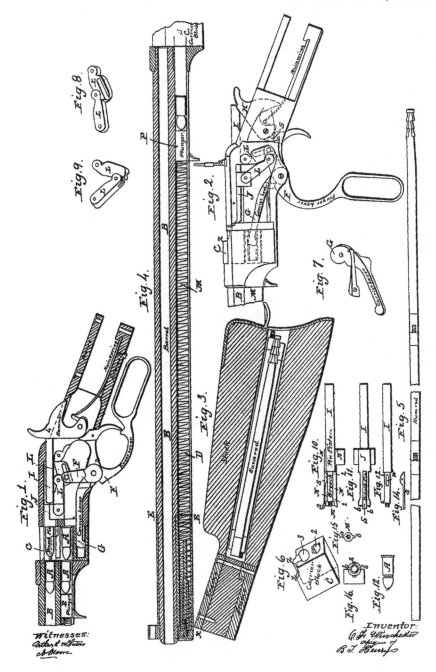

Witnesses:

Inventor:

The Zeppelin

Count Ferdinand Zeppelin was born in Konstanz in the State of Baden in 1838. He had a career as an army officer, which included serving as a military observer with the Union forces in the American Civil War (when he first went up in a captive balloon in 1863 in St Paul, Minnesota) as well as in wars against Austria and France, before retiring in 1890 to devote himself to the idea of the dirigible. From 1874 onwards his diaries had notes on the idea. Others before him had thought of the idea of a dirigible, but he was the first to work out most of the problems, admittedly with the help of an engineer, Theodore Kober. Hot air balloons were at the mercy of the wind, while his lighter than air dirigible would be independent. Numerous bags were each filled with hydrogen and encased within a rigid skin 128 m long. Hydrogen is lighter than air, and it is the difference between the mass of the hydrogen and that of the air that gives the dirigible the ability to lift cargo. The drawing shows two cars for crew at (g), each with a 12 kilowatt engine geared to two propellers, positioned as shown in Figure 2. These enabled the dirigible to drive forward. A rudder enabled it to move horizontally. A sliding weight (b) moved along the keel so that the bow would rise or sink. This produced vertical movement. The bow was hauled up before landing. A gangway below the dirigible gave access to all parts of the ship by rope ladders.

Zeppelin showed the plans to the German Military Commission but they were not interested, saying that such a ship would be too slow and too weak. A company was formed in 1898 to manufacture the first model along the patent's design, the LZ-1, which made its maiden flight from a floating hanger on Lake Constance on 1 July 1900. Zeppelin himself was at the controls and, although it was damaged, on landing it caused a sensation. For the first time a flight had been made under power. Donations poured in and Zeppelin's funds were helped by permission to run a lottery. The third model, LZ-3, in 1906, was a success. This caused alarm among many, and H. G. Wells's novel *The war in the air*, published in 1908, about an attack by German dirigibles on the USA, was one result. Later modifications included stabilising fins, the removal of the sliding weight idea and much more powerful engines. Regular flights began to be carried out between several German cities with 24 passengers travelling in great comfort.

When World War I broke out Zeppelin urged using his dirigibles as well as huge aeroplanes to bomb Britain. A hundred 'Zeppelins' were used for bombing, and some were able to fly for 4 days before descending. They made huge targets for anti-aircraft guns and opposing aircraft. Ferdinand Zeppelin died in 1917 in Charlottenburg near Berlin. After the war the *Graf Zeppelin* and later the *Hindenburg* made flights across the Atlantic and around the world in 1929. Their great failure was using hydrogen, which, although it does not explode, burns. Helium has only 92% of its lifting power but does not burn. Britain, Germany and the USA all lost dirigibles with loss of life due to storms, instability and fires. Even a helium-filled dirigible such as the USA's *Shenandoah* was destroyed in a storm in 1925 owing to design defects. The end for rigid (but not non-rigid) airships came with the burning of the *Hindenburg* in Lakenhurst, New Jersey in 1937.

No. 621,195.

Patented Mar. 14, 1899.

FERDINAND GRAF ZEPPELIN.

NAVIGABLE BALLOON.

(Application filed Dec. 29, 1897.)

(No Model.)

4 Sheets—Sheet 1.

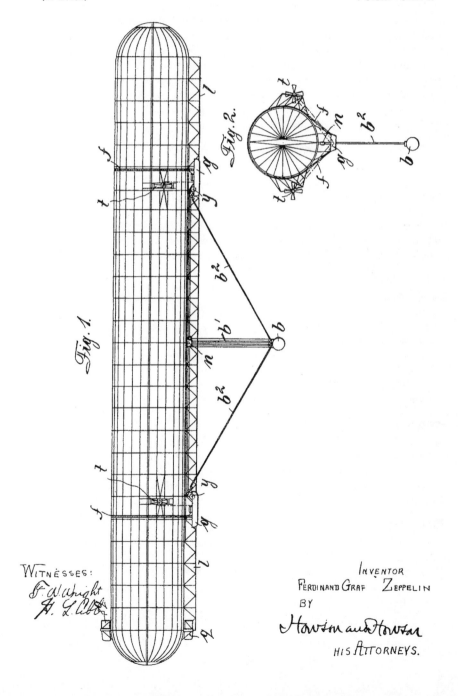

INVENTOR

FERDINAND GRAF ZEPPELIN

BY

Howson and Howson

HIS ATTORNEYS.

WITNESSES:

F. W. Wright

H. L. Abb.

FURTHER READING

The patent specifications held at the British Library were the main source for this book but there were too many others to list. Different sources often contradict each other and I had to make hard choices on what to include. Primary sources such as archives are better than second-hand accounts, but they are usually impossible to identify. For those who wish to read further the actual patent numbers have been freely used in this book. Many books do not quote patent numbers, which can make it difficult to find the patent. Several books useful for research into the history of inventions, websites and the patent libraries that can be visited in Britain and the United States are given below. The only books listed which regularly mention patent numbers are marked *. They also include extensive reproductions, mainly of drawings, from the patents themselves.

Books arranged by broad topics

The book of inventions and discoveries 1992. V.-A. Giscard d'Estaing. 1991, Macdonald.
The evolution of useful things. P. Petrovski. 1993, Knopf.
The new Shell book of firsts. P. Robertson. 1994, Headline. [An excellent starting point. Includes an index by place.]
Patent applied for: a century of fantastic inventions. F. Coppersmith and J. J. Lynx. 1949, Co-Ordination (Press & Publicity) Ltd. [A superb source of engravings of strange inventions, but without citations of any patents.]

Books arranged alphabetically

The Guinness book of innovations: the 20th century from aerosol to zip. G. Tibballs. 1994, Guinness.
*Historical first patents: the first United States patent for many everyday things. T. Brown. 1994, Scarecrow Press.
*New and improved: inventors and inventions that have changed the world. R. Baker. 1976, British Library.
They all laughed . . . from light bulbs to lasers: the fascinating stories behind the great inventions that have changed our lives. I. Flatow. 1993, Harper Perennial.

Books arranged chronologically

The Harwin book of inventions, innovations, discoveries from pre-history to the present day. K. Desmond. 1987, Constable. [No detail, but an excellent index by specific topic so a good way to identify the inventor and the date.]
*Inventing the 20th century: 100 inventions that shaped the world. S. van Dulken. 2000, British Library/New York University Press. [Companion volume to this one.]

Other books

Inventors at work. K. A. Brown, 1988, Tempus Books. [Interviews with prominent American inventors.]
The sources of invention. J. Jewkes, D. Sawers and R. Stillerman. 2nd ed., 1969, Macmillan. [Really a textbook, but includes numerous case studies on the development of inventions.]

Other books on invention are normally classified at 608 or 609 in the Dewey sequence in public libraries. *Victorian inventions* by L. de Vries (1971, John Murray), while very interesting, consists of attractive illustrations from contemporary magazines of crazy ideas without mention of patents. Not quite in our period is R. Dale's *Edwardian inventions, 1901–1905* (1979, W. H. Allen) which features illustrations and summaries of hundreds of British patents. He also either wrote or co-authored seven short profusely illustrated books, published by the British Library in the early 1990s, which quote patent numbers. These are *Early cars, Early railways, Home entertainment, The industrial revolution, Machines in the home, Machines in the office* and *Timekeeping*. H. Dale wrote *Early flying machines*. The *Dictionary of American biography*, 20 volumes, 1928–36 and the *American national biography*, 24 volumes, 1999 give detailed information on many American inventors. Both cite sources for further reading and list inventors who are covered by articles. The British *Dictionary of national biography* has far less information on inventors. The *Encyclopaedia Britannica*'s Micropaedia is a good source for biographies.

This author's *British patents of invention, 1617–1977: a guide for researchers* (1999, British Library) is a detailed, practical guide for research into the British patent system or approaching its patents by subject, name or number. No such book exists for any other patent system. Background books on British patent history include N. Davenport's *The United Kingdom patent system: a brief history* (1979, Kenneth Mason), J. Hewish's *Rooms near Chancery Lane: the Patent Office under the Commissioners, 1852–1883* (2000, British Library) and the older *Patents of invention: origin and growth of the patent system in Britain* by A. A. Gomme (1946, British Council), which concentrates on the period to 1852, and H. Harding's *Patent Office centenary: a story of 100 years in the life and work of the Patent Office* (1953, HMSO). D. J. Boorstin's *The Americans: the democratic experience* (1973, Random House) is an authoritative survey of mainly American innovation (some being unpatentable concepts such as mail ordering) with extensive bibliographies. H. J. Habbakuk's *American and British technology in the nineteenth century: the search for labour-saving inventions* (1962, Cambridge University Press) is really an economics textbook. The history of the American Patent Office to the end of the Civil War in 1865 is well covered by K. Dobyns' *The Patent Office pony: a history of the early Patent Office* (1994, Sergeant Kirkland's Museum and Historical Society). Women's inventions are covered by A. Stanley's lengthy *Mothers and daughters of invention: notes for a revised history of technology* (1993, Scarecrow Press).

The Internet holds a great deal of information on old patents but this is often difficult to find. Information about the numeration of old patents and the number ranges, mainly British, is at **http://www.bl.uk/services/stb/patents/history.html**. Old patents can only be seen in numbers at one site, **Esp@cenet**, through for example its British portal at **http://gb.espacenet.com**. The 'worldwide' option must be chosen. All German patents from 1877 can be seen here provided that Adobe Acrobat is loaded on your PC. Some 20th century material for France, Britain and the USA is also available there. American patents from 1790 can be seen on the USPTO Web Patent Database at **http://www.uspto.gov/patft/index.html** provided that special software is loaded as explained in the 'Help' key. D. Newton's *How to find information: patents on the Internet* (2000, British Library) is an excellent introduction to this difficult area. For modern patents (mainly), a good starting point is the British Library's own links off the site **http://www.bl.uk/services/stb/patents/home.html**, 'Links to patent and other intellectual property resources', which offers numerous links to databases (many free) of patent data, as well as to general information resources for inventors (these have a British bias). These databases can generally be searched by keyword, classification, company and inventor name. Often Adobe Acrobat software is necessary to see images of the patent specifications. Many sites are difficult to use.

Some useful sites are 'About.Com: inventors' at **http://inventors.about.com/education/inventors**; 'Inventure place' at **http://www.invent.org**; and the 'Jerome and Dorothy Lemelson Center for the Study of Invention and Innovation' at **http://www.si.edu/lemelson**. The National Inventors Hall of Fame describes numerous American (mostly) inventors at **http://www.invent.org/book/index.html**. Also use the Google website, **http://google.com**, by running a search such as <"thomas edison" patents> in the search box. Many people are surprised how quickly relevant material can be found this way. Searches will often also pick up URLs of companies talking about their past successes. Edison's American patents are listed chronologically and by subject at **http://edison.rutgers.edu/patents.htm**, with links to Adobe Acrobat copies of the complete patent specifications. The site **http://www.patentmuseum.com/listing.html** contains many references to attractive American patents, both utility and design, with many being significant firsts. Although the patent numbers are not given the drawings, year, address and name of the inventors are given. For finding out how well known devices such as refrigerators work try **http://express.howstuffworks.com**, Marshall Brain's How Stuff Works, is very useful. The auction house Ebay.com at **http://www.ebay.com** shows photographs of many old devices that are available for sale, some with patent numbers.

However, these sources are of little use if you are unable to construct a good search or to interpret the results. Nearly all of these databases look different from each other and it may be difficult to understand them. Also, older material is generally best searched using manual indexes and abridgments. You should begin at a public patent collection, although many will not have older material. Both Britain and the United States have networks of publicly available patent collections. These are: Britain's Patents Information Network (see **http://www.bl.uk/services/stb/patents/pinmenu.html** or telephone the British Library on 020 7412 7919/20 for details of a nearby library). The United States' Patent and Trademark Depository Library program (see **http://www.uspto.gov/go/ptdl**). Those living in other countries can try the list of patent offices at **http://www.bl.uk/services/stb/patents/polinks.html**.

The British Library can supply copies of specific, known patents. Telephone its Patent Express photocopy operation on 020 7412 7992 or telephone the British Library in America on 800 932 3575. In both cases payment is by Visa or Mastercard. The British Library holds over 44 million patent specifications from 38 countries. Uniquely the national patent collection is not in the Patent Office, but rather in the national library, as this is useful for consultation of the science and technology collections. Illustrated British patent abridgments for 1855 to 1930 were arranged in 146 broad topics or their subdivisions making looking for general concepts such as ships or shoes, as opposed to very narrowly defined ideas, relatively easy. Britain is the only country which produced such a series. The British Library can offer *limited* free help to enquirers on both old and new patents. We cannot provide a free search to see if an idea has been patented before but we can often help with specific, known inventions, especially if they are historical in nature. In other cases we can often provide (non-legal) advice. Please be as specific as possible with any enquiries. Personal visitors who wish to carry out research are welcome but must first obtain a pass. We can be contacted by telephone (UK callers only) on 020 7412 7919/20, fax on 020 7412 7480, e-mail on patents-information@bl.uk or post at Patents Information, 96 Euston Road, London NW1 2DB. A great deal of information about what we do, what we hold and the services we offer, can be found on **http://www.bl.uk/services/stb/patents/home.html**.

For legal enquiries contact the Patent Office on 08459 500 505 (UK callers) or by e-mail on patent-enquiries@patents.gov.uk. Contact the American Patent and Trademark Office on 800 786 9199 (US callers) or by e-mail on usptoinfo@uspto.gov?=subjectPatents.

INDEX

This index covers the 100 inventions and the names of those inventors. The countries of origin or residence are indexed for the inventors of all patents mentioned (for the USA the states themselves are indexed, and for the UK the counties). Other indexing is selective.